Reading Mastery

Signature Edition

Textbook B

Siegfried Engelmann
Susan Hanner

McGraw Hill SRA

A Division of The McGraw-Hill Companies
Columbus, OH

Illustration Credits

Jan Benham, Barbara Counseller, John Edwards and Associates, Simon Galkin, Heidi King, Susan Jerde, Paul Montgomery, Meryl Henderson, James Shough, Jessica Stanley

Photo Credits

7, 61 ©Corbis; **63(tl)** ©Andrew J. Martinez/Photo Researchers, **(tr)** ©Nick Rains/Cordaiy Photo Library Ltd./Corbis, **(b)** ©Robert Yin/Corbis; **64 (t)** ©Elio Ciol/Corbis, **(b)** ©Corel; **126** (tl) ©Andrew J. Martinez/Photo Researchers, **(tr)** ©Nick Rains/Cordaiy Photo Library Ltd./Corbis, **(b)** ©Robert Yin/Corbis; **173** ©NASA; **190** ©Corbis; **217 (tl)** ©Nick Rains/Cordaiy Photo Library Ltd./Corbis, **(tr)** ©Andrew J. Martinez/Photo Researchers, **(b)** ©Robert Yin/Corbis; **239** ©NASA; **322** ©Claude Nuridsany & Marie Perennou/Science Photo Library/Photo Researchers, Inc.

SRAonline.com

McGraw-Hill SRA

A Division of The McGraw-Hill Companies

Printed in the United States of America.

Send all inquiries to this address:
SRA/McGraw-Hill
4400 Easton Commons
Columbus, OH 43219

ISBN: 978-0-07-612582-1
MHID: 0-07-612582-3

5 6 7 8 9 10 QPD 13 12 11 10 09

The McGraw-Hill Companies

Table of Contents

A

1	2
1. Maria Sanchez	1. unusually
2. deserve	2. spoon
3. dipped	3. rice
4. opening	4. purred
	5. meowed
	6. hamsters

B

Teaching Animals a Hard Trick

In the last lesson, you learned the main rule for training an animal to do a trick. Sometimes you reward the animal. Sometimes you don't reward the animal. The animal learns that the only way to get the reward is to do the trick. The animal wants the reward, so the animal does the trick.

Sometimes, the animal is not able to do the trick that you want it to do. Maybe you want the animal to jump up in the air and do a somersault before it lands on its feet. When you teach a hard trick, you don't follow the rule for teaching simple tricks. Here's why: The animal can't do the trick at first. So the animal will not receive any rewards for doing the trick. If the animal doesn't receive any rewards, the animal will stop trying to learn the trick.

Here is what you do when you're teaching the animal a trick it can't

Picture 1

Picture 2

Picture 3

do at first: You help the animal do the trick. And you reward the animal for <u>trying</u> to do it. You keep rewarding the animal for getting closer to doing the trick. To teach the animal how to somersault in the air, you put a belt around the animal so the animal won't fall on its back. Then you reward the animal each time the animal <u>tries</u> to do the trick. At first, you may give the animal a reward if the animal just jumps up in the air. After a while, you may reward the animal for jumping up in the air and trying to lean backward. If the animal just jumps in the air, you don't reward it anymore.

Later, you may reward the animal if the animal turns upside down in the air. Later, you may reward the animal if the animal turns almost all the way around in the air. Later, you may reward the animal for turning all the way around in the air. At last, you reward the animal if the animal does the trick without the belt around it.

Remember, if the animal can't do the trick at first, you reward the animal for <u>trying</u> to do the trick. When the animal gets better, you don't reward the animal unless the animal comes closer to doing the trick.

By rewarding animals for trying, you can teach an animal amazing things. You can teach a dog to ride a bicycle. You can teach a dog to turn a doorknob and to open a door. You can teach a dog to get the newspaper and bring it to you.

C

The Pet Shop

The owner of the pet shop was named Maria Sanchez. She loved the pet shop, but it was not making money. Each month she had less money. She knew that if things didn't change, she would have to close the shop very soon. She had tried different ways to interest more people in buying pets. She put ads in the newspaper, and she did a lot of other things.

Maria Sanchez usually spent a lot of time thinking about how to make her pet shop more interesting and about how she could make the pet shop earn more money. But she had never thought of cooking up the kind of food that Waldo made. She stood there in the kitchen of her pet shop, watching Waldo pour different things that he had cooked into a big bowl. She couldn't believe what was happening. Birds and squirrels were looking in the window. Dogs and cats were running around outside the window. The animals in the pet shop were howling and screeching and jumping around.

"What makes the animals act that way?" she asked Waldo.

He smiled and looked up from his cooking. "My food," he said. "They love it."

She picked up a large spoon. "Do you mind if I try some?" she asked.

"No," he said. "It's very good food."

She dipped her spoon into the bowl, filled it with food, and put it in her mouth. She tried not to make a sour face, but the food tasted bad—very bad. "My," she said, trying to smile, "that certainly has an unusual taste." She wasn't really lying. The food did have an unusual taste—unusually bad.

Waldo finished cooking some corn and rice. He dumped the corn and rice into the bowl with the other things he had cooked. Then he began to whistle. He walked into the pet shop with his food. Maria followed. Waldo began opening the bird cages. "No," Maria shouted. "We'll never be able to catch them."

"They won't fly away," Waldo said. And he was right. They landed on his shoulders and on his head. Two of them tried to get into the bowl of food, but he brushed them away with his hand. Those two birds landed on his shoulder and sat there.

Next, Waldo went to the cages with the cats. He opened all the cages. "No," Maria shouted. "They'll go after the birds."

"No, they won't," Waldo said. And he was right again. The cats rubbed against Waldo's legs. They put their tails high in the air. They meowed and purred loudly.

Next, Waldo opened the cages for the dogs. “No,” Maria started to say. Then she stopped and said, “I know. They won’t chase the cats.”

“Right,” Waldo said. The dogs didn’t pay any attention to the cats. They barked and wagged their tails and jumped up to get the food from the bowl. Waldo held the bowl high so they couldn’t reach it.

Then Waldo opened all the other cages. Rabbits and hamsters and other animals came out and tried to get close to Waldo.

Maria couldn’t believe what she saw. Here was Waldo holding a bowl of food above his head. More than fifty animals were around him and on him.

Waldo said, “Now we can show people the pets that you have for sale.” Waldo walked to the front window of the pet shop. He sat down with his back to the window. The animals crowded close to him and tried to reach the bowl, but he held it above his head.

Maria looked outside the window. People who were passing by the pet shop stopped and looked. They smiled and pointed to the different animals. At first there were only

four or five people standing in front of the window. But soon there was a large crowd of more than thirty people.

Waldo was now feeding the animals. He held a little bit of food high in the air. The birds flew from his shoulders and his head. They flew around and took the food from his hand. Maria watched. The other animals watched. The people outside the window watched. The birds went back to Waldo's shoulders and head. Then Waldo fed the dogs and cats and rabbits and hamsters and all the other animals. The people outside were laughing and pointing.

D Number your paper from 1 through 21.

Skill Items

Use the words in the box to write complete sentences.

deserved	boring	adult	anxious	aimed
audience	incredible	fancy	disturbed	whales

1. The _____ _____ made them _____.
2. The _____ speaker _____ the _____.

Review Items

3. What runs an electric eye?
4. Which planet is largest?
5. Which planet is the next largest?
6. How many times larger than the earth is the sun?
7. How many suns are in the solar system?
8. How many planets are in the solar system?
9. What's the largest city in Japan?
10. When you're training an animal, what do you do each time the animal does the trick?
11. What do you do if the animal does not do the trick?

12. Gravity is the force that ____.
13. What happens to people and things when there's no gravity?
14. If something weighed 100 pounds on Earth, how many pounds would it weigh on our moon?
15. The pilot of Traveler Four turned off the engines when the spaceship was out in space. Did the ship slow down?
16. If you drop an object on Earth, it falls to the ground. What makes it fall?
17. The arrow on the map goes from San Francisco to ____.
18. Which ocean does the arrow cross?

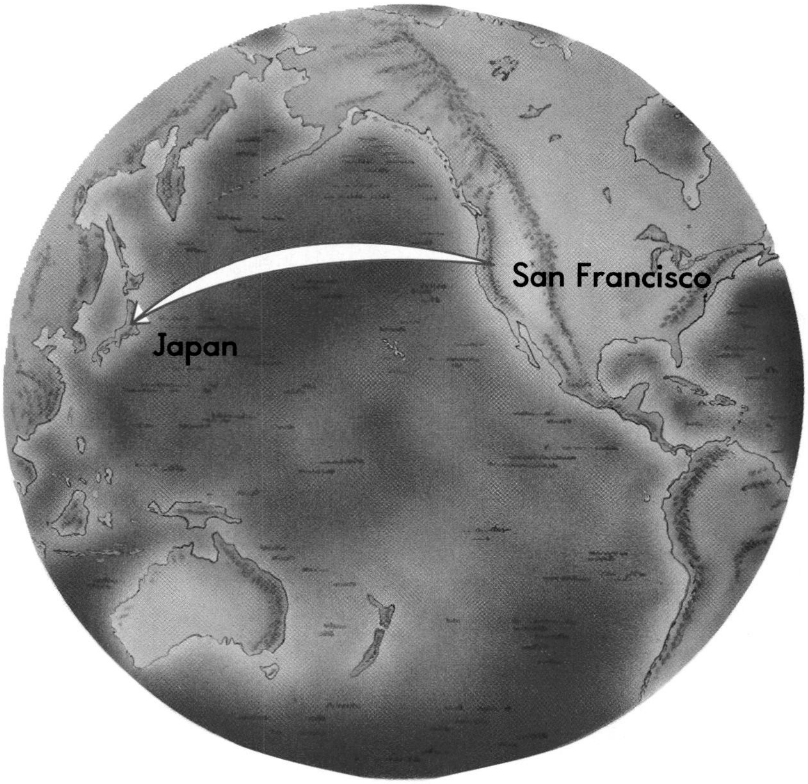

19. What planet is shown in the picture?
20. Which is bigger, the "eye" of the planet or Earth?

21. Write the letters of the 5 things that tell about Jupiter.
    a. It's small.
    b. It's beautiful.
    c. It has 4 moons.
    d. It's huge.
    e. It has stripes.
    f. It has more gravity than Earth.
    g. It's green and blue.
    h. It's brown, orange and white.

72

A

1	2	3
1. library	1. seventeen	1. o'clock
2. taught	2. isn't	2. yucky
3. music	3. puppies	3. mommy
4. somersault	4. reward	4. deserves

B

Maria and Waldo Make a Deal

Usually, Maria Sanchez sold eight pets a week. On the first day that Waldo cooked, she sold seventeen pets. And all those animals were sold in less than one hour. By the time Waldo had finished cooking, it was already four o'clock. The pet shop closed at five o'clock. But during that time, Maria had sold more pets than she usually sold in two weeks.

As Waldo sat in the window of the pet shop with birds, and dogs, and cats, and other animals, people gathered to watch. They pointed and laughed and said things like, "Oh, look at that striped kitten. Isn't it cute?"

Some of the children watching the show said things like, "Mommy, can we get that little dog with the long ears? Please?" The mothers and fathers were saying things like, "Well, I don't know if we should have a pet," but the children kept saying, "Please. Can we just go inside and look at it?"

So the parents and the children would go inside the pet shop. And once they picked up one of the animals and petted it, they usually bought the animal. Parents and children were holding cats that were purring and puppies that were licking faces and wagging tails. They were giving little bits of Waldo's food to parrots and rabbits. And Maria was very busy. When the pet shop closed at five o'clock, she turned to Waldo and said, "If you want a job here, you've got it. In fact, I'll make a deal with you. I'll give you 20¢ for every dollar that I make when I sell a pet."

Waldo jumped up and down. "All right!" he shouted. "This is great!" After he and Maria talked some more, Waldo ran home. On the way, he thought about how he would change his plans about cooking in the garage.

Waldo was out of breath when he got home. His mother said, “Waldo, what happened to you? You’re nearly an hour late.”

Waldo said, “I’ve got a new job. I’m going to work in a pet shop.”

Waldo’s father said, “That sounds fine. What are you going to do at the pet shop?”

Waldo said, “I’m going to train the animals and show them off so that people will want to buy them.”

Waldo’s mother said, “How are you going to do that?”

Before Waldo could answer, his sister Fran said, “I know what he’s going to do. He’s going to cook up some of that yucky food. Don’t let him do it.”

Waldo’s brother said, “Yeah, make him stop cooking.”

Waldo’s sister said, “Yeah, and make him answer the phone.”

“Wait a minute,” Waldo’s father said. “Let Waldo talk.”

Waldo said, “I’m going to cook, but I won’t cook around here. I’ll cook at the pet shop.”

Waldo’s brother said, “That place will stink so much that nobody will come in it.”

Waldo started to get angry. "I'm a good cook," he said. "I can't help it if the only people who like my food are not people."

Waldo's sister laughed and said, "Oh, that makes a lot of sense. The only people are not people. Make him stop cooking."

Waldo's father said to Fran, "Just be quiet and give Waldo a chance to tell us about his job."

Waldo explained, "I'll cook at the pet shop and I'll make a lot of money. The owner of the pet shop told me that she would give me 20¢ for every dollar that she made from selling a pet. I'll be rich."

"Yeah," his brother said. "But how are people going to buy pets if they're holding their noses all the time?"

"Be quiet," Waldo's mother said. "I think Waldo deserves a chance to cook again if he cooks at the pet shop."

Waldo said, "There's a kitchen in the back of the pet shop and I can cook everything I need there. And I did it today." Waldo went on to explain how he had cooked the food, let the animals out of their cages, and sat in the window with them. "The pet shop was mobbed," he concluded. "And people were buying pets like crazy."

"I think that's very nice," his mother said.

"I think it stinks," his sister said. "You should make him..."

"That's enough," Waldo's father said.

Waldo said, "I think I'm going to start training some of the animals to do tricks. I don't know much about training animals, but I'll get some books and read them. I know that the animals will do anything to get my food. So I'll use the food as a reward. And I think I can train the animals to do some really good tricks."

Waldo's father said, "As long as you don't cook around the house, I think your plan sounds very good. You may work in the pet shop."

A Number your paper from 1 through 18.

Review Items

1. Name the planet we live on.
2. What's in the middle of the solar system?
3. Name the only part of the solar system that's burning.

4. In what part of a spaceship are the engines?
5. The sound of the engines can't reach the passenger section because the spaceship ___.
6. If an object weighed 20 pounds on Earth, would it weigh more than 20 pounds on our moon?
7. Which is larger, Earth or Saturn?
8. If an object weighed 20 pounds on Earth, would it weigh **more than 20 pounds** or **less than 20 pounds** on Saturn?
9. A person weighs 100 pounds on Planet A and 300 pounds on Planet B. Which planet has stronger gravity?
10. Planet A has stronger gravity than Planet R. On which of those planets would you weigh more?
11. When you teach an animal a simple trick, when do you reward the animal?
12. When don't you reward the animal?
13. Let's say that you want to teach an animal a very hard trick. Can the animal do the trick at first?
14. What will happen if the animal doesn't receive any rewards until it does the trick?
15. So when you're teaching the animal a hard trick, what do you reward the animal for doing?

Let's say you're training a dog to jump up in the air and do a backward somersault. **Use the words below to finish each sentence.**

- jumping up and leaning backward
- jumping up in the air
- jumping up and turning upside down

16. At first, you would reward the dog for ___.
17. Later you would reward the dog for ___.
18. Later you would reward the dog for ___.

73

A

1	2
1. admission	1. tightrope
2. fantastic	2. library
3. experience	3. taught
4. tour	4. somersaults
5. music	5. peppy
	6. rewarded

B

Waldo Starts Training Animals

The man at the library looked at the stack of books that Waldo had and he said, "What are you going to do with all those books on animal training?" Waldo explained.

He had so many books that he was tired of carrying them by the time he got home. He took them to his room, and he started to read. And he kept on reading during every spare minute he had. Some books told about training your pet dog. Others told about training horses. Others told about training birds. Others told about training monkeys.

Within a month, Waldo had read all the books. But he didn't wait to finish the books before he started to train animals at the pet shop. At first he taught the animals easy tricks. He found out that the easiest animals to teach are birds. The day after he read a book on how to train pigeons, he trained three pigeons to tap dance.

Here's what he did. He took one pigeon from a cage. He put the pigeon on a table. He waited for the pigeon to turn its head to one side. When it turned its head, he gave it a tiny bit of food. Then he waited for the pigeon to turn its head and move its feet. Again, he gave the pigeon a bit of food. Then Waldo waited until the pigeon turned its head, moved its feet and flapped its wings.

Within a few minutes, the pigeon was doing a dance with its wings out to the sides. Now Waldo attached little buttons to the pigeon's feet. Each time the pigeon took a step, the buttons on its feet made tapping sounds. Now Waldo turned on a CD player. The music he played was very peppy. Whenever the pigeon moved its feet in time with the music, Waldo gave it a little bit of food. Within half an hour, the pigeon was tap dancing in time with the music. The training for the second pigeon was a little different. Waldo left the music on and let the first pigeon keep dancing. From time to time, Waldo gave the first pigeon a bit of food. Waldo rewarded the second pigeon each time it did something the first pigeon did. Within a few minutes, the second pigeon was holding its wings out to the sides and dancing in time with the music.

Waldo kept the music playing and brought out the third pigeon. When Maria came out of the back room and saw what the pigeons were doing, her eyes became very large. "I've never seen anything like this in my life," she said. The three pigeons were dancing in time with the music.

Waldo moved the table to the front window and turned the music on very loud. Within a few minutes, a large crowd gathered. They were clapping in time with the music and smiling at the animals.

Within a few more minutes, people were coming into the pet shop and trying to talk to Maria over the loud music. "Are those pigeons for sale?" they asked.

Maria answered, "No, they're not. But if you want a dancing pigeon, we can train one for you." That day, she took orders for eight dancing pigeons.

After the shop closed, Maria said to Waldo, "If you can train animals to do things like that, we should put on some shows. People would pay to see tap-dancing birds."

Waldo smiled. "That's a great idea," he said. "But let's not just have tap-dancing birds. Let's have cats that ride bicycles, and dogs that do somersaults in the air, and rabbits that walk tightropes."

"Do you know how to train animals to do those tricks?" she asked.

Waldo explained that he had books that told how to teach hard tricks and that he would study those books and learn how to train the animals.

So Waldo read during all his spare time. And when he went to the pet shop, he worked with the animals. The first thing he did was train a rabbit to walk on a tightrope. Actually, he had two tightropes side by side. First he stretched two thick ropes out on a table. Each time the rabbit stood with all four feet on the ropes, he gave the rabbit a bit of food. (Look at picture 1.) When the rabbit got good at doing this part of the trick, Waldo changed the rule for rewarding the rabbit. Now he gave a reward if the rabbit kept all four feet on the ropes while walking forward. Then Waldo stretched the ropes out a few centimeters above the table. He put a little belt around the rabbit and held on to the belt so that the rabbit wouldn't fall if it missed the ropes. (Look at picture 2.) Waldo rewarded the rabbit for trying to walk on the ropes. Soon the rabbit could walk without any help from Waldo. Then Waldo put up thin ropes instead of thick ones.
1 (Look at picture 3.) When Waldo finished training the animal to walk on the thin ropes, he decided to make a super trick. So he trained four mice to sit on the back of the rabbit as the rabbit walked along the tightropes. (Look at picture 4.)

C Number your paper from 1 through 16.

Skill Items

A lot of folks mobbed around the cute singer.

1. What's another word for **good-looking and charming?**
2. What's another word for **people?**
3. What's another word for **crowded around?**

Review Items

4. How long ago did dinosaurs live on the earth?
   - a hundred years ago
   - a hundred million years ago
   - a million years ago
5. Here's how an electric eye at a store works. When somebody walks in the door, the person's body stops the beam of light from reaching the ______.

The picture shows two electric eye beams on the side of doors. The number **1** shows the beam that is broken first. The number **2** shows the beam that is broken next. Write the letter of the correct arrow for each doorway.

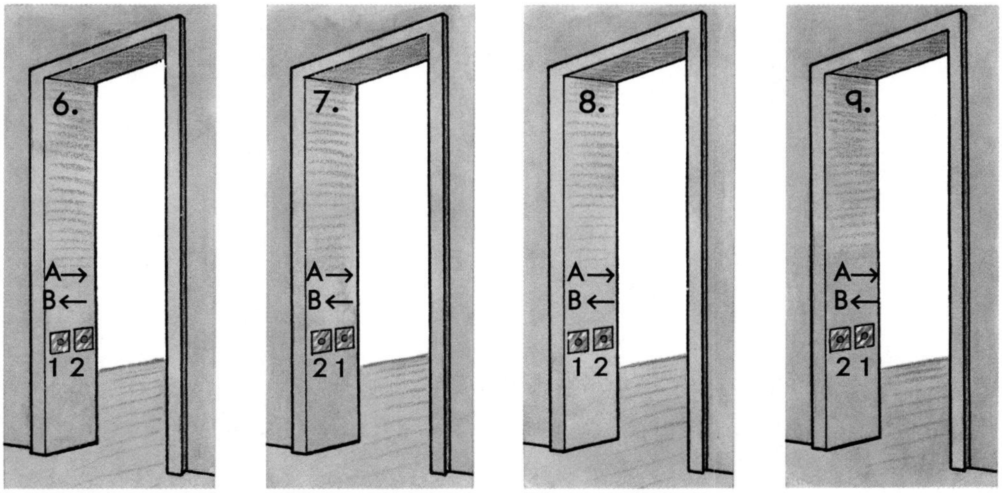

Write the words that go in the blanks to tell about the steps you take to invent something.

10. You start with a _____.

- need
- electric eye
- solution

Then you get an idea for an invention.

11. Then you build a _____ of the invention to show how it works.
12. Then you get a _____ to protect your invention.
13. What are businesses that make things called?
14. Write the letter of the best deal for an inventor.
15. Write the letter of the best deal for a manufacturer.
    a. 8 thousand dollars and two dollars for every copy sold
    b. 8 thousand dollars and six dollars for every copy sold
    c. 8 thousand dollars and four dollars for every copy sold
16. Name 2 things you could give a dog to reward it.

A

1	2	3
1. tune	1. applauded	1. song
2. lamb	2. Homer	2. admission
3. beak	3. sidewalk	3. reminded
4. experience	4. you'd	4. stove
	5. fantastic	5. tour

B

The Animal Show

During the third week that Waldo worked at the pet shop, Maria put this sign in the window of the pet shop:

Every day that week, a large crowd gathered in front of the pet shop after school. Maria would walk outside and say, "Today we'll show you some of the things that you'll see in the show this Friday night." Then she would introduce Waldo to the crowd. She would say, "This is Waldo Greem. He's the person who trained these animals."

Waldo would wave to the crowd and feel embarrassed as they applauded. Then Waldo would bring some animals outside, and the animals would put on one of the tricks. One day, he brought out one of the trained dogs. This dog held a little hammer in its mouth. Waldo put a row of glasses in front of the dog. Each glass had some water in it, but no two glasses had the same amount of water. When the dog tapped a glass with the hammer, the glass made a ringing sound. Here's the rule about the sound each glass made: The more water the glass has, the lower the sound it makes. If the glass is almost empty, it makes a high ring. If the glass is almost filled with water, it makes a very low ring.

Maria told the crowd, "This dog is named Homer. And Homer is going to play 'Mary Had a Little Lamb' on these glasses." Waldo patted the dog on the head and said, "Play the tune." The dog started to tap different glasses. The crowd recognized the song and started to sing as the dog tapped: "Mary had a little lamb, little lamb, little lamb . . ."

When the dog finished playing the song, it stood up on its hind legs and tossed the hammer high into the air. Waldo caught the hammer and threw a little bit of food high into the air. The dog caught the food. The crowd clapped and cheered. "Do it again," some people said. Then other people joined in. "Yes, do it again. Do it again. Do it again."

"Okay," Waldo said. "We'll do it one more time." Waldo gave the hammer back to Homer, patted Homer on the head, and said, "Play the tune."

And the dog played the tune again, without making one mistake.

The crowd clapped. Maria held up her hands to quiet the crowd. "Remember," she said, "this is just

one of the acts that you may see this Friday night at Samson High School. Bring your friends and your family."

On the following afternoon, Waldo had two parrots do tricks on a little swing. The parrots did some amazing things. They held on to the swing with their beaks. They did somersaults on the swing. One parrot stood on the head of the other parrot, and both parrots did a giant somersault. Then one parrot held on to the tail feathers of the other parrot and they spun around and around as the swing went back and forth. From time to time, Waldo would toss a little bit of food to the parrots. They would catch the food with their beaks.

Again the crowd went wild. Again Maria reminded the crowd that the pet shop would put on a full show that Friday night at Samson High School. She reminded the people to bring their friends and family. "Remember," she said, "the admission is only $1.00."

• • •

Waldo looked at the people who were lined up outside Samson High School.

"Wow," he said. "I think they all brought their friends and their families." There was a line of people that went all the way out to the sidewalk and halfway around the block.

Maria said to Waldo, "The show will start in less than an hour. So you'd better go inside and start cooking your food."

"Right," Waldo said. He had brought all the things that he needed to cook. There was a large kitchen in the high school. So he and Maria had decided to do the cooking in the high school. They thought that

plan would be better than cooking in the pet shop and then bringing the food over in a car. Maria had pointed out, "If you cook at the high school, we won't have a thousand animals following the car over to the high school."

So Waldo went to the kitchen of the high school. He laid out the things that he wanted to cook. Then he turned on the stove and waited for it to get hot. He waited and waited. Suddenly, he realized that the stove was not working. He ran from the kitchen and found Maria. "I can't cook," he said. "The stove doesn't work."

Maria didn't say anything for a moment. Then she said, "I'll go back to the pet shop and get some pet food that is supposed to be really good. I just hope the animals will work for that food."

"Me, too," Waldo said.

C Number your paper from 1 through 20.

Skill Items

Use the words in the box to write complete sentences.

folks	disturbed	screeched	cute	audience
delivered	boring	peppy	mobbed	attract

1. The ______ speaker ______ the ______.
2. A lot of ______ ______ around the ______ singer.

Review Items

3. What's the name of geese that are gray and black and white?
4. What's the name of geese that are all white?
5. What color are all geese when they are born?
6. In which direction do geese fly in the fall?
7. What is this trip called?

8. When geese learn to fly, do they start in the water or on the land?
9. They run with their ______ out to the side.

10. The earth is shaped like a ______.
11. The hottest part of the earth is called the ______.
    - pole
    - desert
    - equator

12. How long ago did dinosaurs live on the earth?
    - a hundred years ago
    - a hundred million years ago
    - a million years ago
13. Most of the things that we use everyday were invented after the year ______.
    - 1900 • 2000 • 1800

14. What does an inventor get to protect an invention?
15. Special lawyers who get protection for inventions are called ______.
    - patents
    - dentists
    - patent attorneys

16. Why don't smart manufacturers act interested in the inventions that they want? **Write the letter of the answer.**
    a. because they are at the fair all day long
    b. because they want to pay more for the invention
    c. so they don't have to pay as much for the invention
17. If an invention wins a prize, would a manufacturer have to pay money for it?

Study Items

- Get two glasses that look the same. The glasses must be made of glass, not plastic or paper.
- Fill one glass half full of water.
- Tap the glass and listen to the sound it makes.
- Now fix up the second glass so that it makes the same sound as the first glass.

Write the answers to these items.

18. How much water is in the second glass when both glasses make the same sound?
19. Change the amount of water in the second glass so it makes a sound that is lower than the sound of the first glass. Did you **add water** to the second glass or **take water away?**
20. Find out how a xylophone works and tell how its keys are like glasses of water.

A

1

1. chant
2. flop
3. jammed
4. carrot
5. Gormer
6. lowest
7. pecked

B

A Big Crowd

The large hall in Samson High School was jammed. Maria told Waldo that there were nearly two thousand people in the hall. Some people had come from over thirty miles away to see the show. And when Maria walked out on the stage to announce the first act, the crowd cheered and applauded.

But the show was a complete flop. Each trick started out pretty well, but then the animals stopped performing. The first act was Homer. He played "Mary Had a Little Lamb" without making one mistake. Then he tossed the hammer into the air. Waldo caught it and tossed an ordinary dog treat into the air. The dog caught it, took one bite of it, and spit it out.

The crowd began to chant, "Do it again. Do it again."

"All right," Maria said. "Here is 'Mary Had a Little Lamb' one more time." Waldo handed the hammer to Homer. Waldo patted Homer on the head and said, "Play the tune." Homer looked at Waldo, hit the glass that made the lowest sound three times, and dropped the hammer on the floor. Waldo tried again. He gave the hammer to Homer, patted him on the head, and said, "Play the tune," one more time. This time, Homer just dropped the hammer on the floor and looked down.

Maria came out on the stage smiling. "He's just a little tired, folks. But don't worry, we have other acts."

The other acts were even worse. Gormer the rabbit was next. Here's how Waldo usually rewarded Gormer and the four mice for doing the trick. First, Gormer would stand on the table with his front legs on the tightrope, waiting for the four mice to get on his back. Waldo always gave Gormer a little bit of special food for waiting without moving. As the mice climbed onto Gormer's back, Waldo gave each mouse a little bit of food. Then after the rabbit had walked all the way across the tightrope, Waldo would reward all the animals again with a little bit of food.

This time, Waldo rewarded the rabbit with little pieces of carrot, and he rewarded the mice with little bits of cheese. Here's what happened: Gormer got in place with his front feet on the tightrope. Waldo gave Gormer a little piece of carrot. The rabbit sniffed the carrot and then started to look around.

The four mice climbed onto Gormer's back. As each mouse got in place, Waldo gave the mouse a bit of cheese. Not one of the mice ate the cheese. The first three mice just sniffed it and looked away. The fourth mouse sniffed the cheese and then took a bite out of Waldo's finger. Waldo jumped back very suddenly. The rabbit jumped. The mice jumped and started fighting. The rabbit leaped into the air and ran off the stage. One mouse was still hanging on to Gormer. The others were on the table, still fighting.

The people in the audience started talking to each other. "What's going on?" some of them were saying. "This isn't a very good show at all."

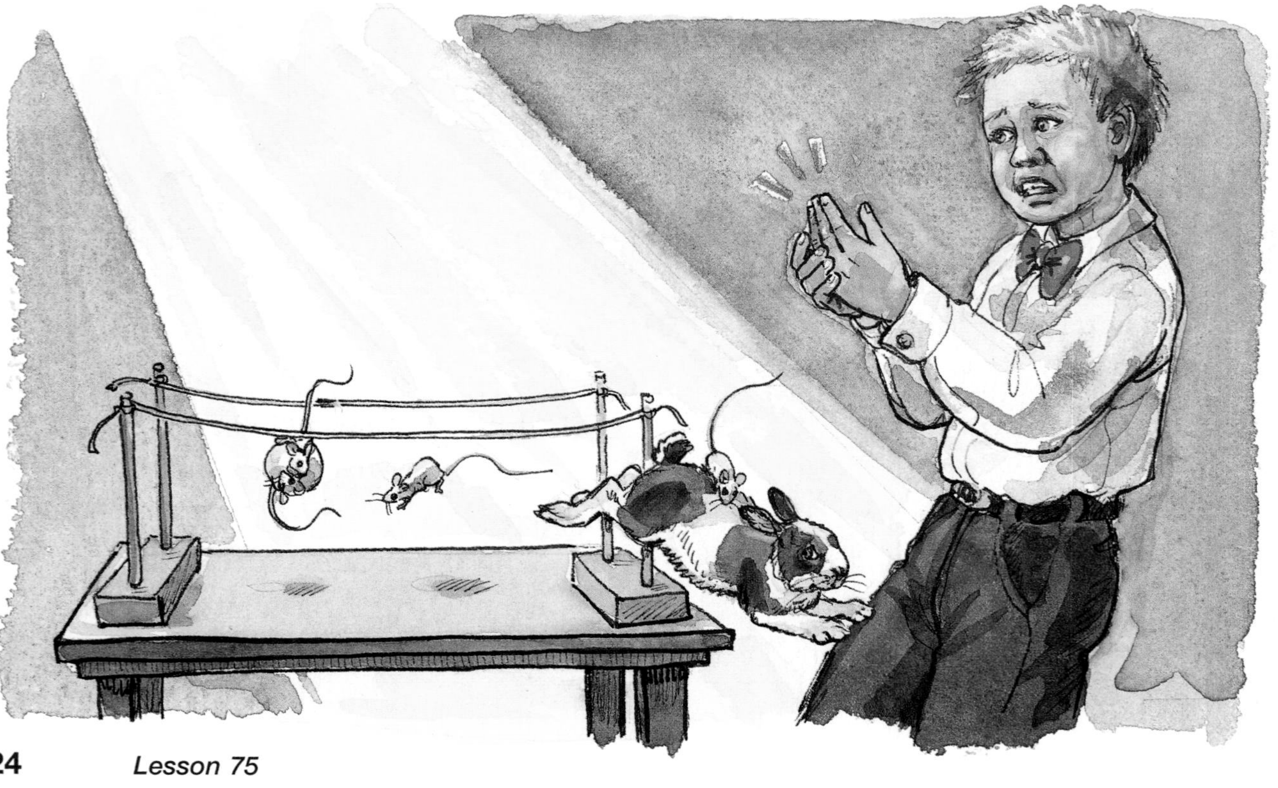

Maria came onto the stage again. "Sorry about that, folks," she said. She was trying to smile. "But you know how animals are. Let's hope our next act will do a little better. This act is one of the most amazing acts you will ever see. If you've never seen pigeons tap dance, this act will be a real treat for you. And here they are, ladies and gentlemen, the tap-dancing pigeons."

The crowd applauded. Some people were saying, "I've seen this act and it is great."

The tap-dancing pigeons weren't very great this time. Waldo brought out the pigeons, turned on the peppy music and gave the birds the signal to start dancing. And they danced quite well, at least for a while. Usually, Waldo would toss them little bits of special food as they danced. This time, he tossed them little bits of bird seed. The birds blinked and spit out the seeds. Before the song was half over, one of them stopped dancing and started to peck at the buttons that were attached to its feet. Then one of the other birds started dancing out of time with the music. Soon that pigeon stopped dancing. It pecked at the third bird. The third bird pecked the first bird. The first bird flew to the back of the hall and landed on top of a picture.

"This is a bad act," somebody shouted from the back of the audience. Again, the people in the audience began to talk to each other. Maria came out on the stage and smiled. She tried to talk, but the people in the audience did not listen. They were busy talking to each other. They were saying things like, "Who said this was a good show?" and "These animals aren't even trained well."

Waldo was thinking, "I hope this show will be over soon."

C Number your paper from 1 through 16.

Skill Items

Here are 3 events that happened in the story. Write **beginning, middle** or **end** for each event.

1. Maria told Waldo that there were nearly two thousand people in the hall.
2. The first bird flew to the back of the hall and landed on top of a picture.
3. Waldo gave Gormer a little piece of carrot.

Review Items

4. The more water the glass has, the ______ the sound it makes.
   - lower
   - higher
5. Write the letter of the glass that will make the lowest ring.
6. Write the letter of the glass that will make the highest ring.

7. The men who invented the first airplane saw a need. What need?

8. What is a person doing when the person makes an object for the first time?
9. The person who makes an object for the first time is called an ______.
10. The object the person makes is called an ______.

11. Whirlpools are made up of moving ______.
12. A whirlpool is shaped like a ______.
13. What happens to something that gets caught in a whirlpool?

14. Things closer to the bottom of the pile went into the pile ______.

15. Does Io move around Jupiter **fast** or **slowly?**
16. It takes Io about ______ to go all the way around Jupiter.

A

1

1. shortly
2. refund
3. angrily
4. softly
5. growl
6. upstairs

B

Problems at the Pet Shop

Half the people left before the show was over. Some of them made comments as they walked out of the large hall. Some said, "This show stinks." Others said things like, "I drove twenty miles to see this show. I should have stayed home."

Maria tried to smile and pretend that everything was going well, but the people in the audience made a lot of noise when she tried to talk. When the show was finished, only a few people clapped. The others just stood up and left.

When the hall was empty, Maria and Waldo went around trying to find the birds and other animals that were hiding. It took them over an hour to find the last animal, Gormer. Then they had to break up a cat fight and another fight between two pigeons.

Waldo felt terrible. "Those people paid money to see this show and it was a terrible flop," he said.

"Well," Maria said and patted him on the back. "I think we've learned something from this experience." Maria continued, "We must make sure that we have the food that you cook. Other food will not work."

"I know," Waldo said and shook his head. "I just feel sorry for all the people who had to sit through our show tonight."

The next day, Waldo had more problems. When he arrived at the pet shop after school, he saw a line of people outside. Each person was carrying one of the trained animals that Maria had sold. The people did not look very happy. Waldo asked a young woman who was holding a trained pigeon, "Is anything wrong?"

"A lot is wrong," she said angrily. "I bought a pigeon that was supposed to dance. It won't dance for me. It danced the first couple of times I turned on the music, but now it just looks at me and blinks. If I try to put buttons on its feet, it pecks me." The woman held out her hand. It had little red marks on it. She said, "See what that bird did to me? I want my money back."

The man who was in front of her said, "I want my money back, too. My rabbit is supposed to walk a tightrope, but the only thing it wants to do is bite me if I try to pick it up."

"We all want our money back," a man near the end of the line said. "Who wants a dog that does nothing but growl at you if you tell it to do a somersault?"

Waldo went inside the pet shop. Maria was busy giving people their money back and putting animals

back in cages. She looked up at Waldo and shook her head. She didn't have to say anything. Waldo knew how she felt.

Waldo didn't put on a show that night. He helped Maria refund money to the people. Shortly before the store closed, they took care of the last person. After that person left, Maria said, "Well, there goes all the money we've made during the last month." She walked to the front window and stared outside for a long time. Then she turned around and said, "Waldo, I don't think our deal is going to work."

"I understand," Waldo said softly. He felt very, very bad. "I understand," he repeated. Then he said, "But I really want to thank you for giving me a chance. I . . ." He couldn't seem to find any more words to say. So he put his head down and walked from the pet shop. He walked home very slowly.

He explained his problem to his parents. His mother said, "Oh, that is too bad."

His father said, "You seem to have a problem, but maybe you can solve it."

"How?" Waldo asked.

"I don't know much about training animals," his father said. "But I think you have a training problem. Your animals will work when you reward them with your special food. But they won't work for any other rewards. Isn't there some way you can train them to work for other rewards?"

"I'm not sure," Waldo said. "But I have a lot of books in my room. I'll read them and find out."

During dinner, Waldo wasn't sad. He could hardly wait to go upstairs and start reading his books. If there was a way to teach the animals to work for other rewards, he would just train the animals that people had returned to the pet shop. Then those animals would not need Waldo's special cooking anymore. During dinner, he kept saying to himself, "I just hope there is a way to train those animals to work for other rewards."

"Waldo," his mother said, "you're hardly eating anything."

His sister said, "He doesn't like any cooking unless it's <u>his</u> cooking."

"That's not true," Waldo said. "I just . . ."

"That's enough," Waldo's father said. "Let's not argue while we're eating."

When dinner was finished, Waldo ran to his room and started looking through his books. "I just hope there is a way," he said to himself.

C Number your paper from 1 through 19.

Skill Items

The tour to the islands was a fantastic experience.

1. What word describes each thing you do?
2. What's another word for a **trip to several places?**
3. What's another word for **wonderful?**

Review Items

4. Which is smaller, Alaska or Japan?
5. Is Japan a **state** or a **country?**
6. How many people live in Japan?
   - 127
   - 127 million
   - 127 thousand
7. Which planet has more clouds around it, Earth or Mars?
8. Which planet is smaller?
9. Which planet is colder?
10. Why is that planet colder?

Use these names to answer the questions:
Tyrannosaurus, Triceratops.

11. What is animal **G?**
12. What is animal **H?**

13. Captain Parker's ship passed through a place where hundreds of ships have sunk or been lost. Name that place.

14. Which came **earlier** on Earth, dinosaurs or horses?

15. Which came **earlier** on Earth, strange sea animals or dinosaurs?

16. Name 3 animals that are warm-blooded.

17. Name 3 animals that are cold-blooded.

18. The picture shows half a hailstone. How many times did the stone go through a cloud?

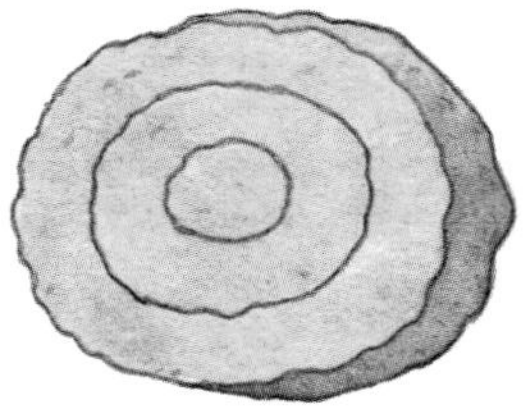

19. How long does it take Jupiter to spin around one time?

77

A

1	2
1. upstairs	1. waste
2. backyard	2. changing
3. tightrope	3. pyramid
4. sidewalk	4. demonstrated

B

Changing the Rewards

The first book that Waldo looked through did not tell about how to train animals to work for new rewards. The second book didn't, either. But there was a big part in the third book. The title of that part was: "Training an Animal to Work for New Rewards."

"Wow," Waldo said, and started to laugh. "I found it! I found it!"

Then he started to read. He kept reading until his mother came into his room and told him that it was very late and that he had to go to bed. He didn't go to sleep right away.

After the lights were turned off, he kept thinking about the things that he had read. In his mind, he began to make up a plan about how he would train the animals to work for new rewards.

He kept remembering the rule that the book gave for teaching animals to like new rewards. Here is that rule: **You slowly change the reward.** The book explained how to change the reward. "You start with the reward the animal will work for. Then you start to change it a little bit at a time. You keep changing it until it is the new reward."

The book told about how to teach a dog to work for a pat on the head. At first the dog will do the trick for a food reward. But the trainer wants the dog to work for a pat on the head. The trainer starts slowly changing the food reward. At first, the trainer gives the dog the food reward, and at the same time, the trainer pats the dog on the head. Later, the trainer starts giving the dog less food each time the dog does the trick and gives the dog more pats on the head.

After a while, the trainer does not give the dog a food reward each time the dog does the trick. Sometimes, the trainer gives the food reward.

But every time the dog does the trick, the trainer gives it pats on the head. After a while, the dog works for just the pats on the head. The trainer does not have to give the dog the food reward.

The next morning, Waldo got up very early and went to the pet shop before going to school. The shop wasn't open yet. He knocked and knocked on the front door until Maria answered. "I was in the back," she said. "I guess I didn't hear you knocking."

Waldo said, "I think I've worked out a solution to our problem. I think I can train the animals to work for regular food. Or maybe I can train them to work for no food at all."

"Do you really think you can do that?" Maria asked.

"I think I can," Waldo replied. "At least I've read part of a book that explains how to do it."

Maria smiled and then shook her head no. "Maybe we'd better not try," she said. "We've had two very bad experiences with your special food rewards."

"Please," Waldo said. "Please, give me one more chance. If it doesn't work, you won't have to pay me. But I really want to try to train those animals so that other people can get them to do their tricks."

Maria smiled again. Then she said very slowly, "Well . . . all right. Let's try to do that."

"Okay," Waldo said, and laughed. "Wow. I can hardly wait until school is over today." Waldo was going to use the rules that he had read about for teaching animals to work for new rewards. The book told which reward you start with. The book then told what you do to that reward. And the book told when you stop changing that reward.

Waldo was going to use these rules. He was going to start with the reward that the animals would work for. Then he was going to slowly change that reward. He was going to keep changing the reward until the animals were working for regular food.

The school day seemed to drag on and on. Waldo looked at his watch every five or ten minutes. Each time, he said to himself, "Will this school day ever be over?"

It seemed as if a whole year passed before the last bell of the school day rang. The kids rushed from their classroom. Waldo was one of the first outside. He ran to the pet shop. When he arrived there, he was out of breath. But he didn't waste a second. He went into the kitchen and fixed some food. He didn't pay much attention to the three dogs and the goat that were looking in the kitchen window. Then he took his food inside the pet shop. The animals were jumping around and making a lot of noise.

Maria looked at him, and he looked at her. With a smile, he said, "Well, I sure hope it works."

Maria said, "We'll soon find out." And they did.

C Number your paper from 1 through 17.

Skill Items

Use the words in the box to write complete sentences.

waste	cute	fantastic	refund	folks
shortly	deserved	experience	tour	mobbed

1. A lot of ______ ______ the ______ singer.
2. The ______ to the islands was a ______ ______.

Review Items

3. Write the letters of 3 types of products that are used in the United States and manufactured in Japan.

   a. books
   b. cars
   c. rugs
   d. TVs
   e. furniture
   f. CD players
   g. Mr. Light Saver

4. Two things happen to melted rock when it moves down the sides of a volcano. Name those two things.
5. What is it called when the earth shakes and cracks?
6. Which uses up more oxygen, sleeping or jumping?
7. What's another name for hot, melted rock?
8. What color is lava when it's very hot?
   - brown
   - orange
   - gray
9. What color is lava after it cools a little bit?
10. What color is lava after it's completely cooled?

11. Which has more gravity, Jupiter or Io?
12. Which is smaller than Earth?
13. Where can you jump 8 feet high?

14. Which has a stronger gravity, Earth or Jupiter?
15. So where would you feel lighter?

16. The earth makes a circle around the sun one time every ___.
17. How many days does it take the earth to make one full circle around the sun?

78

A

1	2
1. retrained	1. regular
2. resold	2. hungry
3. returned	3. couple
4. remind	4. contacted
5. refund	

B New Rewards and a New Super Trick

Waldo took one of the tap-dancing pigeons from its cage. He put the pigeon on the table and gave it a little bit of special food. Then Waldo turned on the peppy music. The pigeon danced and Waldo rewarded it with another tiny bit of special food.

Then Waldo put his hands in the bowl of special food and rubbed the food all over the palms of his hands.

"What are you doing?" Maria asked.

"I'm going to fix up the regular bird seed so that it is more like my special food."

Waldo picked up a handful of birdseed and rubbed until each seed was coated with a little tiny bit of special food. "Let's see if the pigeon likes this bird seed," he said. He tossed one seed in front of the pigeon. Before the seed hit the table, the pigeon caught it in the air with a snap.

Waldo turned on the CD player, and the bird held its wings out and danced in time with the music. When the song was finished, Waldo dropped a couple of coated seeds in front of the pigeon. "Snap, snap." The seeds were gone in an instant.

The bird worked for the new reward. Again Waldo played the tune, and again the pigeon danced. After the song was finished, Waldo gave the bird two coated seeds and one seed that was not coated with special food. "Snap, snap, snap."

Waldo gave that pigeon a rest while he worked with the second pigeon. That pigeon also liked the coated seeds. After it danced, he gave it two coated seeds and one seed that was not coated. "Snap, snap, snap."

Waldo went back to the first pigeon. This time he gave the pigeon one coated seed and two regular seeds. "Snap, snap, snap."

Before Waldo went home that night, all three pigeons were working for three regular seeds.

Waldo trained the other animals the same way he trained the pigeons. To train the rabbit to work for regular food, he rubbed his hands over bits of carrots. When the rabbit first did the trick on the tightropes, he gave it a tiny bit of his special food. Next, he gave it two pieces of coated carrots. "GULP, GULP." The next time the rabbit did the trick, he gave it two pieces of coated carrots and a tiny piece of carrot that was not coated. "GULP, GULP, gulp."

By the end of the day, the rabbit was walking the tightrope for three pieces of regular carrot.

"I think it's going to work," Waldo announced.

"I think you're right," Maria said.

Before Waldo and Maria left the pet shop that night, Maria called the people who had returned the trained pigeons and the trained rabbit. "I think we've fixed the problem," she told them. "Why don't you stop by and we'll show you how that animal performs now. You don't have to buy it back if you don't want to. But that animal will do the trick now."

The next day, all the people who had returned pets came back to the pet shop. Maria demonstrated how the retrained pets would work for regular food. All the people bought their pets back.

As soon as Waldo got to the pet shop after school, he started to train some animals to do a super trick. Waldo got the idea for the super trick from working with the mice that sat on Gormer's back. Waldo said to himself, "Why not make a super trick with many, many animals piled up?" His first idea was to make a regular pyramid of animals. For a regular pyramid there would be a row of animals standing on the floor.

On top of the bottom row would be another smaller row of animals. On top of the smaller row would be a row that was even smaller. At the top of the pyramid would be one animal.

This picture shows a regular pyramid of animals:

The more Waldo thought about the regular pyramid, the less he liked the idea. The trick seemed too easy. So Waldo started to think of a better trick. After a few moments, he got the idea for a pyramid that was upside-down. This pyramid wouldn't have one animal at the top of the pyramid. It would have one animal at the bottom. Two animals would stand on that animal. Four animals would stand on top of the two animals. And eight animals would stand on top of the four animals.

This picture shows that upside-down pyramid:

It was after four o'clock when Waldo got the idea for the upside-down pyramid, so he didn't have much time to work on it before the shop closed. He started with the animal that would stand at the bottom of the pyramid. That animal was a great big dog, strong enough to hold many, many animals. He took the dog from its cage and trained it to stand still in the middle of the floor. The training took only a few minutes and a little bit of Waldo's special food.

Now Waldo brought out two smaller dogs. First he put them on the back of the huge dog. When all the dogs stood still, he rewarded all of them with a bit of special food. Next, Waldo trained the smaller dogs to jump onto the back of the larger dog. He trained the black dog to stand with its paws on the huge dog's head. He trained the spotted dog to stand on the huge dog's rear end.

After the three dogs were trained, Waldo started to work on the harder part of the trick. He had to train four animals to stand on the dogs. He decided to train cats to do this part of the trick. Dogs don't usually like to have cats standing on their backs, and cats don't usually like to stand on dogs. But Waldo used his special food to reward the animals. So before the shop closed, Waldo had trained three dogs and four cats for the first part of the super trick.

C Number your paper from 1 through 21.

Story Items

1. Why didn't Waldo like his idea of making a regular pyramid?
2. What super trick is Waldo training the animals to do?
3. What animal will be at the bottom of that pyramid?
4. What was the first animal that Waldo trained for the super trick?
5. The two smaller dogs had to jump to a special place on the big dog's back. Which dog stood with its paws on the huge dog's head?
6. Which dog stood on the huge dog's rear end?

Review Items

7. When you teach animals to work for new rewards, do you change the reward **quickly** or **slowly?**
8. When you teach an animal to work for a new reward, what kind of reward do you start with?
9. Then what do you do to that reward?
10. When do you stop changing the reward?
11. When you teach an animal a simple trick, when do you reward the animal?
12. When don't you reward the animal?
13. Let's say that you want to teach an animal a very hard trick. Can the animal do the trick at first?
14. What will happen if the animal doesn't receive any rewards until it does the trick?
15. When you're teaching the animal a hard trick, what do you reward the animal for doing?

Write the name of each animal in the picture.

16.

17.

18.

19.

20.

21.

79

A

1

1. Greeley
2. upside-down
3. spoke
4. shown
5. perfectly
6. whistled
7. information

B

Colorado and Utah

In a later lesson, Waldo and Maria go to two states in the United States—Colorado and Utah. First they go to two cities in Colorado—Denver, Colorado, and Greeley, Colorado. Then they go to the state of Utah.

The map shows these places. The map also shows the great mountains that Waldo and Maria drive over when they go from Colorado to Utah. These mountains are called the Rocky Mountains.

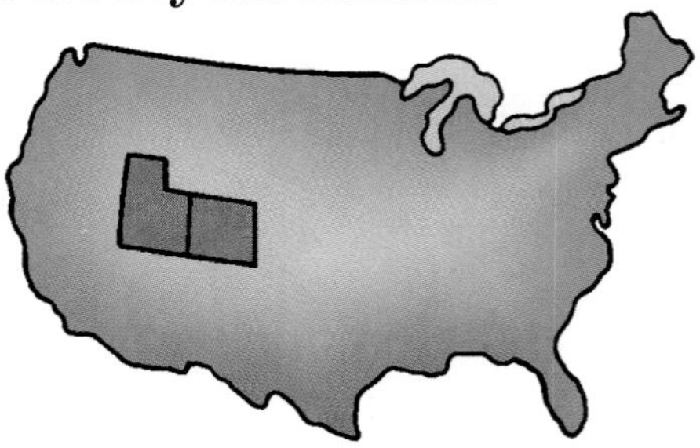

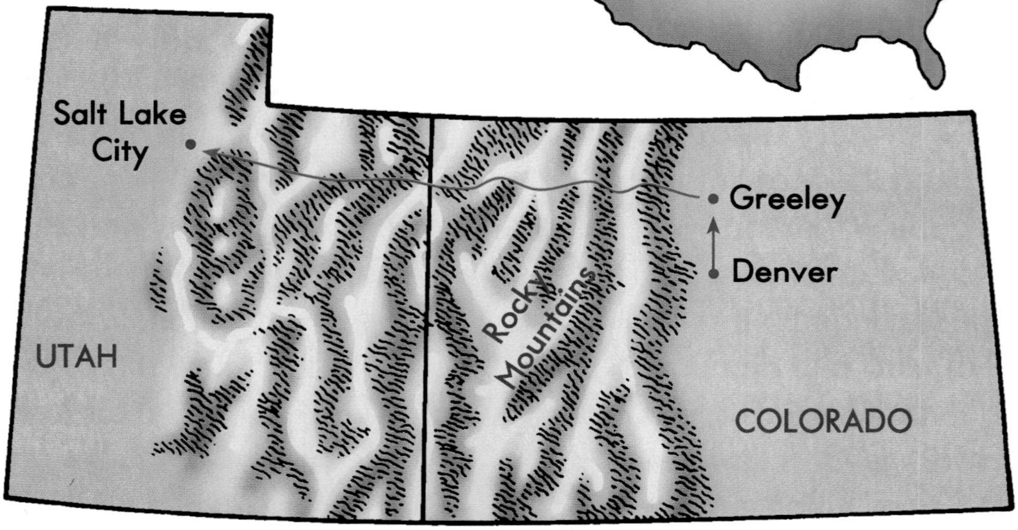

C

A Great Show

Just before the pet shop closed, Waldo showed Maria the animals he had just trained. "Watch this," he said. He used his hand to give the large dog a signal. The large dog walked to the middle of the floor and stood still. Waldo then signaled the black dog and the spotted dog. They ran up to the huge dog and jumped on its back. Then Waldo signaled the four cats. Two of them jumped on the back of the black dog and two of them jumped on the back of the spotted dog.

Maria said, "That's amazing."

"Yeah," Waldo said. "And that's just the first part of the trick. But watch this."

Waldo turned to the animals and said, "Speak!"

All the animals spoke. The huge dog spoke with a very deep "Woof." The dogs on top spoke with sharp barks: "Ruf, ruf." The cats on top of the dogs spoke with loud meows.

Maria laughed. "Oh, that's a great trick," she said.

Waldo said, "Just wait until I train the rest of the animals for that upside-down pyramid. We'll have a super trick."

Waldo went on to explain how he planned to complete the pyramid. He told her that he planned to train eight squirrels to stand on the four cats and sixteen pigeons to stand on the eight squirrels. Waldo concluded by saying, "The next time we put on a show, it will be the greatest animal show that anybody ever saw."

Maria said, "I hope so. Every time I think of the first show we put on, I feel like dying."

Waldo said, "It will be different next time."

And he was right.

• • •

The hall at Samson High School was packed again. For a week before the show, Maria and Waldo had shown some of the acts that would be in the show. Each day, outside the pet shop, they showed a different act. There was one that they didn't show—the upside-down pyramid. Waldo didn't want anybody to see this act before the show.

Just like the first show at Samson High School, some people had come from thirty miles away to see the show. But Waldo didn't worry about cooking his special food this time, because all the animals had been trained to work for regular food. When Waldo trained animals for a new trick, he used his special food because the animals would do anything to get that food. So the animals that made the upside-down pyramid had started out with special food, but now they worked for regular food. So did all the other animals in Waldo's acts.

Maria walked onto the stage at Samson High School and the audience applauded. She bowed and waved. Then she announced the first act, the dancing pigeons. They danced in time with the music. The audience went wild. "Again," they shouted. And Waldo gave the pigeons the signal to dance again. They did it without making a mistake.

The next act was Homer the dog. He played "Mary Had a Little Lamb" without a mistake. People in the audience clapped in time with the music. "Again," they shouted after the act was finished. So Waldo gave Homer the signal to do the trick again and Homer performed without a mistake.

After each animal performed, Waldo rewarded it with some bits of regular food.

The next act was Gormer the rabbit, who walked the tightropes with four mice on his back. They performed perfectly. "Again," the crowd shouted, and the animals did the trick again.

Then Waldo brought out a new act. This act had been shown in front of the pet shop. It was a very good act, but not a super act. Three striped cats howled and meowed in time with the music. Waldo put on a CD. As soon as the music started, the cats sang. As they sang, they sat up with their front paws under their chin. The audience laughed and wanted the cats to perform again. So Waldo played the CD again, and again the cats howled and meowed in time with the music.

Next was the dog that did backward somersaults in the air. First Waldo held out a stick and signaled the dog to jump over the stick. Then Waldo signaled the dog to roll over, to sit up, to speak and to walk on its hind legs. Then Waldo signaled the dog to do the backward somersaults. When the dog started to do the somersaults, the people in the audience counted together, "One . . . two . . . three . . . four . . . five . . . six." Then the people applauded, as Waldo tossed some dog treats to the dog.

Now came the super act.

D Number your paper from 1 through 16.

Story Items

1. Did Waldo use his special food to reward the animals during the animal show?
2. What did he use?
3. One act was the dog that did backward somersaults. What did the audience do while that dog did somersaults?
4. How many somersaults did the dog do?
5. What act comes right after the dog that does somersaults?

Skill Items

Here are 3 events that happened in the story. Write **beginning, middle** or **end** for each event.

6. Waldo gave the pigeons the signal to dance again.
7. Just before the pet shop closed, Waldo showed Maria the animals he had just trained.
8. Next was the dog that did backward somersaults in the air.

Review Items

Fill in each blank with the word **top** or the word **bottom.**

9. A regular pyramid has one animal at the ______ of the pyramid.
10. An upside-down pyramid has one animal at the ______ of the pyramid.

Let's say you're training a dog to jump up in the air and do a backward somersault. Use the words below to finish each sentence.

- jumping up and turning upside down
- jumping up and leaning backward
- jumping up in the air

11. At first, you would reward the dog for ______.
12. Later you would reward the dog for ______.
13. Later you would reward the dog for ______.

- On planet A you can jump 10 feet high.
- On planet B you can jump 30 feet high.
- On planet C you can jump 5 feet high.
- On planet D you can jump 20 feet high.
- On planet E you can jump 3 feet high.

14. Write the letter of the planet that has the most gravity.
15. Write the letter of the planet that has the least gravity.

16. Could you see very far on Jupiter with bright lights?

Number your paper from 1 through 26.

1. When you teach an animal a simple trick, when do you reward the animal?
2. When don't you reward the animal?

3. Let's say that you want to teach an animal a very hard trick. Can the animal do the trick at first?
4. What will happen if the animal doesn't receive any rewards until it does the trick?
5. So when you're teaching the animal a hard trick, what do you reward the animal for doing?

6. The more water the glass has, the ______ the sound it makes.
   - lower
   - higher
7. Which glass will make the lowest ring?
8. Which glass will make the highest ring?

A B C D E F

9. When you teach animals to work for new rewards, do you change the reward **quickly** or **slowly?**
10. When you teach an animal to work for a new reward, what kind of reward do you start with?
11. Then what do you do to that reward?
12. When do you stop changing the reward?

Fill in each blank with the word **top** or the word **bottom.**

13. A regular pyramid has one animal at the ______ of the pyramid.
14. An upside-down pyramid has one animal at the ______ of the pyramid.

15. In what country are the states of Colorado and Utah?
16. Name the mountains you drive over to get from Colorado to Utah.
17. In which direction do you go to get from Colorado to Utah?
18. Name **2** cities in Colorado.
19. Name one city in Utah.

20. Which letter shows Colorado?
21. Which letter shows Utah?

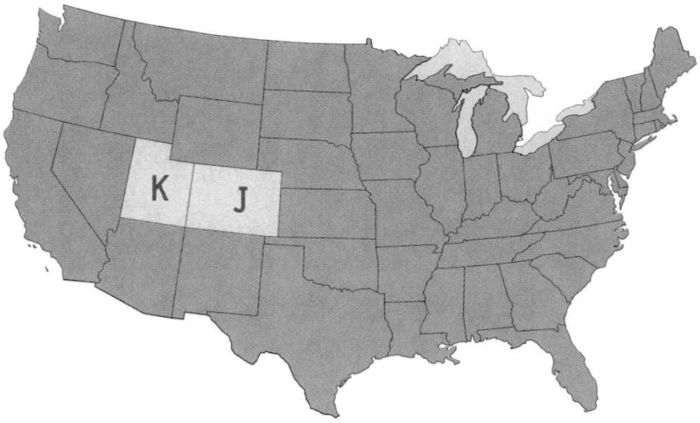

Skill Items

For each item, write the underlined word from the sentences in the box.

A lot of folks mobbed the cute singer.
The tour to the islands was a fantastic experience.

22. What underlining means **wonderful?**
23. What underlining means **good-looking and charming?**
24. What underlining describes each thing you do?
25. What underlining means **crowded around?**
26. What underlining means **people?**

A

1	2
1. success	1. woman's
2. Christmas	2. trailer
3. fantastic	3. tours
4. hire	4. schoolwork
5. officer	5. contacted

B

Plans for a Trip

Maria walked out to the middle of the stage. "Ladies and gentlemen," she said. "You know that dogs don't like cats and cats don't like squirrels and squirrels don't get along well with birds. You're going to love this next act because it involves dogs, cats, squirrels and birds. All these animals will work together to form an upside-down pyramid. So welcome all these animals and watch them work together." The audience welcomed the animals by clapping very loudly.

All the animals came onto the stage and faced the audience. First the large dog walked out and stood in the middle of the stage.

Then the two smaller dogs walked out and took their places, one on each side of the huge dog.

Then the four cats came out. Two went on one side of the stage and two went on the other. The squirrels came out next. The audience laughed as the squirrels took their places with their long tails held high in the air.

The last animals to come out on the stage were the birds—sixteen pigeons. When all the animals were lined up facing the audience, Waldo gave them a signal and all of them bowed. The animals with four legs bowed by lifting one front paw and then bending forward. The birds crossed their legs and bent forward. People in the audience laughed and shouted.

Then Waldo gave a signal to the two smaller dogs. They jumped onto the back of the huge dog. Next, Waldo signaled the cats. They took their place. People in the audience were pointing and laughing and talking. Waldo felt very good.

Next, Waldo signaled the squirrels. When they took their place, the audience applauded so loudly that it sounded like thunder. Maria walked to the middle of the stage and said, "And now for the top of the pyramid, sixteen pigeons."

Waldo signaled the pigeons. They took off and flew over the audience. They circled the hall three times. Everybody watched them. Then Waldo whistled loudly and all the birds landed on top of the squirrels. At first the audience didn't clap. Everybody just went "Ohhh," and "Oooo," and "Wow." Then the people clapped and cheered and stood up and cheered louder.

Waldo said to himself, "That's a good trick."

• • •

For a few days after the big show at Samson High School, Waldo felt very excited. People stopped him on the street and said things like, "We saw your show. It was fantastic." Waldo always thanked the people, but he felt a little embarrassed.

Things were very busy at the pet shop. Maria didn't have enough pets to fill the orders for trained dogs, trained pigeons and trained cats. Some people put in special orders. One man wanted a cat that would ring a bell when it wanted to go outside. An old woman wanted a dog that would keep rabbits and birds out of her garden.

A truck driver wanted a trained cat that would ride in the truck with her and honk the truck horn when the woman gave it a signal.

So Maria was on the phone most of the time taking orders, and Waldo was busy training animals. One day, Maria told Waldo, "We've never had this much business, not even at Christmas time."

Five days after the big show at Samson High School, Maria asked Waldo, "How would you like to go on a tour?"

"What's that?" Waldo asked.

"A tour is a traveling show." She continued, "We go to one city and put on a show. Then we go to the next city and put on a show. The tour that I'm thinking about would take about a month. We'd put on shows in over thirty cities."

"Wow," Waldo said. "That's great." Then he hesitated. "But . . . "

Before he could tell Maria what the problem was, she said, "I know what you're thinking. You're wondering how you'll do your schoolwork if you're on this trip."

"That's right," Waldo said. "If I'm out of school for a month, I'll be far behind in my schoolwork."

"I've already taken care of that," Maria said. "I've called your school and told them about the tour. They're going to tell me what work will be covered in the classes that you're taking. On the tour, I'll go over that work with you. I'll be your teacher."

Waldo smiled. "Do you mean we'll study on the tour?"

"Sure," she said. "We're going to take a small truck and a big trailer. The animals will be in the trailer. You and I will be in the truck. We'll hire a driver to drive the truck. So you and I can study as we go from city to city."

Maria went on to explain that a person who puts on tours for good shows contacted her and set up the places they would go. "And we'll make a lot of money," Maria said. "All we need now is permission from your parents."

• • •

"Waldo, you're hardly eating," Waldo's mother said. "What's the matter?"

Waldo's sister said, "Oh, he doesn't eat any food unless he . . ."

"That's enough," Waldo's father said. Then he turned to Waldo and said, "I feel that you're trying to tell us something. What is it?"

"Well," Waldo said slowly. "Can I go on a tour and put on shows in over thirty cities with the animals?"

Waldo's mother sat up very straight and put her fork down. "What are you talking about?" she said. "What tour? Which cities?"

So Waldo explained the tour. Then he added, "I'll get my schoolwork done. The school has given permission. Everything is all set if you give me permission. Can I go?"

C Number your paper from 1 through 11.

Skill Items

She will contact the person we want to hire.

1. What word tells about giving somebody a job?
2. What word tells about getting in touch with somebody?

Review Items

3. When you're training an animal, what do you do each time the animal does the trick?
4. What do you do if the animal does not do the trick?
5. Name **2** things you could give a dog to reward it.

Write the name of each animal in the picture.

6.

7.

8.

9.

10.

11.

A

1	2	3
1. emergency brake	1. platform	1. success
2 confidence	2 haven't	2. hooked
3. conversation	3. understood	3. tires
4. avoid	4. pickup	4. pressed
5. bare	5. steering	5. winding
6. gear		

B

On the Tour

Waldo had just asked his parents an important question.

Waldo's father said, "I'd like to talk to Maria and get a little more information about this trip. But if the tour is like you say it is, I don't see any problem."

Waldo's father stood up. "I'll call her right now." He walked toward the phone. Before he could pick it up, it rang. He answered, "Hello." Then there was a long pause. "No," he said. "We haven't seen any goats around here for days. If I see one with a red collar, I'll be sure to let you know." He hung up the phone.

Then Waldo's father called Maria. "Tell me about this tour," he said. He talked on the phone for about five minutes. He didn't say much except, "Yes, yes," and "Well, that sounds fine," and "Oh, I see."

After he hung up, he went into the other room with Waldo's mother.

He came back and called Maria again. “That sounds like a very good tour,” he said. “We’ll let Waldo go on it.”

Waldo jumped up from his chair. “I’m going!” he said. “I’m going on a tour! Oh, boy!”

Waldo’s brother said, “I’ll bet Waldo will want to make a lot of food before he goes. Don’t let him cook here.”

Waldo’s mother said, “Don’t worry, dear. Waldo can do all his cooking at the pet shop. And you should try to be nice to your brother, because he’s going to be gone for a month.”

• • •

The tour was a fantastic success. The halls in all the cities were sold out. People were lined up for blocks outside some of the halls. There were posters and ads in the newspapers. At the top of the posters and ads were the words: “The most incredible animal show on Earth.”

The tour took Waldo and Maria to Denver, Colorado. That was their sixth show. From Denver, they went to another city in Colorado—Greeley. Then they started the long drive over the Rocky Mountains. Their next stop was in the state of Utah, on the other side of the Rocky Mountains.

After leaving Greeley, Waldo and Maria were trying to study in the truck as the driver took them up the winding mountain roads. Waldo had trouble keeping his mind on the work, because the view outside was incredible. Waldo had never seen mountains like these before. Their tops were covered with snow, and they were so big and steep that he could hardly believe what he was seeing. From time to time, the truck would go near the edge of the road and Waldo could look down. Each time he looked down, he would get an uneasy feeling. The mountains seemed to go almost straight down, down, down. Every now and then he caught himself thinking, “If the truck ever went over the edge . . .” Then he would stop himself and try to think about how beautiful the mountains were.

After a while, Maria said, “I’ll tell you what. Let’s stop trying to study for a while. Let’s just look at the mountains.”

An hour later, the truck was still winding its way through the mountains. Now the truck was near the top of the highest mountains. Deep banks of snow were on either side of the road. A mountain goat was standing on some bare rocks that were sticking out of the snow.

Then the truck came to a sign that said, “Check your brakes—long downgrade.”

“What does that sign mean?” Waldo asked.

The driver said, "We're going to start going down the other side of the mountain now, and we'll be going down for a long, long time. You don't want to go down this part of the road unless you have good brakes."

The pickup truck started down the winding road. At first it moved slowly. Then Waldo noticed that the truck was gaining speed. Waldo looked over at the driver. The driver's face had a serious expression, and Waldo noticed that he was holding the steering wheel so hard that parts of his hands were white.

Maria asked, "Aren't you going a little fast for this road?"

The driver said, "The trailer brakes aren't working." The driver continued, "The truck brakes are all right. But they're working very hard, and they'll start to fade out soon."

Waldo remembered back to the time when they were getting ready to leave on the trip. The driver hooked up a line from the trailer to the truck. He had explained to Waldo that the line was connected to the brakes on the trailer. When the driver put on the truck brakes, the trailer brakes would also work. The driver had told Waldo that the trailer was so heavy that it needed its own brakes. Without those brakes, the pickup truck would have a hard time stopping.

Now the truck was going very fast down the mountain. The tires screeched as the truck went around a sharp curve. For a moment, it seemed as if the truck would go over the edge. In fact, the truck went through some stones on the side of the road. Then it came back on the road and continued to gain speed.

The driver said, "The trailer is pushing us, and the truck brakes are gone now."

The truck seemed to be flying down the road. It came up behind a car that was loaded with camping gear. The driver of the pickup truck honked the horn and went around the car like it was standing still. Faster, faster, faster. The truck was now on a long, straight part of the road, but the grade was very steep and the truck was going so fast that the engine sounded as if it was ready to fly apart. Waldo could smell the burnt-out brakes.

Waldo was almost afraid to look outside, so he watched the driver. The driver had his foot pressed down hard on the brake pedal, but the pickup truck continued to speed down the long, straight part of the road. The driver turned on the truck lights and pressed his hand against the horn. Waldo understood what the driver was trying to do. He was trying to warn the other cars on the road that the truck was in trouble. The sounds were terrible—the engine screaming, the horn blasting, the air rushing outside the truck. And the smell of the burnt-out brakes was strong. Waldo felt sick. He tried not to think about what was happening. He tried not to think about his animals in the trailer and what might happen to them.

C Number your paper from 1 through 8.

Skill Items

Use the words in the box to write complete sentences.

experience	regular	fastened	fantastic	hire
couple	tour	contact	remind	difficult

1. The [redacted] to the islands was a [redacted] [redacted].
2. She will [redacted] the person we want to [redacted].

Review Items

3. The pilot of Traveler Four turned off the engines when the spaceship was out in space. Did the ship slow down?
4. Was there any air outside the spaceship?
5. Which planets have stronger gravities, the bigger planets or the smaller planets?
6. A person weighs 100 pounds on Planet A and 90 pounds on Planet B. Which planet has stronger gravity?

7. The arrow on the map goes from San Francisco to [redacted].
8. Which ocean does the arrow cross?

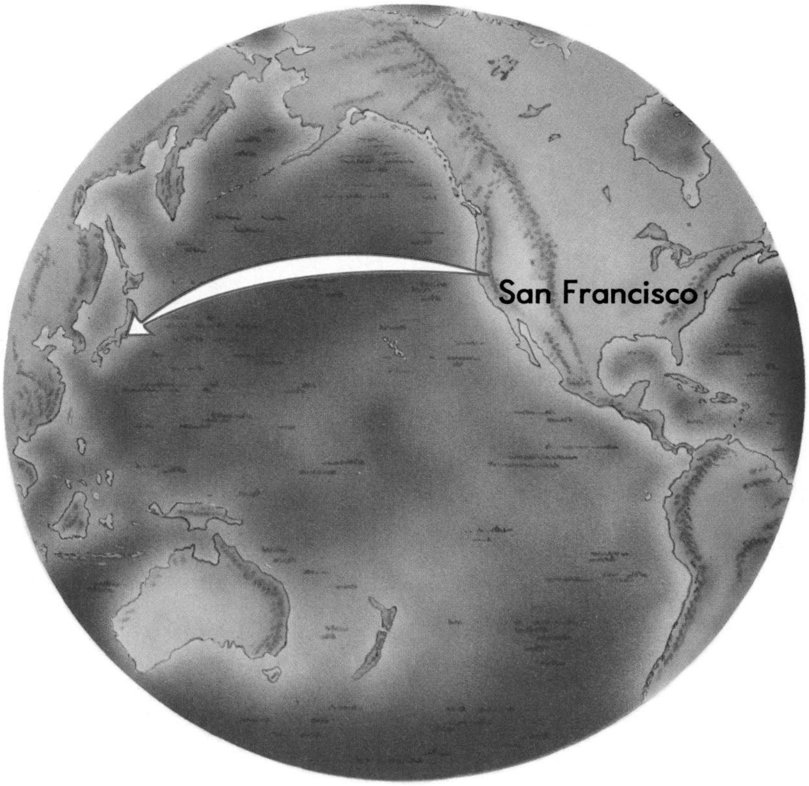

83

A

1	2
1. schoolwork	1. platform
2. understood	2. avoid
3. pickup	3. sharply
4. policemen	4. conversation
	5. emergency
	6. confidence

B

The Pyramid

"Isn't there anything we can do?" Maria shouted.

"There's an emergency brake in the trailer," the driver said. "But I don't know how we can get back there to push down on it."

Waldo turned around and looked at the trailer. It was like a big box with a little window facing the truck. The window was too small for anybody to climb through.

Waldo asked, "How does the emergency brake work and where is it?"

The driver explained, "The brake is on the left side of the trailer. It's on a little platform. But you have to push down on it with a lot of weight to make it work. You have to press down on it with the weight of at least 80 pounds."

The truck was speeding toward another curve. It wasn't a very sharp curve, but the truck and trailer almost tipped over when it went around the curve. The truck started to slide and the tires screeched. The rear wheels of the truck started to slide off the road. Waldo looked down. For a moment he didn't breathe. Then the truck came back onto the road. A car coming the other way was right in front of the truck. The truck driver kept honking the horn. The car turned sharply. The truck just missed the car and continued to fly down the road.

"I'm going to work that emergency brake," Waldo yelled.

He opened the back window of the truck and climbed through it into the pickup bed. Just then, the truck went around another curve. The curve was not very sharp, but the truck was going so fast that

Waldo almost fell out of the truck bed. His heart was pounding and he had trouble breathing, because the wind was blowing so hard.

He crawled to the back of the truck bed, stood up, and leaned against the front of the trailer. The little window was open. Inside, he could see the animals. They looked frightened. They were either lying down or standing with their legs far apart so that they wouldn't fall down. The dogs and cats were panting.

Waldo called the huge dog that stood at the bottom of the pyramid. The dog was lying in the middle of the floor. When Waldo called, the dog stopped panting and looked at Waldo, but the dog did not move. Waldo stuck his hand through the open window and gave the dog a signal to walk to the left side of the trailer. Waldo called the dog three times and gave the signal three times before the dog slowly stood up and followed the signal.

When the dog got near the platform with the emergency brake on it, Waldo gave the dog a signal to put its front paws on the platform. "Up," Waldo shouted. "Get up." The dog looked at Waldo. Then, as the truck trembled and rocked from side to side, the huge dog put one paw on the platform and then the other paw on the platform. The emergency brake was right in front of the dog's paws. "Forward!" Waldo shouted. The huge dog moved its paws forward. Now the dog's two front paws were on the brake pedal, pushing down.

"Good," Waldo shouted. "Good boy."

But the trailer did not slow down. Although the dog weighed more than 100 pounds, the dog did not have all its weight on the brake pedal. Only the dog's front paws were on the brake. So only part of the dog's weight was pushing down on the brake.

"I need more weight on that brake," Waldo said to himself. Waldo turned around to see where the truck was going. Far ahead down the road was a curve—a sharp one. If the truck went into that curve at high speed, the truck would go off the mountain.

Waldo signaled the two smaller dogs. "Make a pyramid," he said, and gave the dogs a hand signal.

The two smaller dogs seemed afraid to try to jump on the huge dog. The spotted dog tried but fell off. The black dog tried and managed to stay on the huge dog's back. Then the spotted dog tried again. This time, that dog stayed on the huge dog's back.

The truck was starting to slow down. It was moving at a terrible speed, but Waldo could feel it start to slow down. Waldo turned around and looked at the sharp curve ahead of the truck. It wasn't far away now, and it was getting closer by the second. The dogs were not putting enough weight on the brake to make the truck stop fast.

"Cats," Waldo yelled. "Cats, get on the pyramid." He signaled the cats. For a moment, they stood without moving. Then, with one great leap, the first cat jumped onto the back of the spotted dog. Then another cat, and another. Finally, the last cat got on the pyramid.

The truck was almost to the curve.

C Number your paper from 1 through 15.

Review Items

1. Does Io move around Jupiter **fast** or **slowly?**
2. It takes Io about ____ to go all the way around Jupiter.

3. What planet is shown in the picture?
4. Which is bigger, the "eye" of the planet or Earth?

5. How long does it take Jupiter to spin around one time?

6. The more water the glass has, the ____ the sound it makes.
   - lower
   - higher
7. Write the letter of the glass that will make the lowest ring.
8. Write the letter of the glass that will make the highest ring.

9. In what country are the states of Colorado and Utah?
10. Name the mountains you drive over to get from Colorado to Utah.
11. In which direction do you go to get from Colorado to Utah?
12. Name **2** cities in Colorado.
13. Name one city in Utah.

14. Which letter shows Colorado?
15. Which letter shows Utah?

A

1	2
1. police officer	1. deathly
2. instructor	2. bravery
3. claws	3. highway
4. screw	4. directing
5. unhappy	5. earrings
6. jewelry	

B

Facts About Coral

When you are underwater in a warm ocean, you may see more than 20 different kinds of coral.

The picture shows three kinds of coral.

Staghorn coral

Brain coral

Red coral

In some places, you'll see underwater hills that are covered with coral. These places are called coral reefs.

Here are some facts about coral reefs:

- The coral is made up of the skeletons of tiny animals.
- Those animals do not swim around. They live and die in one place.
- The coral is easy to destroy but takes years and years to grow back.
- Some kinds of coral, like red coral, are very valuable because they are now very rare. They are used to make jewelry. Here's a picture of earrings made of red coral.

C The Animals' Greatest Show

Inside the trailer, four cats were standing on two dogs. One of the dogs started to howl because the cat was digging into the dog with its claws. But the dog kept its place and the cats kept their place on the pyramid. And the truck was stopping very fast now. In fact, it was stopping so fast that the animals almost fell over. Slower, slower, slower. The truck was at the curve now, but it was hardly moving. Then it came to a stop right in the middle of the curve. The driver jumped out of the truck and opened the back door of the trailer. He ran over to the emergency brake and turned a screw that kept the brake locked in place.

Waldo was right behind the driver. The pyramid was still standing. All the animals were panting. The spotted dog looked very unhappy. One of the cats on that dog's back was the one that was hanging on with its claws.

"Can they move now?" Waldo asked.

"Yeah," the driver said. "The brake is locked."

Cars were stopping in back of the trailer. Two of them were police cars. People were starting to gather around the trailer.

"Okay," Waldo said to the animals. "Get down." The cats jumped from the smaller dogs and the smaller dogs jumped from the back of the huge dog. Waldo hugged the huge dog. "You saved our lives," he said. Then he hugged the other dogs and he petted the cats. He thanked each animal. The animals started to calm down.

A police officer was now looking inside the door of the trailer. "What happened?" he asked. Maria was standing next to him. She explained.

As Maria talked to the police officer, Waldo looked at the animals in the trailer and said, "I'm going to give all of you a special treat." He went to the front of the trailer and opened a pot that was filled with his special food. He gave each animal a treat. Now they were very calm and very happy.

He asked Maria, "Do you think it would be all right if I let them out of the trailer for a couple of minutes?"

"Sure," Maria said.

By now a large crowd had gathered around the truck and trailer. When the dogs, cats, squirrels and rabbits jumped from the trailer, somebody in the crowd said, "I saw this act in Denver. It was great."

"Me, too," some of the other people said.

Now the pigeons were flying from the trailer and starting to circle over it. One police officer said, "Are all these animals trained to do tricks?"

"They sure are," Waldo said.

The driver was talking to two police officers. Two other police officers were directing traffic around the truck and trailer. But nearly all the cars that came by stopped, and the people got out to join the crowd.

Then somebody from the crowd said, "Could you do one trick for us?"

Waldo looked at Maria. She smiled. "I'll show you the trick that I like best," Waldo said.

Waldo signaled the huge dog to stand next to the road. Then he signaled the two smaller dogs. They jumped onto the back of the huge dog. Then came the cats. Then came the squirrels. Finally, Waldo whistled and sixteen pigeons landed on the squirrels. For a moment, the crowd was silent. Then people began to clap and cheer. "That's amazing," some of them shouted.

"Yes," Waldo said. "That's the best trick in the world." It was the best trick in the world because it saved so many lives.

Waldo signaled the pigeons and they flew from the pyramid. The squirrels jumped down, the cats jumped down, followed by the two smaller dogs.

Within an hour, the brakes on the trailer and the truck were fixed, and the truck continued on its way to Utah. A long line of cars followed the trailer.

The show in Utah was a great success. The newspapers carried stories about the experience that Waldo and Maria had in the Rocky Mountains.

Waldo was very pleased with the show. But the show that he remembered as the greatest one his animals ever did took place in a trailer that was speeding down a mountain road.

D Number your paper from 1 through 20.

Review Items

1. If you can see the sun, it is _____ on your side of the earth.
2. What is it on the other side of the earth?
3. The earth turns around one time every _____ hours.
4. What kind of boat do Eskimos use in the summer?
5. Why don't they use those boats in the winter?
6. How long ago did dinosaurs live on the earth?
    - a hundred years ago
    - a hundred million years ago
    - a million years ago

7. Which planet in the picture has more gravity?
8. How do you know?

Planet R   Planet F

9. If an object weighed 20 pounds on Earth, would it weigh more than 20 pounds on our moon?
10. Which is larger, Earth or Jupiter?
11. If an object weighed 20 pounds on Earth, would it weigh more than 20 pounds or less than 20 pounds on Jupiter?

Let's say you're training a dog to jump up in the air and do a backward somersault. **Use the words below to finish each sentence.**

- jumping up in the air
- jumping up and turning upside down
- jumping up and leaning backward

12. At first, you would reward the dog for ____.
13. Later you would reward the dog for ____.
14. Later you would reward the dog for ____.
15. When you teach animals to work for new rewards, do you change the reward quickly or slowly?

Fill in each blank with the word **top** or the word **bottom.**

16. A regular pyramid has one animal at the ____ of the pyramid.
17. An upside-down pyramid has one animal at the ____ of the pyramid.

18. Write the letter of the clouds that have frozen drops of water.
19. Write the letter of the clouds that may stay in the sky for days at a time.
20. Write the letter of the storm clouds.

A B C

END OF LESSON 84 INDEPENDENT WORK

SPECIAL PROJECT

For this project, your group may either decide to train an animal a new trick or write a report that tells how you would train an animal.

If the group decides to train an animal, think about training a pigeon to do a dance. Pigeons learn to dance quite fast. If you train a hamster or a white rat, the training will take more time because these animals will not learn the trick as fast as a pigeon learns to dance. But you may teach a rat to walk a rope or teach a hamster to climb to the top of a tower that you make.

If you train an animal, write a report that tells how you did it. Tell about the rewards that you used to train the animal and tell about the steps that you used in training the animal.

If you do not train an animal, write a report that tells which rewards you would use and how you would use them. Tell all the things you would do to train the animal. Remember, the animal will not be able to do the trick the first time it tries, so you have to reward the animal for trying.

85

A

1	2	3
1. scuba	1. deadly fear	1. panic
2. guide	2. Mrs. Wilson	2. deathly
3. Darla	3. highway	3. Julie
4. badly	4. child	4. sissy
5. instructor	5. bravery	5. reef
6. partner	6. surfaced	6. fought

B

Darla's Fear

Darla Jackson was good at so many things that you wouldn't think she was afraid of anything. But she had one deadly fear. She wasn't afraid of high places. In fact, she loved to go mountain climbing with her older sister, Julie. Together, they climbed some of the highest mountains in California. Darla wasn't afraid of animals. She raised pet mice and for a while she had three pet snakes. She wasn't afraid of beetles or spiders. And Darla wasn't afraid of the dark. She and her sister camped out in places that were so dark at night that they couldn't see anything, although they could hear the sounds of animals that came near the camp.

And Darla wasn't afraid of work. She did very well in school and she worked hard around the house—mowing the lawn, helping paint the house, keeping her room clean.

But Darla had a deadly fear of water. She was so afraid of water that she couldn't even put her face underwater for a second without feeling as if the water was going to choke her. Her sister Julie was a good swimmer. "Come on, Darla," she used to holler from the deep water. "Don't be a sissy. Jump in and get wet." But the closest Darla ever came to swimming was to wade around in water that came up to her chest. When the water got up to her neck, she started to panic. When the water reached her neck, something inside her said, "Get out of here. Get out now." Then she'd become afraid that a wave would come along and splash her in the face.

Several times, she managed to get into neck-deep water, and she fought her fear. But just about the time that she thought she might learn to get used to deep water, a kid would come by and splash her in the face. She would panic, cough and get out of the water as fast as she could. The kids would laugh at her. She would become angry with them, but they would go into deeper water and call to her, "Come and get us."

One day when she went to school, her class was studying bravery and what it means to be brave. Her teacher, Mrs. Wilson, explained, "Somebody might go into a burning building to save a child. That is an act of bravery." Mrs. Wilson continued, "But for the person who goes into a burning building, the act might not take much bravery at all. That person might not be afraid of being close to fire. And that person might have confidence that she will not get hurt." Mrs. Wilson hesitated for a moment. Then she continued, "To be brave, you must do things that are hard for you to do." Mrs. Wilson went on to say, "Sometimes the greatest acts of bravery may not seem very brave to other people. If a person is deathly afraid of high places, climbing a ladder may be a great act of bravery. If a person is deathly afraid of snakes, holding a snake may take an incredible amount of bravery."

Darla almost felt that Mrs. Wilson was talking to her. For Darla, mountain climbing didn't take much bravery. Darla had confidence that she wouldn't fall. She was a very good climber. She figured that climbing a mountain was as safe as driving down a highway in a car. If you make a stupid mistake, you could become badly hurt, but it's not too difficult to avoid these mistakes. Darla felt the same way about the other things that she did. She was very good at them, and other people commented about how amazing and brave she was. But doing these things did not require much bravery for Darla.

After school that day, Darla walked home with Julie. Julie kept trying to start a conversation, but Darla couldn't stop thinking about bravery. Finally, she asked her sister, "Am I brave?"

Her sister laughed and then shrugged. "I never thought about it."

Then Julie continued, "Yeah, I guess you are brave—at least in most things. But you sure are a sissy about going in the water."

"I know," Darla said. Then Darla added, "I'm not really very brave at all, because the things I do are pretty easy for me. Going in the water is sure different, though. If

I just start thinking about it, I get scared."

"So you're a sissy about the water," her sister commented. "You'll probably get over it some day."

Darla said, "If I were brave, I'd get over my fear of water right now."

Julie looked at Darla, and the two girls fell into silence as they walked along the sidewalk. The sunshine was bright and warm. The girls walked for about a minute without saying anything. Suddenly, Darla stopped and said, "Julie, I've got to learn how to swim. I've got to be brave."

Julie smiled. "It's easy, Darla. The water won't bite you."

Darla said, "It's not easy for me. It's going to be the hardest thing I've ever done in my life. But I've

decided that I won't like myself very much unless I'm brave."

Julie said, "I think they're going to give swimming lessons at the high school. I hear that the instructor is very good."

Darla made a face. "Every time I think about it, I get scared. Feel the palms of my hands." The palms were sweaty. Darla said, "I'm scared. But I'll do it."

C Number your paper from 1 through 18.

Skill Items

I have confidence that we can avoid a long conversation.

1. What word describes people talking to each other about something?
2. What word tells what you do when you stay away from something?
3. What word tells that you are sure about something?

Review Items

4. Which globe shows how the earth looks on the first day of winter?
5. Which globe shows how the earth looks on the first day of summer?

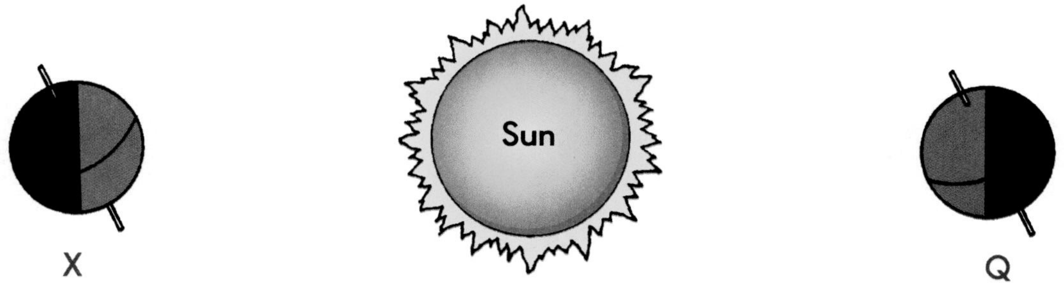

Write the name of each animal in the picture.

6.

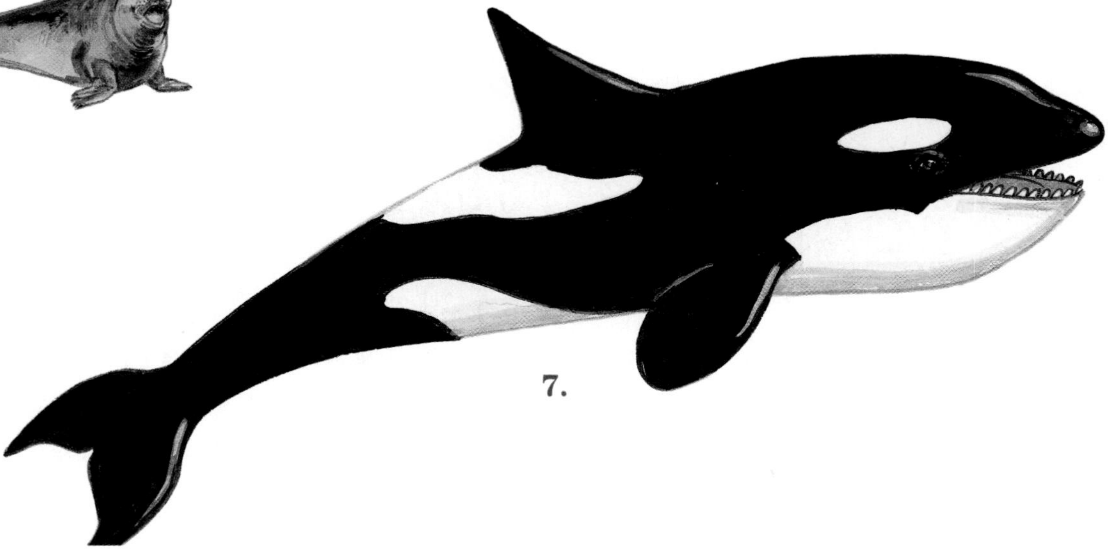

7.

8.

9.

10.

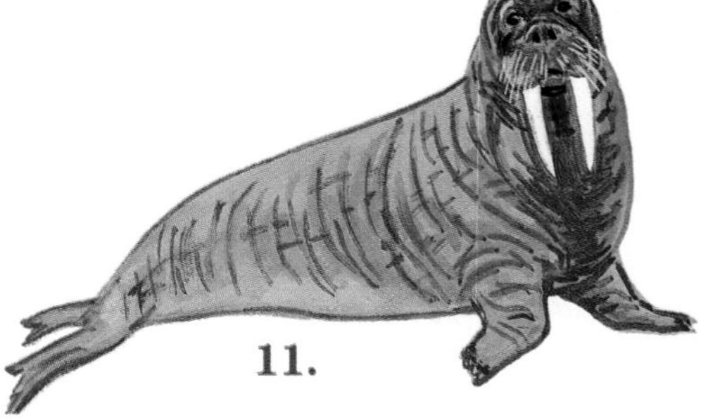

11.

12. Which animal in the picture is the biggest?

13. Which animal is the smallest?

Write the name of each kind of coral.

14.

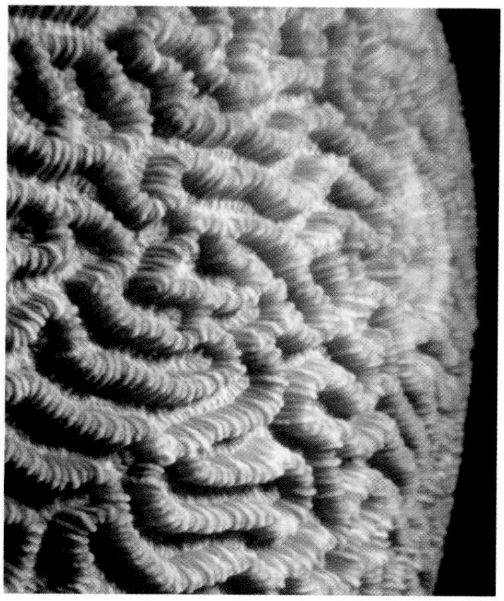

15.

16.

17. Coral is made up of the [redacted] of tiny [redacted].
18. An underwater hill that is covered with coral is called a coral [redacted].

86

A

1	2	3
1. anchored	1. flailed	1. guide
2. separated	2 rapidly	2. hose
3. scene	3. panicked	3. scuba
4. partner	4. mouthpiece	4. quit

B

Facts About Pressure

If you hold a balloon as you go underwater, the balloon gets smaller and smaller the deeper you go.

Here's a balloon when it is 10 feet underwater.

Here's the same balloon when it is 90 feet underwater.

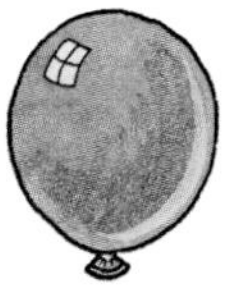

Here are facts about pressure:

- When you are at the surface of the water, there is some pressure on your body.
- When you go 33 feet underwater, the pressure is two times as great as it is at the surface.
- When you go down another 33 feet, the pressure is three times as great as it is at the surface.

C

Getting Ready to Dive

The small boat rolled slowly over the waves. Below the boat, the color of the water changed from dark blue to light green. Places that were light green were shallow. Places that were dark, dark blue were deep.

"Okay," the diving guide said to Darla and Julie and the other five divers who were on the boat. "Check your scuba gear and get ready to dive. This is the place we're going down."

A shot of panic went through Darla, and for a moment she almost said, "No, I'm not going to do it." But then she talked to herself. "There's nothing to be afraid of. You can do it. You can do it."

Darla's hand was trembling as she grabbed the dial that was attached to her air hose. The dial showed how much air was in her tank. The tank was full. Darla checked the rest of her equipment and tried to ignore her fear.

She looked at her sister and smiled, but she was not smiling inside. She was thinking back to the first day she went to the swimming class. She was the oldest person in that class, and the most frightened. She remembered how some of the little kids had laughed at her because she was so afraid to put her face in the water. But she had learned.

She had learned how to float with her face down in the water. She had learned to turn her face out of the water and take a breath while she floated face down. She had learned to kick her feet and to pull with her arms. She had become a fair swimmer by the time she had finished her swimming lessons.

Then Darla had taken scuba diving lessons. For Darla, these lessons were more frightening than the swimming lessons. The first time she had tried to wear a scuba mask, she was in a swimming pool. Water leaked inside the mask. She breathed water through her nose and panicked. As she stood on the deck of the diving boat in the hot sun, she remembered how she had panicked.

Again her mind went back to the first time she wore a scuba mask. She remembered how she flailed with her arms and legs, got a mouth full of water, and came out of the swimming pool coughing. She almost quit her scuba lessons after that experience. She had panicked a

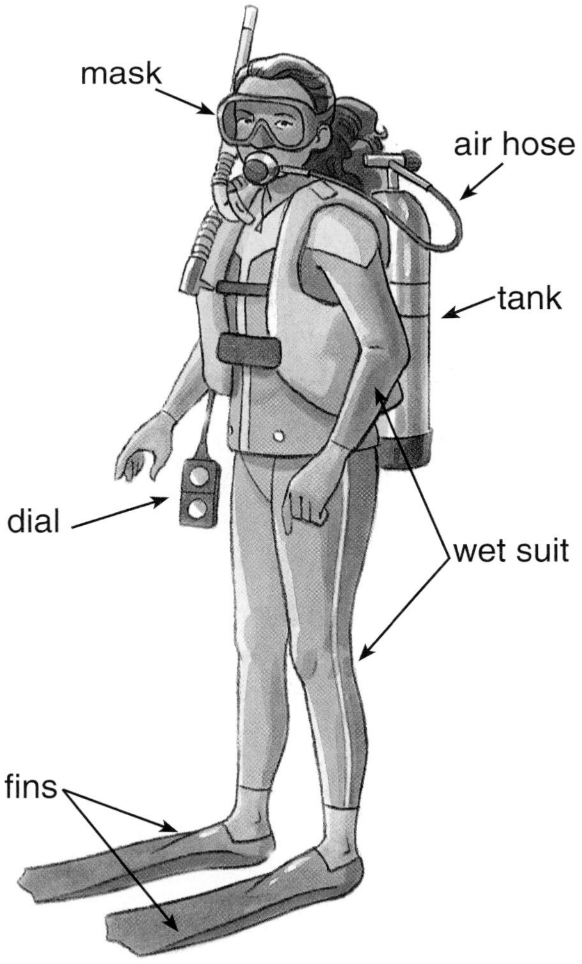

second time when she first tried to use the mouthpiece for the scuba gear. The instructor had told her how to hold the mouthpiece in her mouth so that she would be able to breathe through it. But when Darla went underwater and tried to breathe, water came into her mouth and again, she came out of the pool coughing.

Darla had kept working. She had studied her scuba books very carefully. She had felt that she wouldn't be as afraid of the water if she knew more about it. And she had learned a great deal. She learned about the different animals that live in the oceans, which animals are dangerous and which aren't. She learned all about how to use her scuba gear—how to use the feet fins, the dials and the mask. But the most amazing things she learned about had to do with water pressure. She had never thought much about the pressure of water before she had taken the scuba lessons.

"Are you almost ready?" Julie asked.

"I'm almost ready," Darla said, checking her mask.

Darla's mind went back to the time she had learned about pressure. Darla remembered that there is some pressure on a diver's body when the diver is at the surface. She remembered how deep a diver had to go to have two times as much pressure on the body.

Darla remembered some of the problems a diver may have if the diver comes up too fast. If a diver goes too deep and comes up too fast, the diver can die.

Darla's mind drifted back to the diving boat. Darla shook her head and smiled. She wondered why she was thinking about pressure and about her first scuba lessons. The diving boat rolled from side to side.

The diving guide was standing behind Darla now, checking her air tanks. "You're all set," he said. The diving guide said to the divers, "Remember, we're going down about 100 feet here. So don't try to come up too fast."

A shot of fear ran through Darla again. Her hand trembled as she put her mask in place. The deepest she had ever gone before was fifty feet.

D Number your paper from 1 through 17.

Skill Items

success	avoid	instructor	hire	conversation
confidence	panic	separate	contact	directing

1. She will _____ the person we want to _____.
2. I have _____ that we can _____ a long _____.

Review Items

3. How old are geese when they mate for the first time?
4. After male and female geese mate, how long do they stay together?
5. Most geese live for about _____ years.
6. When you teach an animal to work for a new reward, what kind of reward do you start with?
7. Then what do you do to that reward?
8. When do you stop changing the reward?
9. Which has stronger gravity, Earth or Jupiter?
10. So where would you feel heavier?
11. Which uses up more oxygen, hopping or sleeping?
12. What's another name for hot, melted rock?
13. Write the letters of the 6 things that tell about Jupiter.
    a. It has more gravity than Earth.
    b. It's brown, orange and white.
    c. It's small.
    d. It's huge.
    e. It has stripes.
    f. It has 16 moons.
    g. It's green and blue.
    h. It's beautiful.
14. Let's say that you want to teach an animal a very hard trick. Can the animal do the trick at first?
15. What will happen if the animal doesn't receive any rewards until it does the trick?
16. So when you're teaching the animal a hard trick, what do you reward the animal for doing?
17. Name **2** acts of bravery.

87

A

1
1. buoyant
2. buoyancy device
3. barracuda
4. especially

2
1. trailed
2. entered
3. tilted
4. separated
5. branched
6. anchored

3
1. mass
2. pair
3. hissing
4. scene
5. coral
6. brain

4
1. twilight
2. darting
3. soda
4. stiff
5. rapidly

B

An Underwater World

The diving boat was anchored in a place where the water changed from light green to dark, dark blue. One by one, the divers went down the ladder on the side of the boat and entered the warm water. The boat was about one thousand miles east of the United States, just south of the Bermuda Islands. Darla was the last diver to go down the ladder and enter the warm water.

"Now stick together," the guide said as he floated with his mask tilted back on his forehead. "You've got your partners. Stay with your partner. If you see something you want to look at, signal me. If one person stops, we all stop or somebody's going to get lost."

The guide continued, "If you get separated, go to the surface of the water. Don't try to look for the rest of us. Just go to the surface. And remember, don't go up too fast. Take at least two minutes to go up, or you may get the bends."

The bends. Darla had read about the bends. She knew that a person gets them because of the great pressure of water. When a person

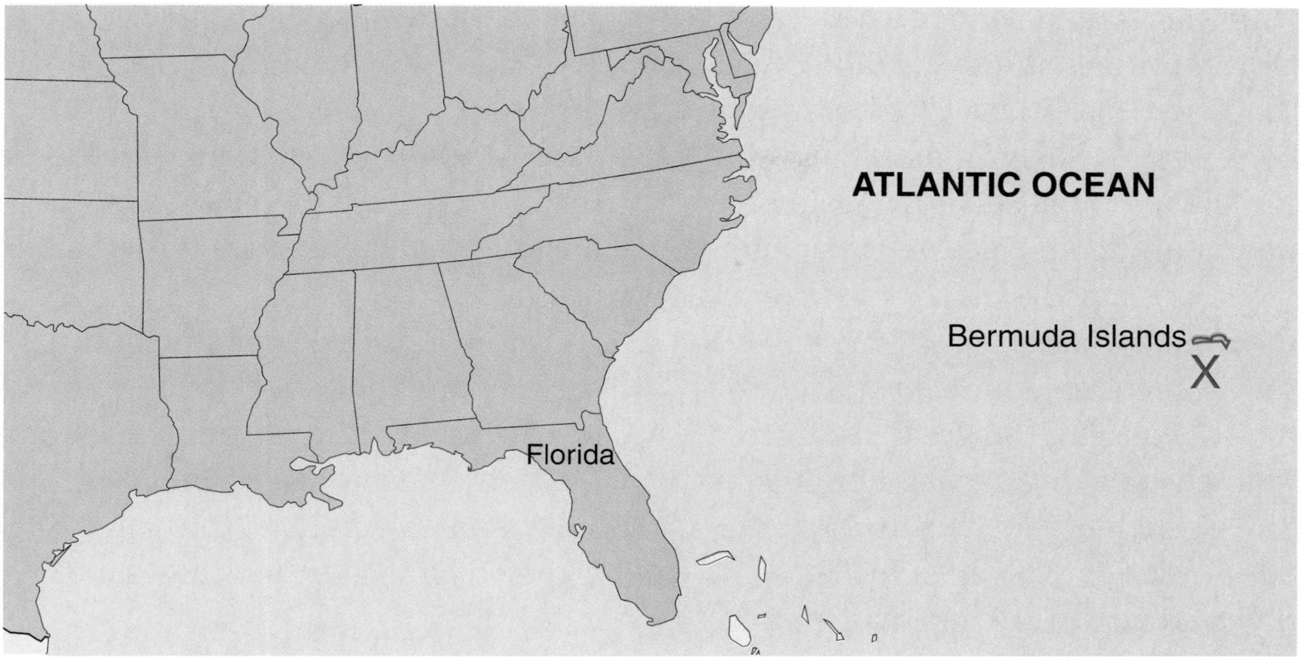

goes 100 feet underwater, the pressure of the water is pushing against the person's body with four times the pressure that would be on a person standing in air. When you're 100 feet down, four times the normal pressure pushes against your body. When a person comes up very fast, the pressure on the body goes down very fast. It goes down so fast that bubbles start to form in the blood, the same way bubbles form in a bottle of soda pop when you open the bottle. There is great pressure inside the bottle when it is capped. When you open the bottle, the pressure inside goes down very fast, and the bubbles form. That's just what happens to the blood when the pressure goes down very fast. Bubbles won't form in the blood if the pressure changes slowly. That's why the divers should take at least two minutes to go up to the surface.

As the diving guide floated on his back, he pulled his mask over his face and held his arm up. Then he pointed down and disappeared below the surface. The other divers followed. Darla's partner was Julie. They swam side by side and they were the last pair of divers to go down.

For Darla, going underwater was like going into a different world. She did not feel comfortable in this world. The sounds were different. She could hear herself breathe. With each breath that she took, the air hose made a loud, hissing sound. Each breath that she let out made the sound of bubbles—blub, blubble, blub. She could hear her heart pounding. Aside from these sounds, everything was silent except for the occasional squeaking or clicking of a sea animal.

In this strange underwater world, Darla floated. She didn't feel the weight of the heavy tanks on her back or the weight of anything. ★ But even though she floated slowly down through the green water, she did not escape from the pressure of the water. When she had gone down only fifteen feet, her ears started to hurt because of the great pressure that was pushing against her body. She could feel the pressure squeeze her mask tightly against her face. She held her nose, closed her mouth, and pushed air out very hard. Her ears felt better now.

When Darla and Julie were about 50 feet below the surface, Darla noticed that Julie was saying something and pointing down. Darla couldn't understand what Julie was saying. It sounded something like "Blulululululu Blulululu." Darla looked down to see what Julie was trying to point out. Below the sisters was an incredible scene. They were right above a great reef that was covered with plants. Some plants had huge leaves that seemed to wave in the water currents. Some coral looked like small trees that branched in all directions, other coral looked like round domes. Darla knew that these were large brain coral.

A school of silver fish was swimming through the coral— darting one way and then another. Next to them were three yellow fish. Above them was a huge black fish, swimming slowly in the other direction.

Darla smiled to herself. Her face felt stiff because the mask was pushing against her face with great pressure.

Darla and Julie hesitated above the reef and looked at the coral and the fish. The other divers were about fifty feet ahead of Darla and Julie, so Darla pointed at them and signaled her sister that they should catch up.

The divers followed the reef for about six hundred feet. Then they started down into a valley between two reefs. The water at the bottom of this valley was dark purple, almost black. Darla looked down at the other divers and realized that they looked like insects who were slowly gliding through a purple sky. The only difference was the trail of bubbles that followed each diver. Each time a diver breathed, out came a boiling mass of bubbles that broke into tiny bubbles and trailed up to the surface. The divers were now going down rapidly. Darla had to clear her ears again. Her mask was starting to hurt her face.

The diving guide pointed to the right. Darla searched the ocean to see what he was pointing at. For a moment she couldn't see anything unusual. Then she saw a giant ray fish, slowly flapping its fins as it

glided through the valley. Darla thought, "That ray really looks like it is flying in the air."

Again, the diving guide pointed down and again the group of divers followed him. Darla was no longer afraid, but she didn't feel very comfortable. She told herself that she should enjoy the things around her. She told herself, "Not many people get to see the things that are around me right now. So enjoy them." But this experience was new for Darla.

The group was now down 66 feet. The pressure on Darla was three times the pressure on land.

C Number your paper from 1 through 12.

Review Items

1. What's the name of the line that goes around the fattest part of the earth?
2. What's the name of the spot that's at the top of the earth?
3. What's the name of the spot that's at the bottom of the earth?

4. When you dive down 33 feet, you have ______ times the pressure on you that you have at the surface.
5. When you dive down 66 feet, you have ______ times the pressure on you that you have at the surface.

6. What part of the scuba equipment does the **A** show?
7. What part does the **B** show?
8. What part does the **C** show?
9. What part does the **D** show?
10. What part does the **E** show?
11. What part does the **F** show?
12. What part does the **G** show?

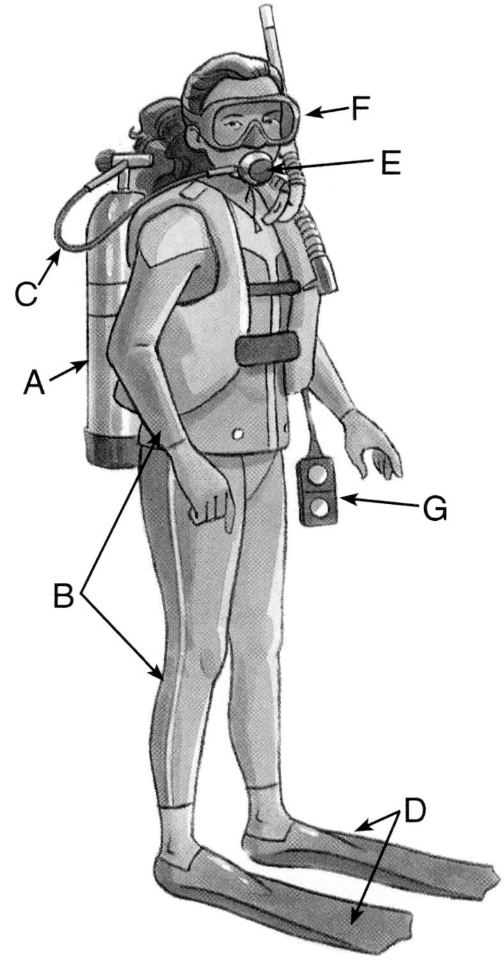

88

A

1	2
1. Iditarod	1. grasp
2. Anchorage	2. especially
3. twilight	3. buoyancy
4. buoyant	4. upwards
5. barracuda	5. struggling
6. teasing	6. suffer

B

An Emergency

About ten minutes after the dive began, the group of divers had reached the bottom of the valley between two long reefs. The bottom was 100 feet below the surface. Here the pressure was four times as great as it was on land. Darla's mask pressed against her face with great pressure. Her ears seemed to ring. Her mouth was dry and she had trouble swallowing. And things looked different. There weren't as many plants as there were above on the reefs. And things were not as bright. When Darla looked up, she could see the sun shining above the surface of the water, but it looked like a light gray circle.

The other divers seemed to be swimming through twilight. A slow stream of dark gray bubbles followed each diver.

Darla and her sister stayed close to each other and tried to stay close to the other divers. However, as they moved through the valley, Darla saw a school of fish above her. They were not tiny silver fish, but large, arrow-shaped fish. She pointed up and said the name of these fish to her sister. "Barracuda," she said. But it sounded like "bububuda."

Darla had read about barracudas. They were dangerous, perhaps more dangerous than sharks or killer whales. Barracudas swim in large schools and they grow to a length of almost two meters. A barracuda's mouth is filled with sharp teeth, and barracudas have been known to attack swimmers and kill them.

The barracudas above Darla and her sister swam swiftly through the water, moving in almost a straight line. Darla and her sister watched

them until they disappeared into the darkness of the water above them. When Darla turned around, she did not see the other divers. She signaled her sister that they should catch up to the others. The sisters began to swim fast along the floor of the valley. Darla could not swim as fast as her sister. As Julie moved ahead of Darla, Julie turned around and motioned for Darla to catch up. Darla could see that Julie was smiling. She was teasing Darla.

Darla kicked harder and pulled harder with her arms, but she couldn't catch up to Julie, who stayed just ahead of Darla. The girls swam rapidly along the bottom for about a minute, but still they could not see the other divers. Darla was starting to feel a little nervous, especially as she moved through a current of very cool water. The water at 100 feet down is cooler than it is at the surface, but every now and then there is a current of water that is very cool. The one that Darla and Julie were going through now gave Darla a chill.

"Where are the other divers?" Darla asked herself.

Darla remembered what their guide had told them to do if they were separated from the group. Darla was just about ready to signal Julie that they should ★ go to the surface. Suddenly, Julie turned around and pointed to the air hose. Darla noticed that Julie had a frightened expression. Then Darla noticed that Julie was not letting out large masses of bubbles. Only a small trail of bubbles was coming out of her mouth.

Julie was excited. She kept pointing at her air hose. Her eyes were wide. Before Darla could think about what was happening, Julie pointed up toward the surface and began to swim toward the surface very fast.

"No!" Darla shouted as loudly as she could. "No!"

But Julie was already about five feet above her and moving very fast.

"I must catch her," Darla thought to herself. Darla used every bit of strength she had. She kicked with all her might and she pulled hard with her arms. Then she remembered her buoyancy device. The device is a little air bag above the air tanks. The diver can fill the buoyancy device with air or let air out of it. When it is filled with air, the diver is very buoyant, which means that the diver floats to the surface very fast. When there is no air in the buoyancy device, the diver is not very buoyant and the diver sinks to the bottom.

Darla pressed the button that filled her buoyancy device with air and she shot upwards very fast. Within a couple of seconds, she caught up to her sister. She grabbed Julie around the waist with one arm. With the other, she pressed the button that lets the air out of her buoyancy device.

Julie was struggling to get free. Her face was turning red. Her eyes were now very wide and she was flailing her arms and legs. Darla knew that if Julie went up too fast, she would suffer from the bends.

Now Darla was faced with one of the most difficult decisions she had ever made in her life. She could share her air hose with her sister. To do that, Darla would take a deep breath, remove the air hose from her mouth and give it to her sister. Her sister would then take a deep breath from the hose and return it to Darla. The decision was difficult for Darla because she started to feel a great panic when she thought about removing the air hose from her mouth, 100 feet below the surface. "I can't do it," she said to herself as she struggled with her sister. "You must do it," she told herself. "If you don't, Julie will die."

Darla gathered all her bravery, took a deep breath, and removed her air hose. Julie grabbed it with both hands and shoved the mouthpiece into her mouth. A few seconds later, she let out a huge cloud of bubbles, and then another, and then another. Darla signaled her sister to give the air hose back, but Julie was holding the hose with both hands and not paying any attention to Darla. Julie was in a state of panic.

C Number your paper from 1 through 16.

Skill Items

The scuba diver and her partner surfaced near the reef.

1. What word describes a person you do something with?
2. What word tells about a ridge that forms underwater?
3. What words tell about someone who goes underwater with a mask and a tank of air?
4. What word tells that a person swam to the surface?

Here are 3 events that happened in the story. Write **beginning, middle** or **end** for each event.

5. About ten minutes after the dive began, the group of divers had reached the bottom of the valley between two long reefs.
6. Darla was starting to feel a little nervous, especially as she moved through a current of very cool water.
7. Now Darla was faced with one of the most difficult decisions she had ever made in her life.

Review Items

8. What does the color of water tell you about the water?
9. If you're underwater 100 feet deep, the pressure is much greater than it is on land. How many times greater is it?
10. When divers are that deep, how long should they take to return to the surface of the water?
11. What may happen to the divers if they go up faster than that?
12. When you open a bottle of soda pop, what happens to the pressure inside the bottle?
13. What forms in the soda pop?

14. Write the letter of the body that has the least pressure on it.
15. Write the letter of the body that has the most pressure on it.
16. Write the letters of all the bodies that have more pressure on them than **P** has on it.

A

1

1. Denali
2. Knik
3. honor
4. command
5. veterinarian
6. thorough

2

1. musher
2. argument
3. grasping
4. bodies
5. married

3

1. overcome
2. Anchorage
3. fourteen
4. pinched
5. examination

4

1. Nome
2. white-capped
3. traded
4. Iditarod
5. fresh
6. locker

B

Facts About the Iditarod

Every year, in early March, a great sled-dog race starts in Anchorage, Alaska, and ends in Nome, Alaska. That's a distance of more than 11 hundred miles. The map shows the route of the Iditarod.

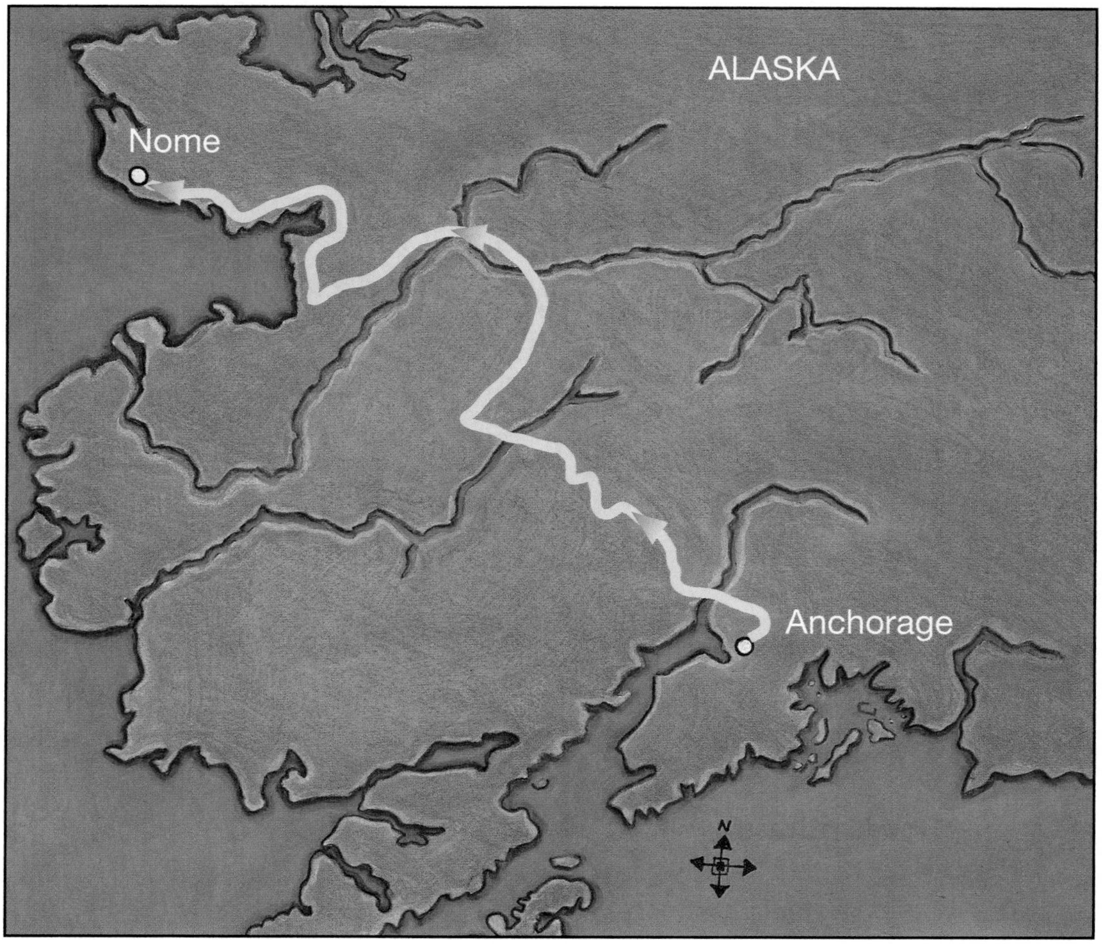

The people who enter the Iditarod race are called mushers. A musher is a person who drives a team of sled dogs. The musher usually stands at the back of the sled and shouts commands to the dogs. The dogs pull the sled. Some sleds have as many as sixteen dogs pulling it. Some sleds have only twelve or fourteen dogs.

The picture shows a sled in action.

The race from Anchorage to Nome takes about 10 days. Sometimes it takes longer. If the weather is very bad, the musher who wins the race may be on the Iditarod trail for eleven days. Even if the winning sled gets to Nome in eleven days, the sled travels about 100 miles per day.

C The Trip to the Water's Surface

Three times Darla signaled her sister to let go of the air hose, but Julie was grasping the air hose with both hands and breathing. Darla was starting to panic now. Darla was running out of air. She pinched Julie's hand and pointed to the air hose. Suddenly, Julie's eyes changed. They had been wide and wild. Now they moved toward Darla. Julie took a deep breath and then handed the air hose to Darla just in time. Darla took a couple of breaths of fresh air, took another deep breath and handed the hose back to Julie.

Darla and Julie traded the air hose back and forth a couple of times. Julie seemed all right now. As she was taking a couple of deep breaths, Darla pointed up. Together, the girls moved up slowly. Darla could feel the difference in pressure as she moved up. Darla's mask was not pressing against her face as hard, and her ears did not have the ringing sound they had when she had been 100 feet down. The girls continued to move up until they were ten feet below the surface. Then they stopped. They would have

to stay here for one minute, until their bodies got used to the lower pressure.

Darla kept looking at her watch as she and Julie took turns using the air hose. The one minute seemed to take one hour. At last, Darla's watch told her that they could move up again.

She signaled her sister that they could go the rest of the way to the surface. Up, up, through the clouds of bubbles. Up, all the way to the surface.

As soon as Darla surfaced, she noticed the sounds of birds and the splashing of water. Julie came up right beside her. Julie pushed her mask back onto her forehead. "Wow!" she shouted. "We made it!"

Darla smiled as she pushed her mask back. "Yeah," she said. "Yeah."

Julie swam over and kissed Darla on the cheek. "Thanks," she said. Darla hugged her sister.

In the distance, the diving boat was moving toward them, making a row of white-capped waves. The girls waved and shouted, "Over here!" Before the boat reached the girls, Julie said, "Well, I guess you're the brave one. When I lost my air, I couldn't think. I just panicked."

"I would have done the same thing," Darla said. "I was scared to death."

Julie replied, "I'm sure glad you stopped me. I guess I didn't know what I was doing. I just had to have air."

Suddenly, Darla realized that she was brave. She remembered how she had felt when she and her sister were slowly returning to the surface. The wait had seemed like a long, long time, but Darla hadn't felt panic.

She looked at her sister and said, "Yeah, I guess I overcame my fear of water."

• • •

Darla walked into the locker room next to the swimming pool. She changed into her swimming suit. Then she walked through the hallway to the swimming pool. A group of people was gathered at the shallow end of the pool. Darla walked to the other end of the pool, where the scuba gear was laid out. She picked up a pair of fins and a mask. Then she checked one of the air tanks to make sure that it was filled.

She carried the fins and the mask as she walked toward the group of people at the shallow end of the pool. As she approached the group she said, "Hello, I'm Darla Jackson, and I'm going to be your scuba diving instructor."

The students told Darla their names. Then Darla said, "To

understand scuba diving you must understand water pressure. The pressure on your body becomes very great when you dive. When you go down 33 feet in water, the pressure on your body is two times as great as it is when you're standing on land. When you go down 66 feet, the pressure on your body is three times as great as it is on land."

As Darla talked, her mind went back to the first time she had gone down 100 feet. Since that dive, she had gone down much farther. She had already taken ten dives below 130 feet and thirty dives below 100 feet. She had gone diving with her sister in the Pacific Ocean and the Atlantic Ocean. She had been swimming with seals, whales and even sharks. She no longer had fear of the water, but she remembered how she had felt on her first deep dive.

"Oh, yes," she said to the group. "Some of you may be afraid of the water. You can overcome that fear if you train yourself to think about the things you must do. I know that you can overcome the fear because when I started out, I was as afraid of the water as anybody that ever lived."

The people in the group smiled, and Darla went on with the instruction.

D Number your paper from 1 through 19.

Story Items

1. What did Darla realize about **herself** when she got to the surface of the water?
2. What kind of job did Darla have at the end of the story?
3. Name **2** oceans where Darla and Julie have gone diving.
4. Darla told her students, "To understand scuba diving, you must understand ______.

Skill Items

partner	twilight	confidence	especially
surfaced	rapidly	conversation	overcame
avoid	scuba diver	mass	reef

5. I have ______ that we can ______ a long ______.
6. The ______ and her ______ ______ near the ______.

Review Items

7. In what ocean is the **X?**
8. About how many miles is it from Florida to the **X?**

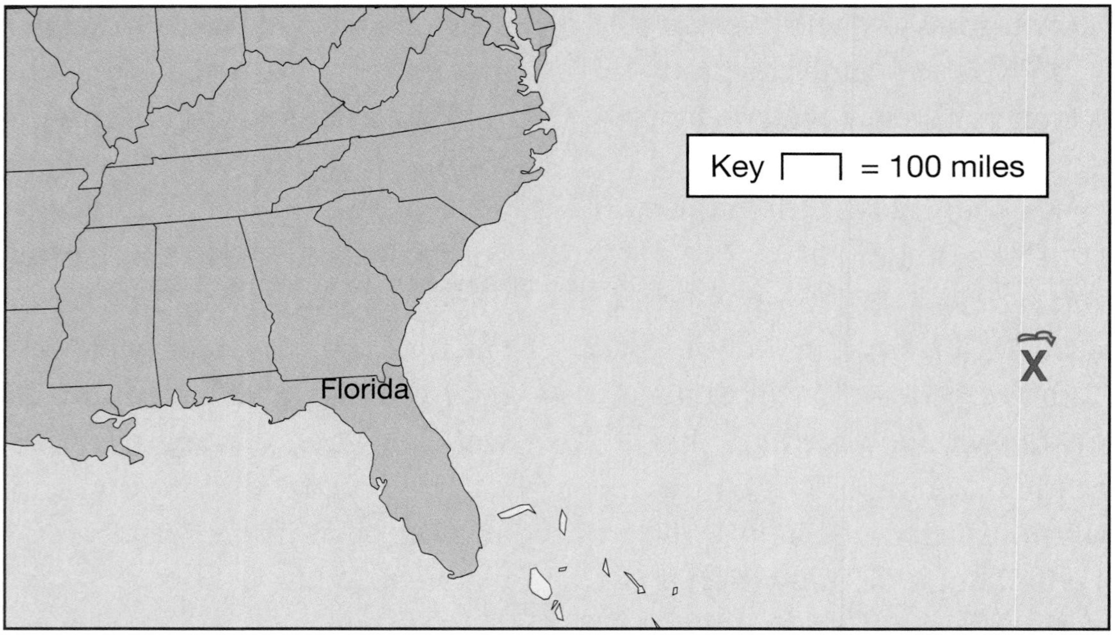

9. If you move up too fast from very deep water, you may get the [redacted].
10. What forms in your blood as you go up too fast?
11. When you go up very fast, is there **more pressure** or **less pressure** on your body?

12. Do things look **light** or **dark** when you're 100 feet below the surface of the ocean?
13. There aren't as many plants down there because there isn't as much [redacted].

14. Name 3 things that great water pressure can do to you.

15. Name an arrow-shaped fish.
16. Write **2** facts about those fish.

17. What do you fill a buoyancy device with?
18. When it is filled up, what happens to the diver?
19. When it is empty, what happens to the diver?

Number your paper from 1 through 36.

1. Coral is made up of the [redacted] of tiny [redacted].
2. An underwater ridge that is covered with coral is called a coral [redacted].
3. When you dive down 33 feet, you have [redacted] times the pressure on you that you have at the surface.
4. When you dive down 66 feet, you have [redacted] times the pressure on you that you have at the surface.
5. What does the color of water tell you about the water?
6. In what ocean is the **X?**
7. About how many miles is it from Florida to the **X?**

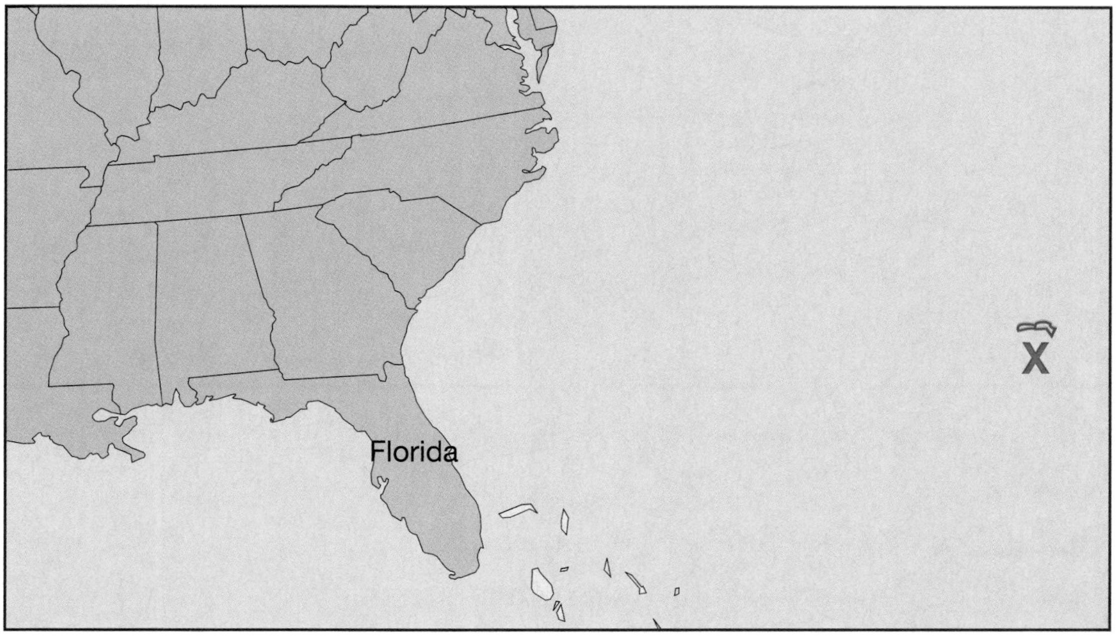

8. Do things look **light** or **dark** when you're 100 feet below the surface of the ocean?
9. There aren't as many plants down there because there isn't as much [redacted].
10. Name **3** things that great water pressure can do to you.

11. Write the letter of the body that has the **least** pressure on it.
12. Write the letter of the body that has the **most** pressure on it.
13. Write the letters of all the bodies that have more pressure on them than **M** has on it.

14. If you move up too fast from very deep water, you may get the ____.
15. What forms in your blood as you go up too fast?
16. When you go up very fast, is there **more pressure** or **less pressure** on your body?

17. When you open a bottle of soda pop, what happens to the pressure inside the bottle?
18. What forms in the soda pop?

19. Name an arrow-shaped fish.
20. Write **2** facts about those fish.

21. Is the water cooler at 100 feet down or at the surface?
22. Is all the water at 100 feet down the same temperature?

23. What do you fill a buoyancy device with?
24. When it is filled up, what happens to the diver?
25. When it is empty, what happens to the diver?

26. In what state is the Iditarod sled-dog race?
27. In which city does it begin?
28. In which city does it end?

29. The Iditarod is about ______ miles from start to finish.
    - 1600
    - 500
    - 1100
30. In most years the race takes about ______.
    - 10 days
    - 2 weeks
    - a week

Skill Items

For each item, write the underlined word or words from the sentences in the box.

> I have confidence that we can avoid a long conversation.
> The scuba diver and her partner surfaced near the reef.

31. What underlining tells what you do when you stay away from something?
32. What underlining describes a person you do something with?
33. What underlining tells about someone who goes underwater with a mask and a tank of air?
34. What underlining describes people talking to each other about something?
35. What underlining tells that you are sure about something?
36. What underlining tells that people swam to the surface?

91

A

1

1. reins
2. Butch
3. gee
4. purpose

2

1. harnessed
2. referring
3. toughness
4. yapping
5. commands

3

1. Uncle Chad
2. parka
3. husky
4. goal
5. leash
6. Denali

4

1. kennel
2. strain
3. Susie
4. crisp
5. Knik
6. honor

5

1. Nome
2. alongside
3. wool
4. whoa
5. zero

B

Sled-Dog Teams

Most sled-dog teams have an even number of dogs—twelve, fourteen or sixteen. In the Iditarod, a musher can't have more than sixteen dogs.

The first pair of dogs in the team are the lead dogs. Lead dogs must be very smart and they must be leaders, so the other dogs will follow them. The pair of dogs just behind the lead dogs are called swing dogs. They are the best dogs at following and they are very fast. When the lead dogs swing to the left, the swing dogs follow closely to make sure the other dogs follow the same path. The pair of dogs closest to the sled are called wheel dogs. Wheel dogs must be very strong because when the sled gets stuck, the wheel dogs are the ones who have to pull it out or turn it so it is free.

The dogs are harnessed together with nylon straps. Each dog wears a criss-cross harness. Each harness is attached to a tug line. All the tug lines are connected to the gang line. That's the long line that runs down

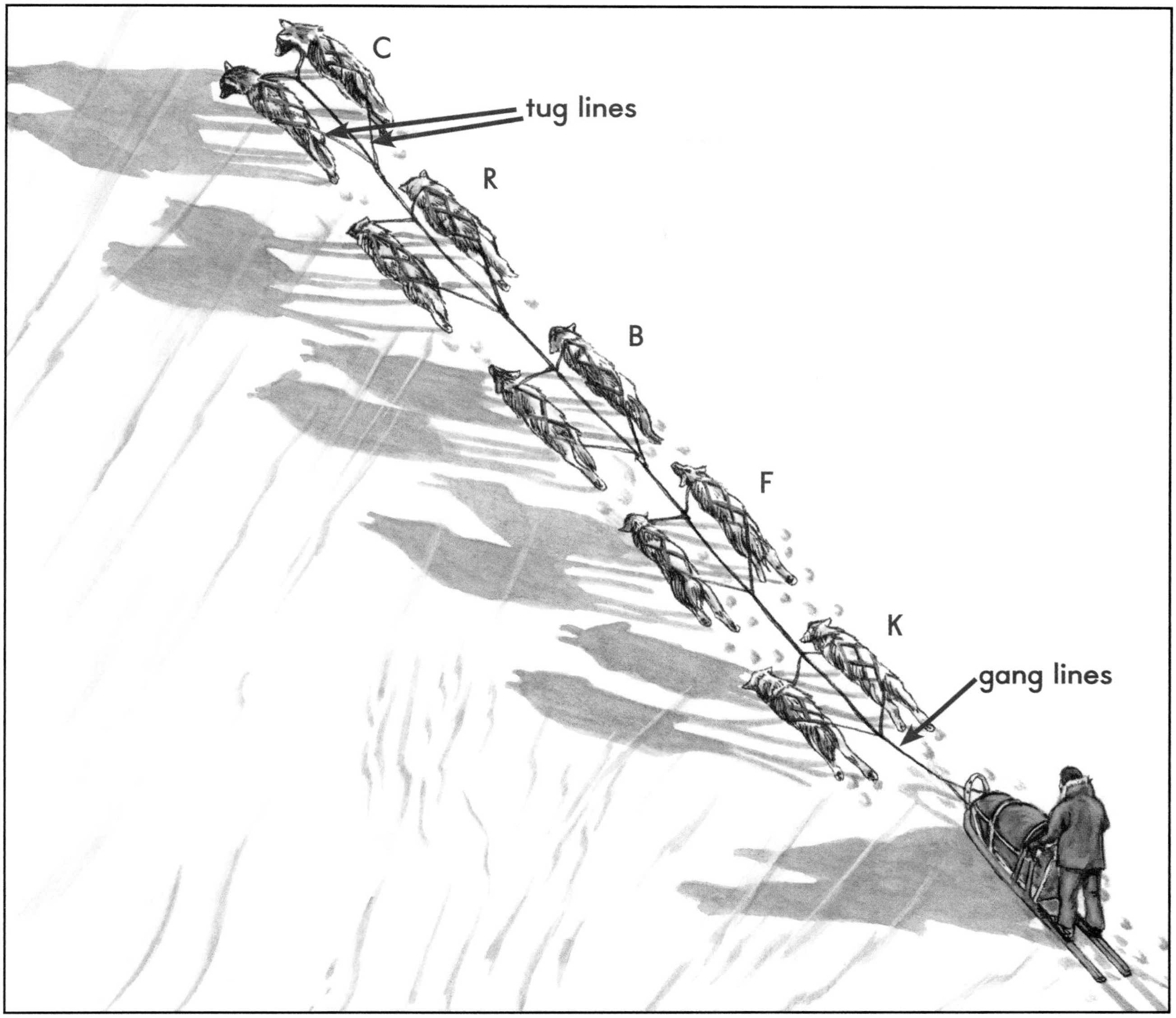

the middle of the team. The gang line is connected to the sled. If there are sixteen dogs, the gang line may be over sixty feet long.

C Susie and Denali

Susie put on her parka and mittens. It was warmer today, about 4 degrees below zero.

Susie went outside and called, "Denali." A large Alaskan husky came running through the crisp snow, stopped in front of her, sat down and wagged his tail. "It will happen in a little more than two weeks," Susie said. Denali licked his chops and looked as if he understood her.

Susie was referring to the Iditarod. This year it would begin on

March 15. Susie's Uncle Chad was going to be a musher in this year's race. He lived less than a mile from Susie's place in Knik, Alaska, and Susie had been working with him for almost a year, getting ready for the race.

Susie harnessed Denali to a practice sled. She stood next to the sled and called out, "Mush."

Denali pulled hard and the sled jumped forward. Susie ran alongside the sled, then jumped on the back. Denali knew that he was going to Uncle Chad's place, and he was eager to get there. The snow squeaked and crunched as Denali pulled the sled along, next to the road.

Susie imagined that she was in the great Iditarod race. She tried to imagine what it was like with fourteen or even sixteen dogs in front of her as they pulled a sled through country that was so wild that there were no roads in many places, just the Iditarod trail. Susie had heard stories about the Iditarod and the dangers mushers had to face—getting lost, being attacked by animals and, the most feared problem of all, freezing.

"Whoa," she called to Denali. Uncle Chad's place was on the other side of the road. A large truck went by. The driver waved to Susie. She waved back and then called out, "Mush." Denali pulled the sled across the road. Some of Chad's dogs were looking at Denali from their kennel. Two of them were barking.

Uncle Chad came out, wearing a wool shirt, gloves and earmuffs, but no coat. He was handsome and, for an instant, Susie wondered why he had never married. She also wondered how he could dress like that in cold weather. He called to her, "Susie, bring Denali around back. Today, we're going to run with a loaded sled."

"Can Denali be one of your wheel dogs?" ★

"Maybe later." He smiled. She didn't.

"Oh, come on," she said. "He's a good wheel dog. He knows all the commands, and . . ."

"Susie," Chad said. "I need to find out how the regular team of fourteen dogs is going to do in really rough country."

Chad walked to the kennel, opened the kennel gate and said, "Into the truck, you guys." The dogs ran around, jumped up on Chad and Susie and then jumped in the back of Chad's truck. Three dogs got into arguments about who would sit closest to the sled, which was already in the truck bed. They growled and snapped.

"Stop that," Chad said, and the dogs settled down. Most of them were a lot smaller than Denali, but they were all very strong, and they were all tough. They would need that toughness when they ran the Iditarod because then they would have to pull the sled all day long—sometimes for more than fourteen hours a day.

Susie had gone on more than a hundred practice runs with Chad, and she knew every dog that he owned—all fifteen of them. Although she knew a lot about mushing, she was always amazed at how much more Chad knew about it. He had been in the Iditarod once before, but he didn't do very well. The sled broke down about 200 miles from Nome, and he didn't finish the race. His goal for this year was to finish. He wasn't thinking about being in first or second place, just finishing. Susie had once told him, "You know so much about mushing, you could win first place!"

He had laughed and said, "Some mushers in that race know more about mushing than I'll ever learn. It's just an honor to be in the same race they are in."

The truck pulled off the road. Down below was Eagle River Valley. It looked very steep. Chad said, "We'll take the sled down into the valley and around the rocky parts."

Chad jumped out of the truck and told the dogs, "Everybody out of the truck." The dogs were glad to obey that command. Some of them looked like they were flying as they jumped out of the truck bed. Through the snow they raced, yapping and running in circles. Then Chad whistled, and they all crowded around him with their tails wagging.

D Number your paper from 1 through 14.

Review Items

1. In what state is the Iditarod sled-dog race?
2. In which city does it begin?
3. In which city does it end?
4. The Iditarod is about ____ miles from start to finish.
   - 1600
   - 500
   - 1100
5. In most years, the race takes about ____.
   - 10 days
   - 2 weeks
   - a week
6. The person who drives a sled-dog team is called a ____.
7. The drivers of the sled-dog teams command the dogs by using their ____.
   - voices
   - reins
   - steering wheels

8. How does water pressure change as you move from deep water toward the surface?
9. How does the light around you change as you move toward the surface?

10. When the diver is ______ feet underwater, the pressure is **two** times as great as it is on land.
11. When the diver is ______ feet underwater, the pressure is **three** times as great as it is on land.
12. When the diver is ______ feet underwater, the pressure is **four** times as great as it is on land.

13. Which letter shows Colorado?
14. Which letter shows Utah?

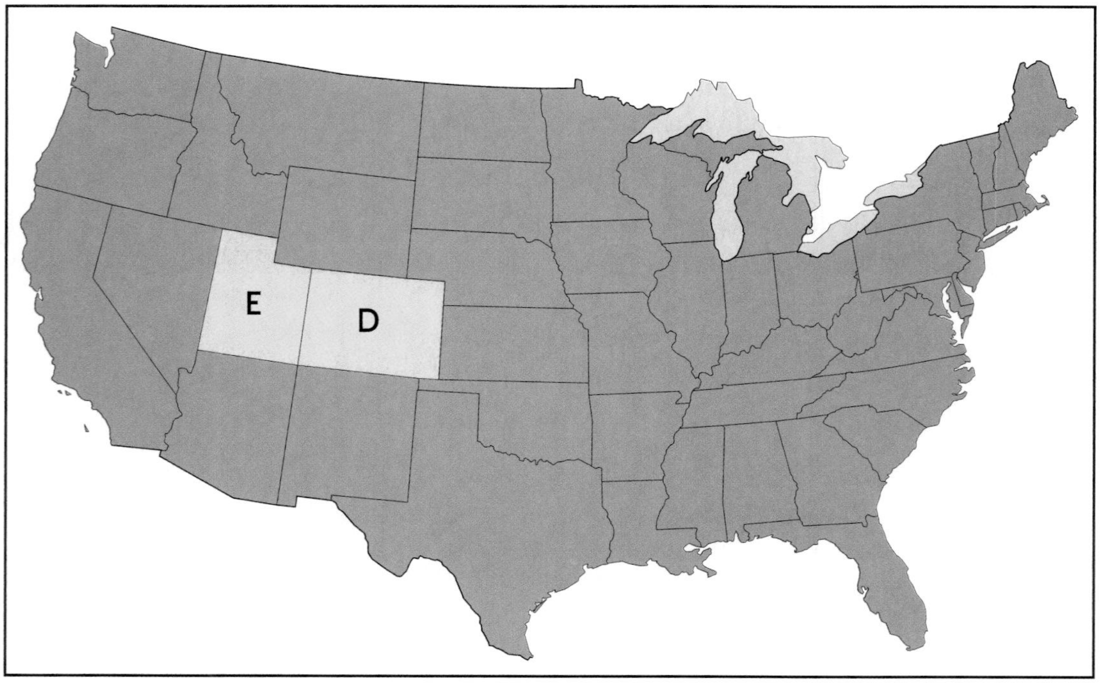

A

1	2	3
1. include	1. booties	1. gang
2. official	2. stiffen	2. reins
3. purpose	3. strained	3. gee
4. leashes	4. huffed	4. haw
		5. canvas
		6. Velcro

B

Booties

The rules of the Iditarod require every dog to wear booties on its feet, and the musher must have a spare set of booties for each dog. Most mushers take along more than 1,000 booties and change them every two days. The booties are designed to protect the dogs' feet. In some places, the dogs go over ice. Without booties, they may get serious ice cuts on their paws. Even if they cut one of their paws while wearing a bootie, the bootie will protect the cut. Also, dogs without booties get balls of snow packed between the pads on their paws. This is uncomfortable for the dogs. When it happens, a dog would like to stop, sit down and chew the snow from between the pads. But there's no time for this kind of stopping during the race. So dogs without booties would suffer. They would also slip around a lot more than dogs with booties.

Not all booties are made of the same material. The booties that Chad preferred are made of canvas. These booties have Velcro flaps.

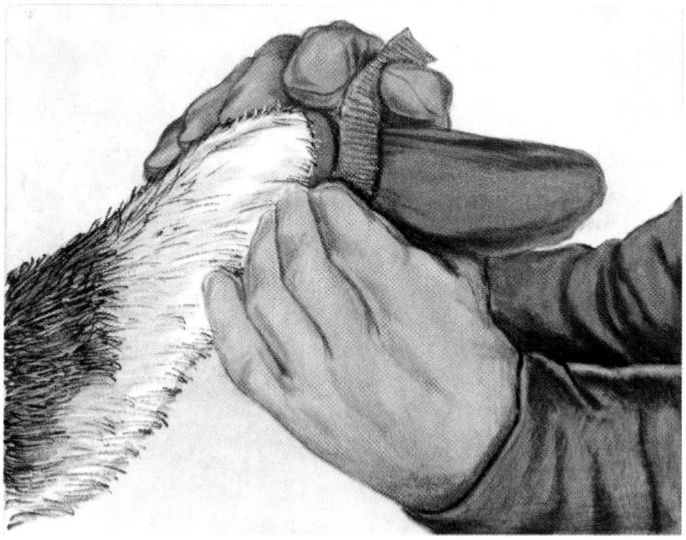

Putting booties on the dogs is tricky. If booties are too tight, the dog's blood cannot circulate around the paws, so the dog's ankles swell up. If the booties are too loose, they fall off. Before putting on the booties, the musher sometimes rubs a special cream on a dog's pads. The cream keeps the pads soft, so they won't crack.

C Getting Ready for a Run

"Let's harness up," Chad said. As he hooked up the dogs to their tug lines, Susie began to put booties on the dogs. Susie and Chad didn't put booties on the dogs for ordinary practice runs in open fields. But the dogs needed booties for a tough run like the one they would do today. Also, Chad wanted to make sure that none of the dogs would have problems with the booties.

Before putting on the booties, Susie rubbed a special cream on each dog's pads. Susie and Chad worked fast, but it took more than 30 minutes to get everything ready. At last, the dogs were lined up in pairs—seven pairs. Each dog's harness was attached to a tug line and each tug line was attached to the gang line. A neck line connected each pair of dogs together. When all fourteen dogs were in place and ready to go, the lead dogs were over fifty feet from the sled.

Steering dogs is tricky. It's not like steering horses because horses have reins. If you move the reins to the left, the horse turns left. Sled dogs don't have reins. The only thing mushers use to steer the dogs is their voice. They shout out commands that the dogs follow. Some of the commands are for only some dogs. So the dogs have to know which commands they are to obey and which commands are for other dogs.

After all the dogs were harnessed, Chad loaded four large sacks of dirt on the sled. He said, "This dirt weighs over ★ 300 pounds, so the dogs will be pulling more weight than they'll have to pull during the race, but I want to see what the team can do in tough places."

Then he jumped on the back of the sled and shouted out, "Muuush, you sled dogs. Muuush."

The dogs put their heads down and their shoulders up. They pulled and strained and wagged their tails. They panted and huffed and pulled harder. At first, the sled moved slowly, but then the dogs began to run—faster and faster. Susie had two dogs on leashes—Denali and

Butch, the other dog that was not on the gang line. They ran behind the sled, but they could not keep up with the sled.

Down the slope the sled went. As it approached the bottom, Chad shouted, "Come gee," and the lead dogs made a circle to the right and headed back up the hill. They slowed down quickly and soon were almost standing still. Chad jumped off and got behind the sled. He pushed while the dogs pulled, and up the hill they went.

"Haw," Chad shouted, and the team turned a little to the left where there were large snow-covered rocks. A moment later, the sled was stuck against a rock. Susie wondered why Chad had led the dogs here when he could have easily directed them to the left or right to avoid the rocks. Then Susie figured out that Chad had done it on purpose. He wanted to get stuck so he could see if the team would have problems getting the sled free.

D Number your paper from 1 through 16.

Review Items

1. What are clouds made of?
2. What kind of cloud does the picture show?
3. What happens to a drop of water at **B?**

4. Which object went into the pile **first?**
5. Which object went into the pile **last?**
6. Which object went into the pile **earlier,** the cup or the pencil?
7. Which object went into the pile **just after** the bone?

Use these words to answer items 8—10:

- **swing dogs** • **wheel dogs** • **lead dogs**

8. These dogs are very smart, and other dogs obey them.
9. These dogs are responsible for freeing the sled when it gets stuck.
10. These dogs are very good followers, and they are smart.

11. Which letter in the picture shows the wheel dogs?
12. Which letter shows the lead dogs?
13. Which letter shows the swing dogs?
14. Which letter shows where the musher is most of the time?
15. Which letter shows the tug lines?
16. Which letter shows the gang line?

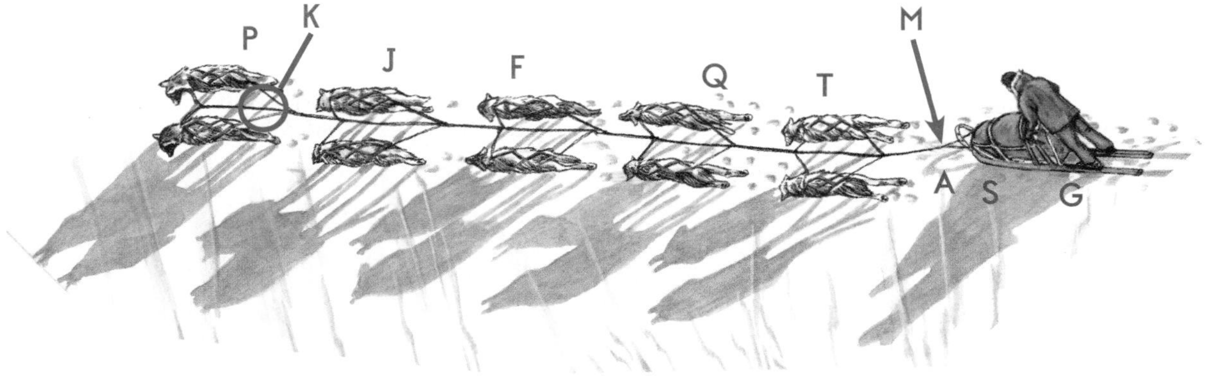

93

A

1	2	3
1. assistant	1. nightmare	1. injure
2. certificate	2. exchange	2. pest
3. health	3. stiffened	3. thorough
4. according	4. backwards	4. included
5. endurance	5. inched	5. officials
	6. examined	6. veterinarian

B

A Practice Run

The sled was stuck against a rock on the slope. Susie patted Denali's head and said, "Watch carefully so you'll know what to do." Denali stiffened up as he tried to figure out what he was to watch.

Chad said, "Wheel dogs, haw." Denali jumped. At the same time, the pair of dogs just in front of the sled pulled hard to their right. The other dogs backed up a little bit. The pulling turned the sled so that it was now facing almost uphill. It was no longer up against a rock.

Now Chad shouted two more commands. "Haw," he called out and the lead dogs moved left. Then he shouted, "Mush," and all of the dogs pulled the sled uphill, away from the rocks.

After the sled had gone a little ways, Chad shouted, "Whoa," stepped on the brake and got off the sled. He ran up to the left lead dog and patted her on the head. Then he patted the wheel dogs and said, "Good job." He smiled at Susie and said, "Not one pair of dogs got tangled up. That was great."

For the next three hours, Chad did everything he could do to get the sled stuck. One time the sled was going across a steep bank when the sled tipped over and Chad went tumbling down the side of the hill. When he stopped rolling, he sat up, spit out some snow and began to laugh. As Susie watched, she forgot that she was supposed to hold the leashes of the two dogs. When they saw Chad rolling down the hill, they thought Chad was playing, so they raced down the hill. Before Chad could get up, the dogs were all over him, licking his face, growling and pretending to bite his boots and

mittens. Some of the dogs on the gang line wanted to join in, but the lead dogs did not move, so the team had to stay where it was.

A few minutes later, the sled was upright and the team was again pulling the sled across the slope. It turned down to the river where he again got it stuck between a rock and a tree. This time, Chad could not free the sled, so he unharnessed the team, unloaded the sled and pulled the sled backwards until it was free.

Before hitching the team to the sled again, Chad said, "Let's try a run with sixteen dogs."

Susie felt a big smile form on her face. When Chad ran sixteen dogs, they included Denali and Butch. Both Denali and Butch were wheel dogs.

With sixteen dogs, the sled went a little faster and could get up the hills with a little less trouble. Chad got the sled stuck against a tree on the slope. Chad gave the dogs the order to wheel. The four wheel dogs pulled and strained and snorted, but the sled didn't turn uphill. "Come on, wheel dogs," Chad called. "Let's see you dig in. Haw, haw." This time the sled inched to the side as the dogs tugged. Then it turned a little

more. After four more tugs, the sled was free.

Chad ran the sixteen dogs up, down and across the slopes of Eagle River Valley. Things went well, except one time, he turned the dogs uphill and some of the dogs got on the wrong side of their partners. They were all tangled up. Finally, the team headed back to the truck. Susie was waiting. She said, "The team looked strong with sixteen dogs." Chad shook his head and made a face. "The team is stronger, all right," he said. "But it's a lot easier for them to get tangled up on the turns."

Just before Chad dropped off Susie and Denali, Susie said, "Are you thinking about running sixteen dogs in the Iditarod?"

"I've thought about it," he said, "but I think a team of fourteen would be a lot easier to handle, and it would be less work."

Susie really wanted Denali to be in the race. She didn't want to be a pest, but it didn't seem fair for Denali not to go.

As Susie walked around the back of the truck to get Denali, Chad called to her. "Remember, tomorrow is examination day."

"I know," she said.

"I'll pick you up at seven in the morning."

That evening, Susie thought about examination day. Before a team can run in the Iditarod, all the dogs must pass a thorough examination. A veterinarian must check them over carefully—their heart, their eyes and ears, their temperature, their legs, their back and their blood. If they don't pass the examination, they don't run in the Iditarod. The officials who run the race set the day for the dogs to be examined. Tomorrow was that day. It would take about twenty minutes for each dog to be examined. Susie figured that examining fourteen dogs would take at least four hours if only one vet examined all the dogs.

Number your paper from 1 through 21.

Skill Items

The veterinarian gave the dogs a thorough examination.

1. What word means **checkup?**
2. What word means **animal doctor?**
3. What word means that nothing is overlooked?

Write the word from the box that means the same thing as the underlined part of each sentence.

harness	partner	deadly	anchored
boxing	separated	mobbed	instructor

4. The teacher wrote a problem on the board.
5. He has a great fear of snakes.
6. The children were no longer together.

Review Items

7. How long does it take Jupiter to spin around one time?
8. What's another name for hot, melted rock?

- On planet M you can jump 15 feet high.
- On planet Q you can jump 5 feet high.
- On planet G you can jump 12 feet high.
- On planet X you can jump 20 feet high.
- On planet T you can jump 2 feet high.

9. Write the letter of the planet that has the most gravity.
10. Write the letter of the planet that has the least gravity.

11. When you teach an animal a simple trick, when do you reward the animal?
12. When don't you reward the animal?

13. Most sled-dog teams have an ______ number of dogs.
    - odd
    - even
14. For the Iditarod, a sled-dog team can't have more than ______ dogs.
15. What do sled dogs wear to protect their feet?

16. Name **2** cities in Colorado.
17. Name one city in Utah.
18. **Write the letters of the 4 items that tell what could happen to a sled dog's feet if they didn't have protection.**
    a. long claws
    b. snowballs between the pads
    c. cuts that do not heal well
    d. stiff legs
    e. slipping on hard snow
    f. icicles on their ankles
    g. cuts from ice and frozen snow

19. What command tells sled dogs to move straight ahead?
20. What command tells sled dogs to turn right?
21. What command tells sled dogs to turn left?

94

A

1	2	3	4
1. visibility	1. assistants	1. alarm	1. hip joint
2. fierce	2. injured	2. blizzard	2. limp
3. miserable	3. according	3. exchange	3. x-ray
4. courage	4. healthy	4. nightmare	4. replace
5. challenging	5. certificates	5. checkpoint	5. Chugger
6. dedicated			

B

Examination Day

Susie didn't like getting up early so she set her alarm clock for 6:40. That gave her only twenty minutes before Chad would pick her up. She dressed quickly, ran downstairs and started gulping down her breakfast. Her mother said, "You're eating faster than Denali. Slow down."

"Mmkay," she said.

The weather reporter on the radio was saying, "Looks as if the Iditarod will be run in winter weather this year. A large mass of cold, cold air is moving in from the north." The report gave Susie a nervous feeling. Bad weather can make the Iditarod a nightmare for the mushers and the dogs.

Five minutes later Susie was standing outside, dressed in her parka. It was seven o'clock. The wind was sharp and ugly and Chad was late. When Chad's truck finally pulled up at 7:10, Susie noticed something very strange. Butch was in the back of the truck. He wasn't one of Chad's regular wheel dogs, so why would he be going for an examination?

"Hey, Uncle Chad," she said. "Why is Butch in the truck?"

Chad replied, "For the same reason that Denali's going to be in the truck."

"What's that reason?"

"I decided to run sixteen dogs."

"Sixteen?"

Susie understood what Chad said as soon as he spoke the words. But it took her a few seconds to realize what she was about to shout. "Denali's going to run in the Iditarod!"

She jumped up and down three times before she ran over to Denali's kennel. She opened the gate and told Denali to get on the truck. Then she opened the truck door, leaned over and gave Chad a great hug. "Yes, yes!" she shouted.

He said, "You're yelling in my ear."

She hugged Chad a few more times, and then her thoughts suddenly changed. She wondered if Denali was really ready for the race. What if he got injured? What if the weather got so bad that the sled got lost? What if . . .

Susie didn't ask Chad these questions. But she had a lot of others, and she asked them—one after another as the truck drove to the examination station. She was still asking questions as she and Chad waited at the station while the dogs were being examined. A veterinarian and three assistants were checking Chad's team. The inside of the station was pretty cold because the dogs were more comfortable in cold than they were in heated places. At last Susie asked Chad her last question. "Why did you decide to run with sixteen dogs?"

"Well," Chad said. "It was a tough decision. A team of sixteen dogs is a headache even if they work well together. But I figured that I would be better off with more dogs. In case something happens, we'll still probably have enough dogs to finish the race."

Susie knew what Chad was referring to. According to the rules of the Iditarod, a musher cannot exchange dogs. If a dog gets injured, the musher must carry it in the sled to the next checkpoint on the trail and leave the dog there. The musher can't replace it with another dog. If too many dogs are injured, the musher can't continue in the race. The rules state that a musher must have at least five dogs on the gang line at the end of the race.

Chad said, "If the team of sixteen is too much trouble to handle, I'll just leave some of them at a checkpoint and go on with either fourteen or maybe twelve dogs. We'll just have to see how well the team of sixteen does on the trail."

The veterinarian and one of her assistants approached Chad and Susie. The assistant was carrying a pile of certificates. The veterinarian handed them to Chad and said, "Fifteen of your dogs check out fine. But the dog named Chugger may have a hip problem. I can't be sure. She doesn't limp, and the x-rays don't show any serious problem, but I'm not sure her hip joint is healthy." She shook her head. Then she added, "But I won't keep her out of the race if you want to keep her on your team."

Now Chad shook his head. Chugger was one of his wheel dogs. She was strong and smart. She was almost nine years old, but she had never had any serious health problems.

The vet said, “I’m telling you about this because I want you to understand that she may have a problem. I’m not sure I would take her if she were my dog.”

C Number your paper from 1 through 19.

Skill Items

Use the words in the box to write complete sentences.

exchanged	truck driver	alarm	thorough
partner	demanded	replaced	reef
veterinarian	scuba diver	surfaced	examination

1. The ____ and her ____ ____ near the ____.
2. The ____ gave the dogs a ____ ____.

Write the word from the box that means the same thing as the underlined part of each sentence.

tune	replaced	according	strained
overcame	pest	shortly	alarm

3. He solved his fear of storms.
4. Darla learned a new song for the party.
5. We're going to eat soon.

Review Items

6. What happens if a sled dog doesn't pass the Iditarod's health examination?
7. If booties on a sled dog are too tight, what could happen?
8. If booties are too loose, what could happen?
9. In what country are the states of Colorado and Utah?
10. Name the mountains you drive over to get from Colorado to Utah.
11. In which direction do you go to get from Colorado to Utah?

12. When you teach animals to work for new rewards, do you change the reward **quickly** or **slowly?**
13. When you teach an animal to work for a new reward, what kind of reward do you start with?
14. Then what do you do to that reward?
15. When do you stop changing the reward?

16. Name 3 things that great water pressure can do to you.

17. The more water the glass has, the ______ the sound it makes.
    - lower
    - higher
18. Write the letter of the glass that will make the lowest ring.
19. Write the letter of the glass that will make the highest ring.

A B C D E F

A

1	2	3	4
1. volunteer	1. competed	1. Mr. Martin	1. endurance
2. blizzard	2. amused	2. feat	2. challenging
3. weary	3. mushed	3. events	3. Hoover
4. photo	4. dedicated	4. courage	4. demanding
5. Sweden		5. unties	

B

Supplies for the Race

The rules of the Iditarod require each musher to bring along supplies that are needed for the musher and the dogs to survive under severe conditions. The rules require the musher to have an ax, a good sleeping bag, snowshoes and enough food for one day. The sled must have at least two pounds of food for each dog and one day's worth of food for the musher. The rules also require the sled to have enough room to carry at least one injured dog.

C

The Big Race

Chad didn't talk much in the truck as he drove back to Susie's place. Susie could see that he was thinking about what to do with Chugger. She didn't say anything. She knew that Chad had to make his own decision because he would be the one who would have to live with it. The only dogs that are more important than the wheel dogs are the lead dogs. Susie knew that Chad did not want to replace either of his regular wheel dogs because they worked well together. As Chad drove, he said, "She hasn't had any problems on the practice runs." A few minutes later he said, "Neither of her parents had hip problems." When the truck was about a mile from Susie's place, he said, "I'll make a decision tomorrow."

When he dropped Susie off, he said, "I've made up my mind about Chugger. I'm going to keep her on the team. I think she'll be fine."

Later that evening, Susie thought about the adventure that Chad was going to have. As she thought about the Iditarod, she looked at a photo on the wall that showed a smiling woman surrounded by sled dogs. The woman was Susan Butcher. She had entered the Iditarod seventeen times, and she actually finished it sixteen times. Not only did she finish the race, but one time, she came in third place. Four times she came in second place. This was an amazing feat for a woman who competed against the greatest mushers in the world in an event that required courage, strength and incredible endurance. Even more amazing than her four second-place finishes was her first-place finish in 1986. And she also finished first in 1987, 1988 and 1990.

Susie wondered how she had done it—four first-place finishes in what has to be one of the most challenging events a person could enter.

• • •

More than 75 teams were ready to start the Iditarod. The weather was miserable. The temperature was near freezing and a thick wet snow was falling. The dogs were panting. They knew that they were going to start something that was very demanding.

The race had started at 10 A.M., but it hadn't started for all the mushers. One musher started at a time. In fact, the first musher who was called to the starting line had died earlier that year. After calling his name, the announcer explained to the crowd that the race was dedicated to him. Two minutes later the first musher left. Everybody cheered. Some of the dogs barked and howled. Others just looked around panting. Two minutes after that musher had left, another musher started.

Musher number 16 amused the crowd, but he didn't do it on purpose. He had tied the back of his sled to a pickup truck. When the announcer called his number, he mushed, the team pulled hard, and as they crossed the start line, the dogs were pulling the pickup truck along behind them. The announcer said, "Now there's a team with some real power. Think of how well they're going to do when Mr. Martin unties them from his truck." Everybody laughed.

It was now after 11 A.M., but Chad hadn't started yet. He was the 61st musher in the race. Just ahead of him was a musher from Sweden. Behind Chad was a musher from Michigan. That musher had run the Iditarod six times.

Chad and Susie were busy getting ready. They were putting booties on the dogs' feet. Chad brought along more than a thousand booties. He figured that he would change booties about every two days and more often if the snow was hard and frozen.

"Number 59," the announcer called from the start line. "Terry North from Colorado. It's your turn, Terry. Good luck." Terry tipped his hat and shouted, "Mush," so loudly that some of the dogs that were not in his team tried to run. One of them was Hoover, a dog in Chad's team.

Chad said, "Take it easy, Hoover. It won't be long now."

Chad and Susie checked the supplies one last time. They had already done it three times earlier, and if something was missing now, there wasn't much they could do about it because of the most important rule of the Iditarod. Once the race starts, all mushers are on their own. They can't try to get help from anybody who is not in the race. They can't use a phone, a radio or any other device that would allow others to help them. When they are on the trail, they must do the best they can without help from anybody.

D Number your paper from 1 through 25.

Review Items

1. During the Iditarod, what does a musher have to do with any dogs that are injured?
2. According to the Iditarod rules, there must be at least how many dogs on the gang line at the end of the race?
3. If you're underwater 100 feet deep, the pressure is much greater than it is on land. How many times greater is it?
4. When divers are that deep, how long should they take to return to the surface of the water?
5. What may happen to the divers if they go up faster than that?

6. Is the water cooler at **100 feet down** or **at the surface?**
7. Is all the water at 100 feet down the same temperature?
8. Name 2 acts of bravery.
9. What do you fill a buoyancy device with?
10. When it is filled up, what happens to the diver?
11. When it is empty, what happens to the diver?

12. What part of the scuba equipment does the **J** show?
13. What part does the **K** show?
14. What part does the **L** show?
15. What part does the **M** show?
16. What part does the **N** show?
17. What part does the **0** show?
18. What part does the **P** show?

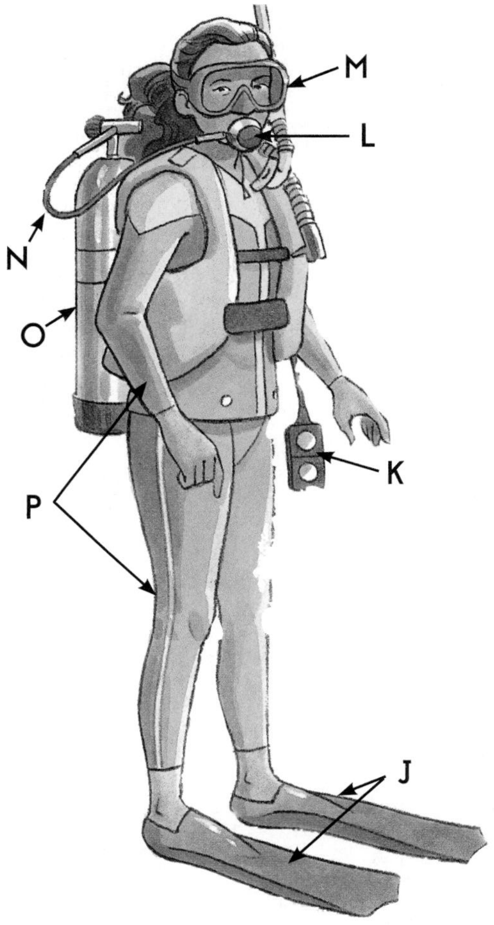

Write the name of each kind of coral.

19.

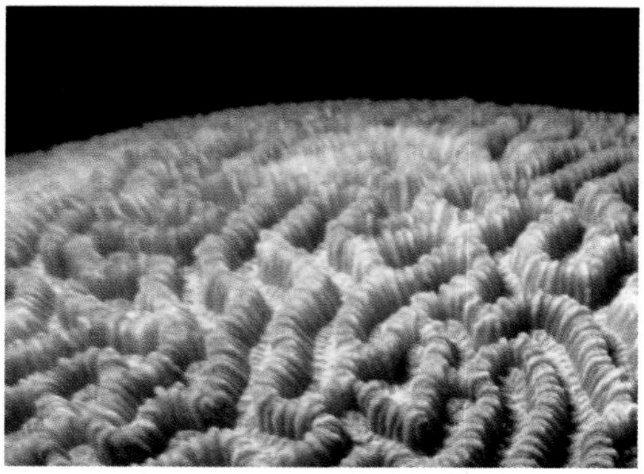

20.

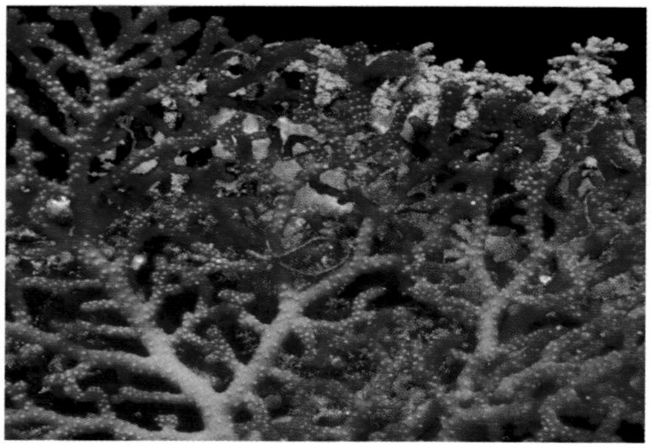

21.

22. Name **2** things you could give a dog to reward it.

23. What color is lava when it's very hot?
    - brown
    - orange
    - gray
24. What color is lava after it cools a little bit?
25. What color is lava after it's completely cooled?

A

1	2	3	4
1. recently	1. trudged	1. Ms. Siri Carlson	1. gust
2. scent	2. rainy	2. Libby Riddles	2. weary
3. cruel	3. stinging	3. Bowman	3. sleeve
4. tempted	4. volunteers	4. evergreen	4. blizzard
5. checkpoint		5. struck	5. birthday
6. handlebar			6. snowmobile

B

Checkpoints

Checkpoints are places along the Iditarod trail where mushers can rest their teams, make repairs and feed their dogs. The places are called checkpoints because race officials check to make sure that all the mushers pass through each checkpoint. If mushers don't get to a checkpoint, the officials send out planes or snowmobiles to find them.

Checkpoints are about 50 miles apart, so there are usually 24 checkpoints from the beginning of the Iditarod trail to Nome. A lot of things happen at these checkpoints. A musher can drop off an injured or sick dog at a checkpoint. Airplanes deliver food for dogs and mushers to most of the checkpoints. Some of the checkpoints have veterinarians and assistants who check the dogs.

C

On the Trail

"Number 60," the announcer called. "From Sweden, in her third Iditarod, Siri Carlson." Susie had talked with Ms. Carlson before the race. "Good luck," Susie called and Ms. Carlson waved to her.

The moment she left, Susie's heart started to pound. This was it. In two minutes, Chad would be off and on his own. He would be challenging cruel weather and fierce winds. And Denali would be out there with him. For a moment, Susie was tempted to grab Chad's sleeve and say, "Don't do it, Chad. It's too dangerous." But instead, she smiled.

Chad looked at Susie, smiled nervously and shook his head. "I'm nervous now," he said. "I always feel that way before a race starts."

A few moments later the announcer said, "Number 61, from the town of Knik, which is just outside the great city of Anchorage, in the great state of Alaska, Chad Bowman. Last time he tried, he didn't have very good luck. This time, I hope his luck will be better. See you in Nome, Chad."

Chad waved, and his sled went down the well-used trail. Then Susie watched it get smaller and smaller as the snow continued to fall. Then Susie could hardly see it. Then . . .

• • •

Hundreds of volunteer workers are needed to make the Iditarod successful. These volunteers do everything from helping injured dogs to flying planes that deliver food to checkpoints. Mushers carry only enough food for about one day on the trail. They get the rest of the food they need at the checkpoints.

Mushers have to do a lot of things and they must do them without help from anybody at the checkpoint. The first thing mushers do at a checkpoint is feed their dogs, then they set up a place for the dogs to rest. Mushers often cut branches from evergreen trees and make beds for their dogs. They must also get water for the dogs. They either heat snow to melt it or haul water from a stream. They check the dogs' paws, booties and harnesses. Then the mushers take a little time to eat, and maybe they'll even take a nap before continuing. After they leave the checkpoint, they usually don't see anything but the trail, the snow and their dogs until they reach the next checkpoint. Sometimes they will catch up to another sled. That sled moves over and lets them pass.

• • •

It was now the third day of the race and Chad's team was in the mountains. On the day before the race had started, the weather reports warned about a great storm moving in from the north. That storm had arrived. Chad was trying to make his way through very rough country. He wasn't riding on the back of the sled. He was walking behind the sled as he held the handlebar, but he wasn't walking very fast. The wind blasted the snow with stinging force and the temperature was around 10 degrees below zero. The snow was hard and icy. The dogs were weary, and so was Chad. He could not see past the wheel dogs.

As a stinging gust of wind struck him, he shook his head and laughed

to himself. He shouted above the wind, “Why do they call this place Rainy Pass? It’s always frozen and cold.” As Chad trudged through the blizzard, he remembered the story of the first woman to win the Iditarod. Her name is Libby Riddles. She won the race in 1985. That was one of the longest races ever because the weather was so bad. The race was stopped twice because the planes could not get to the checkpoints and drop off food. Most of the mushers were at Rainy Pass the first time the race was stopped.

At that moment, Susie was in her warm living room, writing Chad a letter as her mother watched TV. Susie wrote a letter every day. She sent all of them to Nome. She wanted to make sure that when Chad finally arrived there, he would have a lot of mail from Susie. Here’s part of the letter she was writing now:

Do you know that in two days, it will be Denali's birthday? He'll be three years old.

Suddenly, the TV program stopped and an announcer said, "Here's a special report on the Iditarod from Rainy Pass." The picture on the TV showed snow blowing and a reporter who was yelling over the wind. He told about the high winds at Rainy Pass. He said, "The winds are blowing so hard that some of the mushers are lost because they can't see the trail. The race officials may have to send out search parties if some of the teams don't show up at the checkpoint pretty soon."

Susie didn't finish the letter she had started. Denali's birthday didn't seem very important anymore. Instead, she wrote another letter.

Dear Uncle Chad,

The weather report from Rainy Pass is scary. I hope you are not one of those mushers who got lost. I hope they found all the mushers who got lost. And I hope their dogs are okay. I hope that your team is doing well.

With love,

Susie

What she really wanted to say in her letter was, "Oh please make sure that Denali is all right. Oh please don't get lost. And if you do get lost, please find your way to the next checkpoint."

D Number your paper from 1 through 19.

Review Items

1. The rules for the Iditarod require each musher to have certain things. Write the letters of those things.

   a. an ax
   b. snowshoes
   c. a tent
   d. firewood
   e. a good sleeping bag
   f. extra shoes
   g. enough food for a day
   h. enough food for a week
   i. booties
   j. extra dogs

2. During the Iditarod, how much food does each dog need every day?
    - 1 pound
    - 2 pounds
    - 3 pounds
3. Each sled in the Iditarod must have room to hold ______.
    - a spare sled
    - another musher
    - an injured dog
4. Name the woman who finished the Iditarod sixteen times.
5. How many times did she **enter** the Iditarod?
6. How many times did she finish in first place?
7. How many mushers start the Iditarod at the same time?
8. How much time passes before the next musher starts?
9. When Iditarod mushers are on the trail, how much help can they get from someone else?
10. Is the water cooler at **100 feet down** or **at the surface?**
11. Is all the water at 100 feet down the same temperature?
12. What do you fill a buoyancy device with?
13. When it is filled up, what happens to the diver?
14. When it is empty, what happens to the diver?
15. If you move up too fast from very deep water, you may get the ______.
16. What forms in your blood as you go up too fast?
17. When you go up very fast, is there **more pressure** or **less pressure** on your body?
18. When you're training an animal, what do you do each time the animal does the trick?
19. What do you do if the animal does not do the trick?

97

A

1	2	3
1. snowmobile	1. compass	1. beware
2. evergreen	2. peered	2. plunge
3. birthday	3. recently	3. visibility
4. checkpoint	4. total	4. scent
5. nightmare		
6. handlebar		

B

Lost

Chad was lost. The snow had been blowing so hard that he had lost the trail to Rainy Pass. He had an idea of which direction he should be going and he noticed that the snow was deep. That meant that nobody had been over the snow recently. The dogs were very tired from plowing through the deep snow. And it was getting dark out. In about half an hour, it would be completely dark.

Chad didn't know if he was left of the trail or right of the trail. So he wasn't sure which way he should head to find the trail. He decided that the best thing to do was not to find the trail but to find the checkpoint. He turned on the light that was on his hat. He took out his compass and looked at the direction his sled was heading. It was going too far to the north. Chad knew that this part of the trail went almost straight west on its way to Rainy Pass. He also noticed that the slopes he was going over were too steep. Both those clues told him that he should just turn left and head straight west. That's what he did.

A half hour later, in almost total darkness, the wind died down. The blowing snow settled from the air. Chad peered to the north to see where the mountains were.

"Yes," he said. The mountains were where they should be. That meant that Chad was going in the right direction. A moment later, he looked ahead and he could see the lights from the lodge at Rainy Pass. "Yes," he repeated. "Yes." He could also see the trail. It was just a little bit to his right.

The dogs seemed to pep up. They could see the lights and smell the

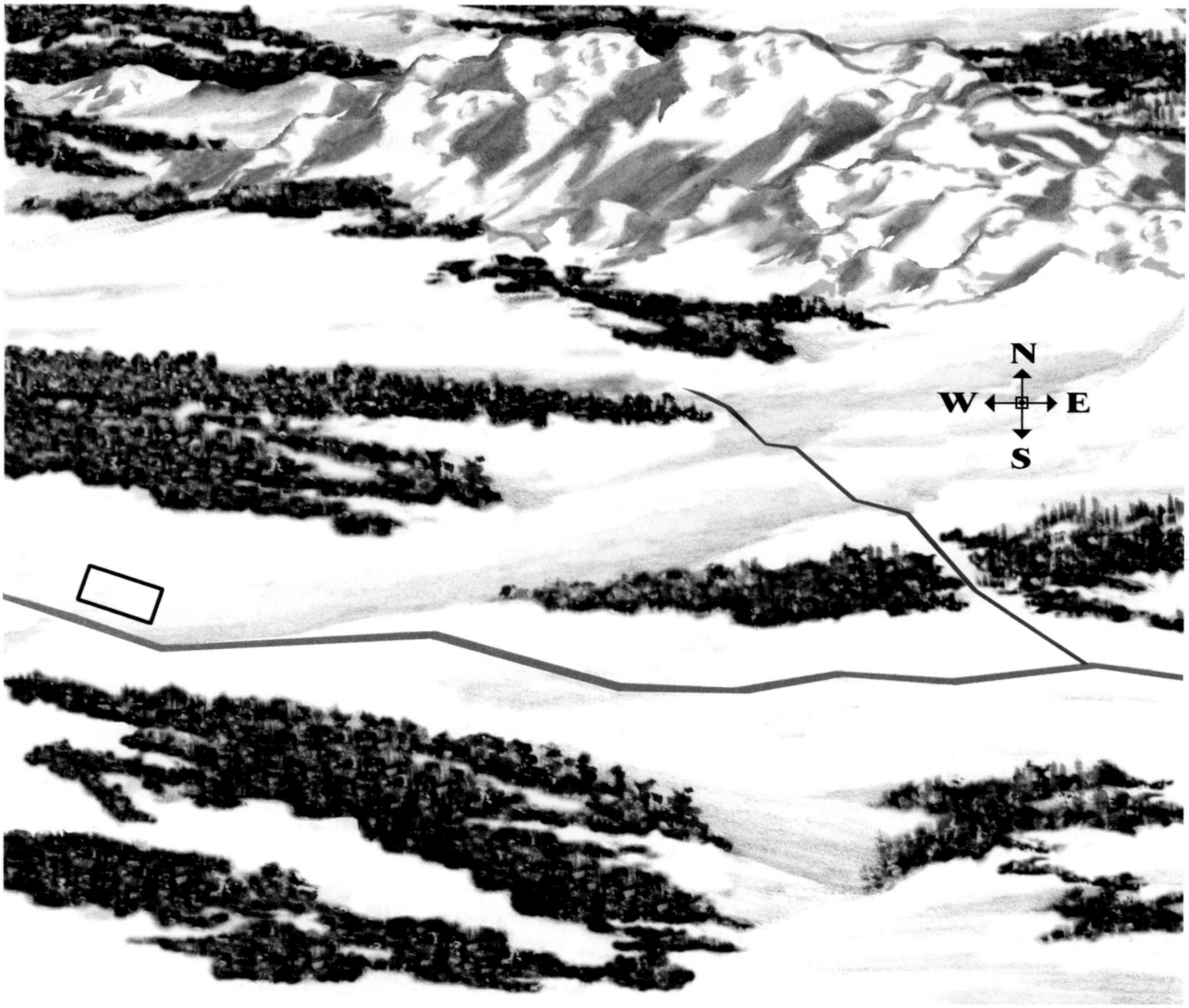

food from the checkpoint. "Mush," Chad yelled and the dogs pulled hard. "You guys are lucky," he said to his team. "If you had just an ordinary musher, you might have to spend all night on the trail. Tonight, you'll have a real treat."

The wind started up again, blowing swirls of snow and making it impossible for Chad to see anything but snow. "Come on, you guys," he said to his team. "The sooner you reach those lights, the sooner we'll be able to rest in real comfort."

About twenty minutes later, Chad entered the checkpoint at Rainy Pass. A lot of people were there, and most of them looked worried. One of the first questions that the officials asked Chad was, "Did you see any other teams?"

"No," Chad said.

"Well, two teams are missing, number 58 and number 60."

Chad explained how he may have passed them without knowing it. "I lost the trail for a while. I went too far north, so I cut back and went west."

"How was the visibility out there?"

"Most of the time I couldn't see my lead dogs."

As Chad was unpacking, unhitching his dogs and feeding them, the officials continued to ask questions. Then they said, "We're going to take some snowmobiles back along the trail and see if we can find 58 and 60. We're thinking of going down the regular trail and also going back along the route that you took. If their dogs pick up the scent of your dogs, they may try to take the same route you took."

Chad tried to describe his route, but he could see that the officials were not able to understand all the things he explained. At last, Chad said, "If you can drive me down the trail a mile or so, I can show you where to go."

A few minutes later, three snowmobiles set out down the trail. Chad was driving one of them. The wind had stopped. When the snowmobiles came to the place where Chad had joined the trail, he pointed out the route he had taken. The other two snowmobiles went back along Chad's trail and the regular trail. Chad drove his snowmobile back to the checkpoint.

As Chad checked the equipment and took care of his dogs, he kept thinking about the lost teams, especially number 60, Siri Carlson from Sweden. What was she doing now? Was she okay? Would they find her?

Chad didn't find out until the next morning. He slept in the lodge that night, on a real bed. What a treat. When he was leaving the lodge in the morning to check on his dogs, he saw her. "Hi," he said and asked about her adventure. She told him that she had lost the trail and the sled had tumbled down a slope. Two of her dogs were injured and a runner on her sled was broken. Chad wanted to help her fix the sled, but that was against the rules. So he wished her good luck. Then he said, "I hope I see you on the trail tomorrow."

She smiled and said, "I'll be there, don't worry."

C Number your paper from 1 through 16.

Skill Items

Visibility was miserable in the fierce blizzard.

1. What word means **terrible?**
2. What word refers to how well you can see things?
3. What word means **very wild?**
4. What word names a snowstorm that is windy and very cold?

Review Items

5. Name **3** things an Iditarod musher does at checkpoints.
6. Why are checkpoints called checkpoints?
7. How does food get to the checkpoints?
8. About how far apart are the checkpoints?
9. About how many checkpoints are there between Anchorage and Nome?
10. During the Iditarod, how do mushers get water for their dogs?
11. What do mushers usually use to make beds for their dogs?
12. What's the name of the first woman to win the Iditarod?
13. In what year did she win it?

Let's say you're training a dog to jump up in the air and do a backward somersault. **Use the words below to finish each sentence.**

- jumping up and leaning backward
- jumping up and turning upside down
- jumping up in the air

14. At first, you would reward the dog for ________.
15. Later you would reward the dog for ________.
16. Later you would reward the dog for ________.

A

1	2
1. arrangements	1. sheltered
2. congratulate	2. tarps
3. beware	3. plunged
4. crust	4. tucking
5. dried	

B

Rest Periods

One rule of the Iditarod is that every musher must take a 24-hour rest at one of the checkpoints and an eight-hour rest at two of the other checkpoints. This rule was put in so that the dogs would not have to work so hard that they collapsed on the trail.

During the first years of the race, a lot of dogs died from injury, starvation and working too hard. During the first year of the race, 1973, thirty dogs died during the race. Even today, with all the care that the mushers take to make sure the dogs are treated well, two or three dogs die during every race. That's not a large number if you remember that there may be 800 dogs entered in a race, but it's still more dogs than anybody wants to die.

Chad had not lost any dogs when he tried running the Iditarod before, but one of Chad's best friends lost two dogs in 1998.

Beware of Streams

It was day nine of the race, and Chad was lost again. After he left Rainy Pass, things went pretty smoothly for three days. Then the weather turned bad again. Chad's team went only about fifty miles one day and fifty miles the next day. The winds and weather were so bad that he didn't feel it was safe to try to go any farther. Today started out a lot better, but about halfway between checkpoints 18 and 19, a terrible storm moved in. Chad could not see the lead dogs and sometimes he

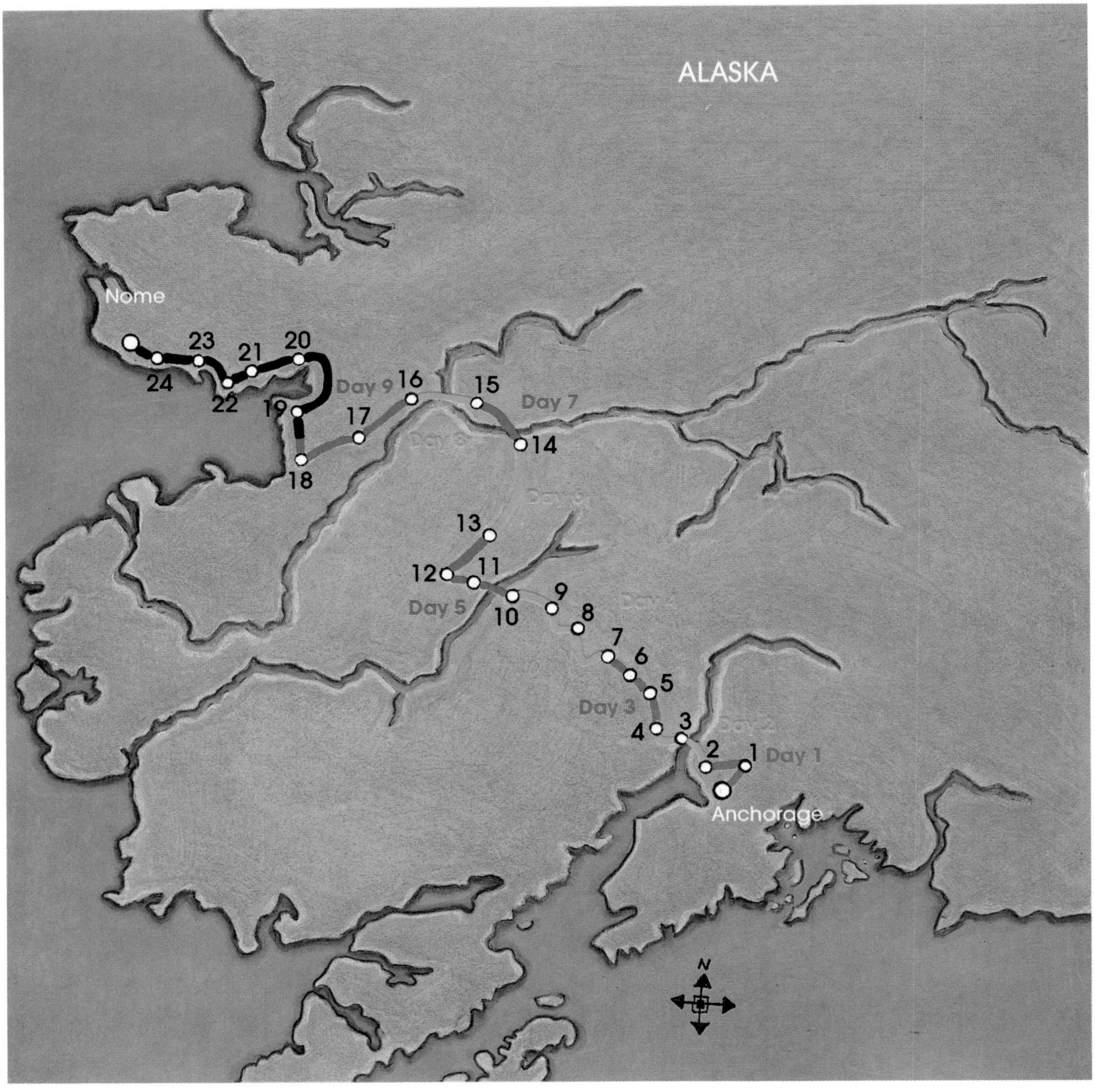

couldn't see the wheel dogs. He found a sheltered place and stayed there for more than two hours. Then he tried to move on. Within an hour he had lost the trail. He headed north along the ocean, hoping that he would find the trail again, but as the team was slowly crossing a low area, one of the worst possible things happened. The sled was going over a thick crust of frozen snow. Below that snow was a fast-moving stream. Chad didn't know that until the back of the sled suddenly broke through the crust of ice and fell into the water below.

The air temperature was around zero. If a person gets wet at that temperature, that person could easily die by freezing. Chad got wet. The rear end of the sled plunged into the water. The front end of the sled was pointing up. As Chad was trying to climb up to the front of the sled, the snow cracked again and the wheel dogs fell into the water. Chugger let out a cry.

The team stopped. Denali and Butch looked back. Chad was up to his chest in the water. He had to get the sled out of the water quickly. Denali and Butch were the dogs that

had to pull the sled out. "Mush," Chad shouted. "Mush, Denali. Mush, Butch. Mush . . ." They did. They got low and strained as they pulled forward. "Mush."

Slowly, the team dragged Chugger and Buck out of the water. Then the sled came out—with streams of water flowing from it. Chad was soaked. He knew that he had only minutes to get warm or he would freeze. He drove the team to a grove of trees. He noticed that Chugger was not able to pull. Then Chad quickly removed some tarps from the sled and hung them from the trees so they made a tent. He quickly unpacked dry clothes from the sled and some emergency wood. This wood was treated and it would burn even if it were wet.

As the wind howled and the snow blew, Chad built a fire inside the tent. It took Chad only about two minutes to start the fire, but he could feel that his legs were starting to get numb. A minute later the fire was putting out good heat. By now, Chad had taken off his wet clothes, dried himself as fast as he could and started putting on dry clothes.

He stayed inside the tent until the feeling had returned to his legs. Then he went out to check on the

dogs. Chugger could not walk on all four legs. Her back left leg did not work because her hip had failed.

Chad took Chugger off the gang line and carried her into the tent. He dried her off and then put a blanket around her. She licked his face as he was tucking her in. Then he took Buck, the other regular wheel dog, off the gang line. Buck would walk behind the sled until the team reached the next checkpoint. Denali and Butch would be the wheel dogs for the rest of the race.

Chad stayed at the grove for three hours, until the weather cleared. Then he climbed a nearby hill so he could look in all directions for the trail. He didn't have much hope of seeing it, but he thought it was worth trying. To his surprise, he saw a dog sled as soon as he got to the top of the hill. It was a few hundred yards to the east. When he took a closer look, he said, "I know who that is." It was Siri Carlson. Chad whistled and waved.

She waved back and shouted something, but he couldn't hear what she said. He signaled that he would catch up with her. Then he ran back to his team and hitched them to the gang line. He put Chugger in the sled. When Chad told the team to mush, Chugger tried to stand up. Chad patted her and said, "Not you, Chugger. You just take it easy." The team went east over the hills until it reached the trail. Chad could see Siri's team about half a mile ahead of him.

D Number your paper from 1 through 16.

Skill Items

Use the words in the box to write complete sentences.

thorough	courage	examination	visibility
included	injured	purpose	veterinarian
officials	blizzard	miserable	fierce

1. The ____ gave the dogs a ____ ____.
2. ____ was ____ in the ____ ____.

Review Items

3. During the Iditarod, is the snow deeper **on the trail** or **off the trail?**
4. Why?

5. How does water pressure change as you move from deep in the water toward the surface?
6. How does the light around you change as you move toward the surface?

7. In what state is the Iditarod sled-dog race?
8. In which city does it begin?
9. In which city does it end?

10. The Iditarod is about ______ miles from start to finish.
    - 1600
    - 500
    - 1100
11. In most years, the race takes about ______.
    - 10 days
    - 2 weeks
    - a week

12. Name an arrow-shaped fish.
13. Write **2** facts about those fish.

14. What command tells sled dogs to turn right?
15. What command tells sled dogs to move straight ahead?
16. What command tells sled dogs to turn left?

A

1	2	3
1. anxious	1. aimlessly	1. victory
2. Angela	2. lantern	2. award
3. curious	3. arrangements	3. hero
4. insist	4. surprise	4. buddies
5. demand	5. finisher	5. miserable
	6. congratulated	6. fierce

B

End of the Race

Chad's team was on the trail again. Siri Carlson was about half a mile ahead of Chad.

"Come on, you guys," Chad said to his team. "If you want some company, we'll have to go faster than this. Mush, you sled dogs. Mush." Chad pedaled with one foot to help make the sled go faster. The team had only fourteen dogs in it, but they pulled hard. And before long, they caught up to Siri's team.

Chad told her what had happened and how the dogs were able to pull the sled out of the water. She said, "You must have strong wheel dogs."

"I do," Chad said. "Although I don't think Chugger will be pulling sleds from now on." Chad and Siri reached checkpoint 19 about an hour later. They stayed there for eight hours. Chad made arrangements for a plane to take Chugger back to Anchorage. He changed the gang line so that there was one dog in front of Butch and Denali. That dog was Buck.

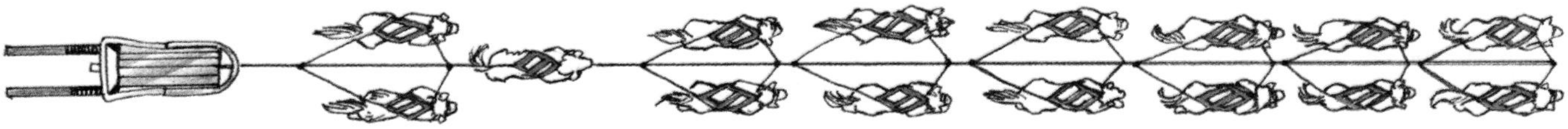

After eight hours of resting, Chad and his team went on the trail again. The weather was cold, but the air was clear and the dogs wanted to run. They made good time. So did Siri's team. Chad was in front of them for most of the trip to Nome.

Chad saw the first signs of the town just after the sun had set the next day. Chad could hardly believe that he had been on the trail for eleven days. In some ways, it didn't seem that long. In other ways, it seemed as if he had been on the Iditarod trail for as long as he could remember.

Siri finished ahead of Chad—in the same order they started. She finished in 34th place. He finished in 35th place. He gave her a big hug. "You're a good musher," he said.

"Thank you!" she said. "It was a wonderful experience, and I hate to see it end."

The words seemed strange. Chad thought how the cruel winds, the fierce weather and the dangers make your days miserable. But when you cross that finish line, you know that you and your dogs worked as a team that battled the cold, the snow, the winds, and you won. You went over 11 hundred miles in only 11 days. This victory was even sweeter to Chad when the race officials told him that the weather for this race had been worse than it had been since 1985.

• • •

The plane from Nome landed in Anchorage the next day at about the same time the last finisher of the Iditarod was crossing the finish line. Every year, the last-place team receives the red-lantern award. This year, the red-lantern winner finished in 12 days, 4 hours.

Chad had taken two showers since finishing the race, and he had slept until after eight in the morning. His clothes were clean, but he hadn't shaved.

The plane was met by a cheering crowd—friends and relatives of the mushers who were flying back with Chad. Susie was there. The day before, she had gone to the airport to pick up Chugger. The vet had told her that there wasn't much she could do to fix Chugger's hip, but that her hip would probably be okay as long as she didn't try to pull sleds or do heavy work.

The first thing Susie did was find Denali and give him a whole lot of hugs and kisses. She whispered to him, "You're a hero. I knew you would be. You're wonderful."

Of course, after Chad loaded his team into his truck, Susie had lots of questions. First she asked whether Chad had received all her mail and read it. He told her that he had received it and had read all of it. Then most of Susie's questions were about Denali. She was most interested in what Denali did when the sled broke through the crust and fell into the water. "Was he the one who helped most to pull you out?"

"Well, you could probably say that," Chad replied. "He didn't slip backwards, and when I told the dogs to pull, he pulled hard."

"He was a hero, wasn't he?" she said.

"Well, I guess you could say that," Chad replied. "I was proud of all the dogs, and Denali certainly did his share, maybe even more than his share."

"He did as well as the older dogs, didn't he?"

"Yes, he did," Chad said. "And if it's all right with you, I'll want him to be a regular wheel dog for next year's Iditarod."

"Well, sure," she said. "I wouldn't want you to go out there without him. You need Denali."

So even before everybody had congratulated Chad on finishing the race, he was making plans about next year's race. Part of the plans included working with Siri Carlson. She planned to do summer training with Chad and his team. And Susie got the idea that Chad and Siri seemed to like each other more than they would if they were just mushing buddies.

She was right. Two years later, Chad and Siri got married. And Denali ran in six more Iditarods. The musher for the first five races was Chad. The musher for the sixth race was Susie.

C Number your paper from 1 through 13.

Skill Items

Write the word from the box that means the same thing as the underlined part of each sentence.

sheltered	darted	plunged	peered
rapidly	recently	trailed	victory

1. The fish moved very fast in the fish tank.
2. We ran down the hill quickly.
3. The kittens followed their mother across the yard.

Review Items

4. The rules of the Iditarod state that every musher must rest for ___ hours at one checkpoint and must rest for ___ hours at two other checkpoints.
5. This rule was put in to protect the ___.
   - race officials
   - mushers
   - dogs
6. In what year was the first Iditarod?
7. During the first running of the Iditarod, how many dogs died during the race?
8. During more recent years, how many dogs die during each race?
9. What do sled dogs wear to protect their feet?
10. **Write the letters of the 4 items that tell what could happen to a sled dog's feet if they didn't have protection.**
    a. stiff legs
    b. snowballs between the pads
    c. cuts from ice and frozen snow
    d. long claws
    e. slipping on hard snow
    f. icicles on their ankles
    g. cuts that do not heal well
11. If booties on a sled dog are too tight, what could happen?
12. If booties are too loose, what could happen?
13. What happens if a sled dog doesn't pass the Iditarod's health examination?

100 TEST 10

Number your paper from 1 through 34.

1. Most sled-dog teams have an _____ number of dogs.
   - odd
   - even
2. For the Iditarod, a sled-dog team can't have more than _____ dogs.

Use these words to answer items 3–5:

- **swing dogs**
- **wheel dogs**
- **lead dogs**

3. These dogs are very good followers, and they are smart.
4. These dogs are responsible for freeing the sled when it gets stuck.
5. These dogs are very smart, and other dogs obey them.
6. If booties on a sled dog are too tight, what could happen?
7. If booties are too loose, what could happen?
8. What command tells sled dogs to turn right?
9. What command tells sled dogs to move straight ahead?
10. What command tells sled dogs to turn left?
11. What happens if a sled dog doesn't pass the Iditarod's health examination?
12. During the Iditarod, what does a musher have to do with any dogs that are injured?
13. According to the Iditarod rules, there must be at least how many dogs on the gang line at the end of the race?

14. The rules for the Iditarod require each musher to have certain things. Write the letters of those things.
    a. firewood
    b. snowshoes
    c. enough food for a day
    d. an ax
    e. a good sleeping bag
    f. extra shoes
    g. a tent
    h. extra dogs
    i. booties
    j. enough food for a week
15. During the Iditarod, how much food does each dog need every day?
    - 3 pounds
    - 1 pound
    - 2 pounds
16. Each sled in the Iditarod must have room to hold ___.
    - a spare sled
    - an injured dog
    - another musher
17. Name the woman who finished the Iditarod sixteen times.
18. How many times did she **enter** the Iditarod?
19. How many times did she finish in first place?
20. When Iditarod mushers are on the trail, how much help can they get from someone else?
21. Name **3** things an Iditarod musher does at checkpoints.
22. Why are checkpoints called checkpoints?
23. How does food get to the checkpoints?
24. About how far apart are the checkpoints?
25. About how many checkpoints are there between Anchorage and Nome?
26. What's the name of the first woman to win the Iditarod?
27. In what year did she win it?

28. The rules of the Iditarod state that every musher must rest for ____ hours at one checkpoint and must rest for ____ hours at two other checkpoints.
29. This rule was put in to protect the ____.
    - race officials
    - mushers
    - dogs

Skill Items

For each item, write the underlined word or words from the sentences in the box.

> The veterinarian gave the dogs a thorough examination.
> Visibility was miserable in the fierce blizzard.

30. What underlining means **very wild?**
31. What underlining refers to how well you can see things?
32. What underlining means **animal doctor?**
33. What underlining means that nothing is overlooked?
34. What underlining means **terrible?**

END OF TEST 10

SPECIAL PROJECT

Things to be found:

- A photograph of the finish line in Nome.
- A map that shows the Iditarod trail and all the checkpoints.
- A magazine article that tells something about the Iditarod.
- A chart that shows how long it took all the mushers in the last Iditarod to finish the race.
- An article that explains who the dog Balto was and how he was related to the Iditarod.

A

1	2	3
1. familiar	1. aimlessly	1. chilly
2. galaxy	2. demanded	2. insisted
3. anxious	3. creepy	3. anywhere
4. Angela	4. surprised	4. agreeing
5. stir		5. midnight
6. curious		

B Go Anywhere—See Anything

Al hadn't done well on the test that he had taken in school that day, but Al was not really very disappointed. Al didn't like school very much, so he wasn't anxious about doing well on tests. He didn't care much about the test, and he didn't feel good about school or about himself. As Al walked from school with his older sister Angela, she was trying to talk Al into playing baseball.

"No," Al replied. "You play. I'm going to walk around for a while." That's just what Al did.

He walked aimlessly down one street and then down another. Now and then a very cold wind would swirl between the buildings and stir up the scraps of paper in the streets. From time to time Al felt chilly, and he thought about the colder weather that was on its way. In two weeks it would be Christmas. Al wasn't paying much attention to where he was going, but he wasn't worried about getting lost. He knew that he'd be able to find his way home from just about anyplace in the city.

Al wasn't sure how he got to that strange street with the strange store, but suddenly he noticed a sign in a dirty window of an old store. The sign said, "GO ANYWHERE. SEE ANYTHING."

For some reason, that sign caught Al's attention. "What does that mean?" he asked himself. He pressed his nose against the dirty window and looked inside. He saw nothing but darkness.

Suddenly a voice asked, "Would you like to go anywhere or see anything?"

Al turned around quickly and saw a very tall old man next to him. The old man was smiling. Al shrugged and looked away. "I don't have any money," Al said softly.

The old man laughed and then replied, "Money? You don't need money." He spoke very loudly. Al glanced around to see who was watching him, but he was surprised to see that the street was empty—no people, no cars. The old man continued, "This is my store. And you don't need money in my store."

The old man motioned to Al. "Come in," he said in a loud voice as he opened the door. A strange little bell rang—ding, ding. The old man held the door open and repeated, "Come in, my friend. Come in."

Al shook his head no and said, "I've got to go home. I . . ."

"Come in," the old man insisted. "You know that you are curious about what's inside and how you could go anywhere and see anything."

The old ★ man was right. Al looked in both directions down the street. Then he slowly followed the old man inside. The inside of the store was dark, quiet and creepy.

The door closed behind Al and the bell rang again—ding, ding. The old man said, "Where do you want to go?"

Al said, "Well, I—I don't know."

The old man laughed. Suddenly, he stopped and bent over so that his face was right in front of Al's. Al could see all the lines in the old man's face. The old man said, "My friend, would you like to go inside a volcano? Would you like to visit another planet? Would you like to swim with whales? Just name anything that you want to see and you will see it. What do you want to see? Where do you want to go?"

Al said, "I would like to see a movie."

"No!" the old man shouted. "I don't show movies. You can see a movie anywhere. I can show you things that movies can't show. I can take you inside the brain of a person. I can take you to the bottom of the ocean."

Al said, "But I told you I can't pay you anything."

The old man smiled. "You don't pay with money. You pay by passing a test."

"A test?" Al asked.

"Yes," the old man replied. "I will take you anywhere. I will show you anything. And then I will give you a test on what you saw. If you do not pass the test, I will never take you to another place or show you another thing. If you do pass the test, then you may go on another trip with me."

The store became silent. Al thought the old man was crazy, and part of Al's mind was telling him to get out of the store. Al kept looking around the inside of the store, but he couldn't see anything because it was too dark.

"Where do you want to go? What do you want to see?" the old man repeated.

Al responded, "I would like to go in a racing car."

"Why?" the old man demanded.

Al answered, "I like to go fast."

The old man smiled. "Speed. That's what you want to see. Speed. You want speed, and I will show you speed. But you must remember everything you will see so that you can pass the test."

"Okay," Al said, but he wasn't sure what he was agreeing to or why he agreed. Maybe he was curious to find out how the old man could show speed.

C Number your paper from 1 through 20.

Skill Items

Write the word from the box that means the same thing as the underlined part of each sentence.

rocket	whether	incredible	silly
suppose	business	device	however

1. She made a machine for making snowballs.
2. They decided if they would have a party.
3. He saw an amazing animal.

Review Items

4. What's another name for hot, melted rock?
5. During the Iditarod, how do mushers get water for their dogs?
6. What do mushers usually use to make beds for their dogs?
7. During the Iditarod, is the snow deeper **on the trail** or **off the trail?**
8. Why?
9. In what year was the first Iditarod?
10. During the first running of the Iditarod, how many dogs died during the race?
11. During more recent years, how many dogs die during each race?
12. Which is bigger, Alaska or Japan?
13. Is Japan a **state** or a **country?**
14. How many people live in Japan?
    - 127
    - 127 million
    - 127 thousand

15. Write the letters of 3 types of products that are used in the United States and manufactured in Japan.
    - a. TVs
    - b. books
    - c. cars
    - d. rugs
    - e. furniture
    - f. CD players
    - g. Mr. Light Saver
16. The person who drives a sled-dog team is called a ______.
17. The drivers of the sled-dog teams command the dogs by using their ______.
    - voices
    - reins
    - steering wheels
18. How many mushers start the Iditarod at the same time?
19. How much time passes before the next musher starts?
20. The ______s are the coldest places on the earth and the ______ is the hottest place on the earth.

102

A

1	2
1. science	1. swooping
2. confused	2. racer
3. observed	3. racetrack
4. galaxy	4. speeded
5. familiar	5. crackling
6. speedometer	6. midnight

B

The Speed of Light

Here are facts about light:

- Light is the fastest thing there is. Light travels millions of miles in an hour. In only one second, light travels 186 thousand miles.
- If you could travel at the speed of light, you would go around Earth almost eight times in one second.
- The sun is 93 million miles from Earth. But light from the sun reaches Earth in only eight minutes.

Remember, nothing goes faster than light, and light travels at the speed of 186 thousand miles per second.

C

The First Trip

Al was inside a strange dark store on a strange street, but he wasn't sure why he was inside that store. And Al wasn't sure whether the old man who owned the store was crazy. That old man had just told Al that he would show Al about speed, and that Al would have to pass a test on everything the old man showed him. Al agreed, but he wasn't sure what he agreed to or why.

Suddenly, Al noticed that the inside of the store was getting light. It got lighter and lighter and lighter. Then suddenly the walls seemed to melt. He could hardly believe what was happening.

Al was no longer standing inside the store, but next to a racetrack. There was a big red racing car right in front of him. The sun was shining and everything was bright.

Al said, "Where—where are we?"

The old man replied, "You are safe when you're with me. Don't worry. You will be home in time for supper."

"How did we get here?" Al asked. "I don't know what happened."

The old man said, "I told you that I would take you anywhere and show you anything. You want to know about speed. This is where we start. Get in the racer."

Al got in the racing car. The old man got behind the wheel and started the engine. "Rrrrrrrooooaaaarrrrr."

The old man said, "Put on your helmet and your safety belt. And get ready for speed."

"Rrrrrroooooaaaarrr," went the engine.

"Squeeeee," went the tires, and the car jumped forward. The car sped down the racetrack. The sound of the wind became very loud as the car went faster and faster.

"Now we are going 100 miles per hour," the old man shouted above the wind. "If we kept going at this speed, we would go 100 miles every hour."

Suddenly, the car speeded up. Things were racing by Al so fast that he could hardly see them. The old man hollered above the roar of the wind and the screaming of the engine, "Look at the speedometer. Tell me how fast we are going now."

Al yelled, "One hundred and thirty miles per hour."

"Right," the old man yelled. "What does that mean?"

Al answered without taking his eyes off the road. "We would go one hundred and thirty miles in an hour."

"Good," the old man shouted. "Now let's go really fast."

The car went faster and faster. It went so fast that Al could hardly breathe. The engine was screaming. Al glanced at the speedometer. It read 200, which meant that the car was going two hundred miles per hour.

"Slow down," Al shouted.

"Slow down?" the old man yelled. Then he laughed above the roaring wind. "You wanted to find out about speed. And we are still not going very fast. In fact, we're hardly moving at all."

Al sat back in the seat and closed his eyes. He did not want to see what would happen next.

Suddenly, there was a crackling sound over the racetrack. Al looked up. A jet plane was swooping over the racing car. In only a few seconds, the plane sped past the racing car and was a mile in front of the car.

"Wow!" Al shouted. "That plane passed us up like we were standing still."

"Yes," the old man hollered. "This car is really very slow. Let's get into something that has some more speed."

"I think I better go home," Al yelled. "It's getting late and . . ."

Suddenly, Al was no longer in the racing car. He was in the front seat of a jet plane. Everything was quiet inside the plane. There was no howling wind or screaming engine noise. There was just a soft humming sound.

Al looked out the window. He could see the racing car below. He could see the track.

Al shook his head. "How did we get here?"

The old man said, "Never mind that. Look at the speedometer and tell me how fast we are going."

Al looked. He couldn't believe it. "Five hundred miles per hour," he said.

D Number your paper from 1 through 22.

Review Items

1. Name the largest planet in the solar system.
2. If something weighed 100 pounds on Earth, how many pounds would it weigh on our moon?
   - 17 pounds
   - 117 pounds
   - 14 pounds
3. How long does it take Jupiter to spin around one time?
4. Write the letter of the layer that went into the pile **first.**
5. Which layer went into the pile **earlier,** B or C?
6. Write the letter of the layer where we would find the skeletons of humans.
7. Write the letter of the layer where we find the skeletons of dinosaurs.
8. Write the letter of the layer where we find the skeletons of horses.
9. Write the letter of the layer we live on.
10. What's the name of layer C?

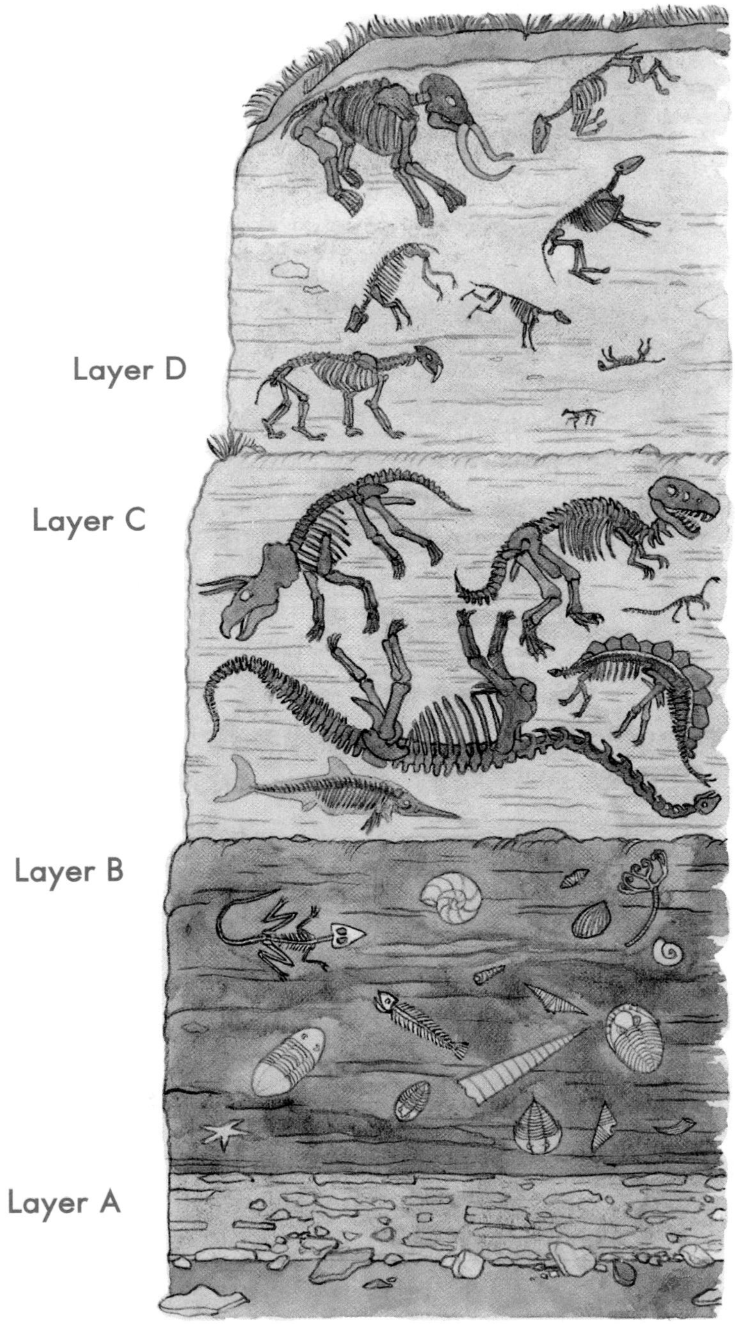

11. What color is lava when it's very hot?
12. What color is lava after it cools a little bit?
13. What color is lava after it's completely cooled?

- orange
- gray
- brown

14. The solid arrows show how many times people went into the room. How many people went into the room?
15. The dotted arrows show how many times people left the room. How many people left the room?
16. Are the lights on in the room?
17. How many more people would have to leave the room before the lights go off?

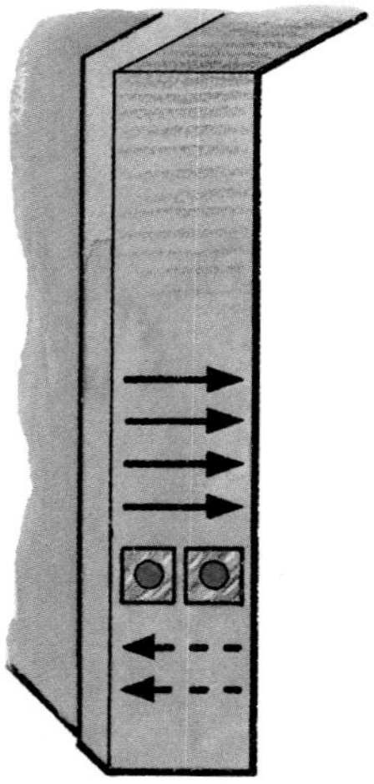

18. Name the woman who finished the Iditarod sixteen times.
19. How many times did she **enter** the Iditarod?
20. How many times did she finish in first place?

21. When Iditarod mushers are on the trail, how much help can they get from someone else?

22. The rules for the Iditarod require each musher to have certain things. **Write the letters of those things.**
    a. a good sleeping bag
    b. firewood
    c. extra dogs
    d. booties
    e. an ax
    f. enough food for a day
    g. snowshoes
    h. extra shoes
    i. a tent
    j. enough food for a week

A

1

1. narrow
2. level
3. puddle
4. rocket

B Al Learns More About Speed

Al and the old man were in a jet plane speeding above the racetrack at 500 miles per hour.

"Five hundred miles per hour," Al repeated to himself.

The plane turned and then swooped down. It streaked along above the racetrack and then sped past the end of the track. Then it suddenly swooped almost straight up before leveling off.

Al could see a town below. He said, "It doesn't feel like we're going fast. It felt like we were going faster in the racer. It's so quiet inside this plane."

The old man laughed and pulled the handle that made the plane go faster. After a few moments, things became very, very quiet. Al could no longer hear the humming sounds of the engine. The old man said, "Now we are going faster than the speed of sound."

The old man continued, "We are going 900 miles per hour. It's very quiet now because the jet engines of the plane are behind us. The sound from the engines cannot catch up with us. The sound from the engines travels one mile in five seconds. But we are traveling one mile in less than five seconds."

The old man smiled and said, "And now we are going to make this plane go just as fast as it can go."

The old man pulled the handle as far as it would go, and Al watched the speedometer move. Now the plane was going 1,000 miles per hour. Now the plane was going 1,200 miles per hour. Now it was going 1,500 miles per hour.

The old man said, "Think of it. If we keep going at this speed for one hour, we will travel 1,500 miles. We will travel nearly halfway across the United States in one hour."

"Wow!" Al said. "And it doesn't even feel like we're moving fast."

Al watched the towns move by below the plane. He watched the fields and the clouds. Suddenly, something sped past the plane. It was a long, silver rocket ship.

Al said, "That rocket went by us like we were standing still."

"Yes," the old man said. "A rocket is a lot faster than a jet plane. So . . ."

When the old man stopped talking, Al noticed that things had changed. He looked around. He was no longer inside a jet plane. He was sitting in a deep seat. Al and the old man were inside a rocket.

The old man pointed to one of the dials. "Look how fast we're going now."

Al looked at the dial. "Nine thousand miles per hour!"

"Yes," the old man said. "We're not going 100 miles per ★ hour. We're not going 900 miles per hour. We're going 9,000 miles per hour."

The old man continued, "But we are really not going very fast at all." The old man pointed to the sun and continued, "If we kept going at this speed, it would take us over one year to reach the sun."

"Wow!" Al said. "That's a long time."

"Yes," the old man said. "We're still moving very slowly." He laughed and then continued. "If you want to move fast, you have to travel at the speed of light."

Al started to say, "How can we go that fast?" Before he could say the first word of that question, he realized that he was floating in space. The rocket ship was gone. The old man was next to Al. "We're now traveling as fast as light," the

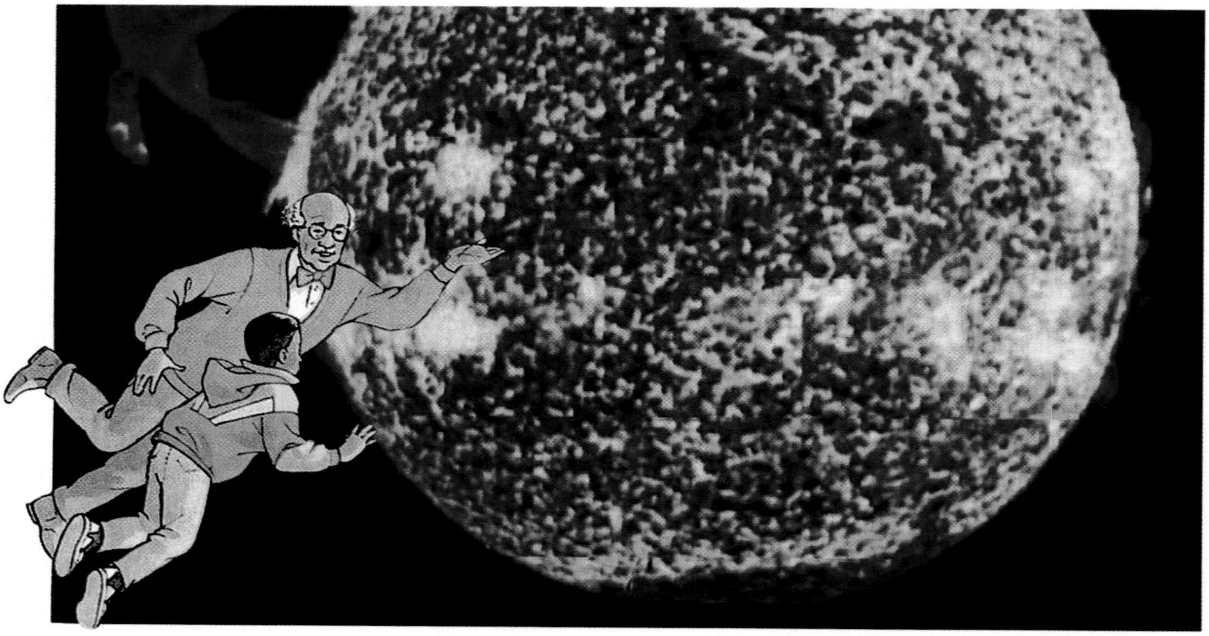

old man explained. "And we're going toward the sun."

Al didn't reply. He just stared at the huge burning ball that was getting bigger and bigger.

The old man said, "Light travels 186 thousand miles every second. At this speed it will take us about eight minutes to reach the sun."

Al said, "It doesn't even feel like we're moving. It feels like we're standing still."

The old man said, "That's because there is no air up here. You can't feel air rush by you."

The sun looked very, very big and very bright. Al could see great flames shooting up from the surface of the sun. He could see a bright star near the sun. He asked, "How long would it take us to reach that star if we kept moving at the speed of light?"

The old man laughed. "Seventy years," he said.

"Wow!" Al said. "I'd be an old man by the time we got there."

Al looked around. In back of him he saw a large cloud of stars. "How long would it take to reach those stars?" he asked.

The old man smiled. "You're looking at a galaxy. It would take 200 million years to reach that galaxy."

"I can't believe it," Al said.

The sun was now very close. It was a mass of burning gas so bright that Al couldn't stand it. He closed his eyes. Suddenly, he felt something under his feet.

When he opened his eyes, he noticed that everything was dark. He was back in the dark store. The old man was standing in front of him. "Come back tomorrow," the old man said. "Come back tomorrow and pay for the trip by passing the test. If you pass the test, I will take you on another trip. Go anywhere. See anything."

C Number your paper from 1 through 27.

Skill Items

Write the word from the box that means the same thing as the underlined part of each sentence.

happy	attached	prepared	thick
level	approached	comfortable	clever

1. The road was flat for many miles.
2. They got ready for the big party.
3. The truck moved toward the cliff.

Review Items

4. In what ocean is the **X?**
5. About how many miles is it from Florida to the **X?**

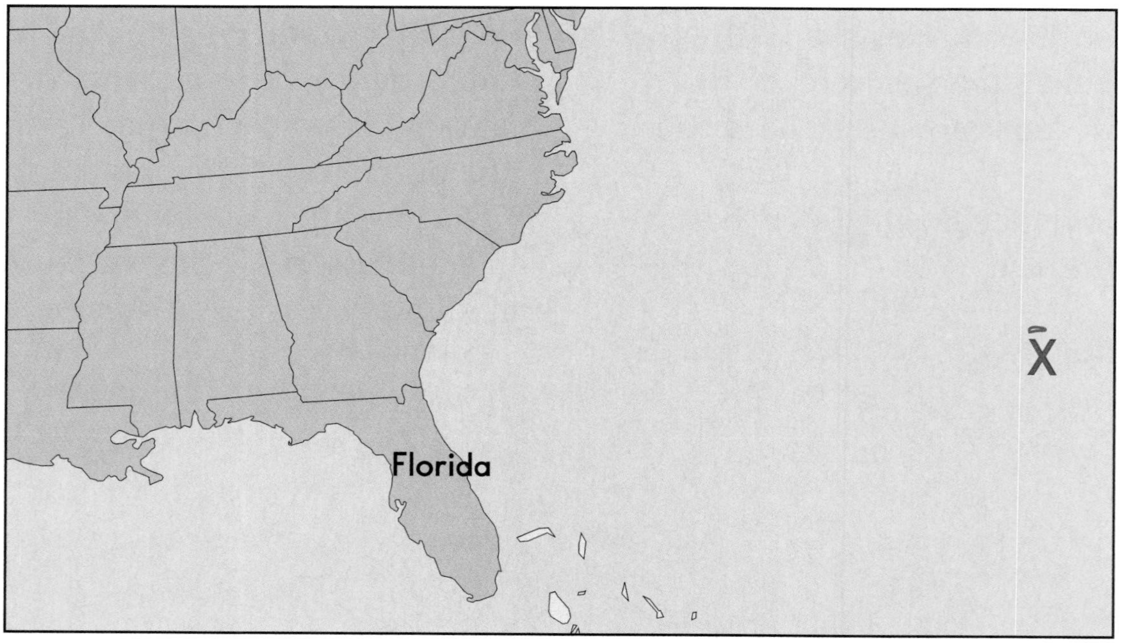

6. A person weighs 400 pounds on planet M and 200 pounds on planet B. Which planet has stronger gravity?
7. Which planets have stronger gravities, the bigger planets or the smaller planets?

8. How many miles does light travel in one second?
   - 186 miles
   - 186 thousand miles
   - 86 thousand miles
9. What else travels as fast as light?
10. How long does it take light to travel from the sun to Earth?
    - 5 seconds
    - 8 seconds
    - 8 minutes
11. Name 2 acts of bravery.
12. What does the color of water tell you about the water?
13. When you open a bottle of soda pop, what happens to the pressure inside the bottle?
14. What forms in the soda pop?
15. Do things look **light** or **dark** when you're 100 feet below the surface of the ocean?
16. There aren't as many plants down there because there isn't as much ______.
17. Name 3 things that great water pressure can do to you.
18. In what state is the Iditarod sled-dog race?
19. In which city does it begin?
20. In which city does it end?
21. The Iditarod is about ______ miles from start to finish.
    - 1600
    - 500
    - 1100
22. In most years, the race takes about ______.
    - 10 days
    - 2 weeks
    - a week
23. How does water pressure change as you move from deep in the water toward the surface?
24. How does the light around you change as you move toward the surface?
25. When the diver is ______ feet underwater, the pressure is **two** times as great as it is on land.
26. When the diver is ______ feet underwater, the pressure is **three** times as great as it is on land.
27. When the diver is ______ feet underwater, the pressure is **four** times as great as it is on land.

104

A

1

1. narrow
2. confused
3. simply
4. science
5. observed
6. staring

B Al Takes a Test About Speed

Al left the store feeling confused. He walked down the strange, empty street until he came to a corner that seemed familiar. Then he began to run. He continued to run all the way home. His experience with the old man was so incredible that he couldn't believe it. He kept thinking about the race car, the rocket, the galaxy and the speed of light.

When he got home, his mother said, "Where have you been?"

Al wanted to tell her, but he didn't say anything because he didn't think that she would believe him. Al simply shrugged and said, "I was out."

"How did your test go in school?" his mother asked.

"I don't know," he said, looking down.

"That test was in science, wasn't it?" his mother asked.

"Yeah, science," Al said. "I don't like science."

Al ate dinner with Angela and his mother. He watched television after dinner. Then he went to bed, but he had trouble going to sleep. He kept thinking about that strange store and that old man.

The next morning, Al left for school very early. He wanted to see what his science book said about speed. He wanted to make sure that he would pass the test and go on another trip with the old man.

When Al read about the speed of light, a funny thing happened. Al had read about the speed of light before. And he had found it very dull. But when he read about it now, it was very interesting.

Another funny thing happened later in the day. The teacher was talking about sound. She asked the class, "Why do you think it is quiet in a jet plane that is traveling 900 miles per hour?"

Al raised his hand to answer the question. Everybody looked at him because Al never raised his hand in school and never answered questions. The teacher called on Al. He said, "It's quiet in a jet because the engines are behind the people in the plane. And the jet is going faster than the sound of the engines. The sound of the engines is traveling a mile every five seconds. But the jet is traveling faster than that."

The teacher looked at Al and blinked. Then she smiled and nodded her head. "That's right, Al," she said.

The other kids were staring at Al with open mouths. For some reason, Al didn't feel embarrassed. He smiled and felt pretty good.

After school Al started to look for the old man's store. He went down one street and then down another. He didn't remember where the store was. Al walked and walked. But he didn't see the store with the sign in the window that said, GO ANYWHERE. SEE ANYTHING.

He was just about ready to go home when he turned down a very narrow street. Al looked at the street sign on the corner. The name of the street was Anywhere Street.

Al walked down the street. Then he saw the sign in the window—GO ANYWHERE. SEE ANYTHING. He ran up to the store. He hesitated and then opened the door. A little bell rang—ding, ding. Al closed the door behind him and stood there in the dark. Everything was very quiet. Then he heard a voice. "I see you have come back to pay for your trip."

Suddenly, the old man's face moved out of the darkness. The old man said, "I will ask you one question. If you answer it, you pass the test. And by passing the test, you pay for your last trip."

Al said, "I'm ready."

The old man said, "Here is the question. What does it mean to go fast?"

Al thought and thought. Then he said, "Maybe I won't give you the right answer. But I don't know what fast means. When we were going in the racing car, it felt like we were going so fast I couldn't stand it. But when we were traveling in space, it didn't feel like we were going fast at all." Al looked at the old man's face. The old man's expression was serious. Maybe Al's answer was wrong.

Al decided to explain what he meant. He continued, "Light travels 186 thousand miles every second. But at the speed of light it would take us millions of years to reach the galaxy we saw. So light isn't very fast at all. And so I don't know what it means to say that something is fast."

The old man's face looked very cold. Then the old man smiled and said, "You are a smart boy. You are a thinking boy. You have passed your test. You have paid for your trip."

The old man bent over so that his face was very close to Al's face. "And where do you want to go for your next trip? Go anywhere. See anything."

Al thought back to the things that his class had been studying. One thing was matter. His teacher had told the class that all things are made of matter and that there are three forms of matter. But Al didn't understand the three forms of matter.

Al looked at the old man and said, "I would like to find out about matter."

C Number your paper from 1 through 21.

Skill Items

At midnight, he saw a familiar galaxy.

1. What word refers to something that is well known to you?
2. What word means **12 o'clock at night?**
3. What word names a group of millions and millions of stars?

Review Items

4. When a person makes an object for the first time, the person ______ the object.
5. How many miles does light travel in one second?
   - 186 million miles
   - 186 miles
   - 186 thousand miles
6. What else travels as fast as light?
7. How long does it take light to travel from the sun to Earth?
   - 12 minutes
   - 8 minutes
   - 12 seconds

8. Why doesn't it feel like you're moving when you're speeding through space?
9. What is a cloud of stars called?
10. How long does it take sound to travel one mile?

Write the name of each animal in the picture.

17. **Write the letter** of the thing that travels the slowest.
18. **Write the letter** of the thing that travels the fastest.
    a. light
    b. racing car
    c. jet plane
    d. sound
    e. rocket

19. When you're training an animal, what do you do each time the animal does the trick?
20. What do you do if the animal does not do the trick?
21. Name **2** things you could give a dog to reward it.

A

1

1. molecule
2. crystal
3. burner
4. billion
5. frying

B

Al Learns About Matter

Al had just told the old man that he would like to find out about matter.

"Matter?" the old man asked. "It is all around you. I am matter. You are matter. The air is matter. Everything is matter."

Suddenly, Al noticed a large frying pan in the middle of the floor. The old man said, "Here's the rule about the three forms of matter. When an object is hard, it is matter in the solid form. When the object gets hot enough, it changes into the liquid form of matter. When it gets much hotter, it changes into the gas form of matter. Remember: solid, liquid and gas."

The old man pointed to the frying pan. "What form of matter is that frying pan?"

"It's solid," Al replied.

"Watch what happens to it when it gets hotter," the old man said.

Al watched. He noticed that the frying pan was starting to glow. He could feel the heat from it.

At first the glow was a very dull red color. Then the color became brighter and brighter. Soon the frying pan was glowing like the burner on a hot, hot stove.

"It's still getting hotter," the old man said.

The frying pan started to turn bright orange. Then bright yellow. Soon it was brighter than a light bulb and the whole room was bright with the light from the frying pan. As Al observed the frying pan, he noticed that it was starting to melt. Al could hardly believe what he saw. He said, "It's melting."

The old man said, "That frying pan is matter. And it's changing from the solid form of matter to the liquid form."

The bright glowing liquid melted into a puddle that was now turning white hot. Suddenly, Al noticed that the puddle was getting smaller and smaller. And Al could see a bright cloud forming in the air.

The old man said, "You have seen the solid form of the frying pan and the liquid form. Now the matter is changing into the hottest form—gas. The gas is going into the air around us. The gas is that cloud that you see."

Soon, the puddle had disappeared, and the room was filled with an amazingly bright light.

The old man said, "The metal is now as hot as the outside of the sun. The metal turned into a gas."

The gas was so bright that Al could hardly look at it. He remembered the great flames that he had seen shooting up from the surface of the sun. Then he realized that those great flames were matter in the gas form.

Al started to say, "The sun is . . ." Before he could finish, he noticed that he was no longer in the store. He was floating in space. The sky all around him was black. In front of him was the sun.

The old man said, "Yes, the sun is matter in the gas form. We are going to fly inside the sun this time."

They flew through the great flames on the surface of the sun. Soon they were inside the sun. Bright gas was all around them. The whole inside of the sun was nothing but bright, bright gas.

The old man held up a rock. "What form of matter is this rock?" he asked.

Al replied.

The old man said, "I will show you how hot it is inside the sun. Watch what happens to this rock when I let go of it."

The old man let go of the rock. In an instant, the rock disappeared. It did not burn or melt. It simply disappeared.

"What happened to it?" Al asked.

The old man said, "It turned into gas. The inside of the sun is so hot that it would turn anything into the gas form of matter."

The old man told Al, "You have seen matter change from solid, to liquid, to gas. Now you will see matter going the other way."

Suddenly, Al and the old man were no longer inside the sun. They were standing in a field on Earth. The old man was holding a huge bottle that had no cap on it.

"What's inside this bottle?" the old man asked.

"Nothing," Al replied.

"Wrong," the old man said. "There is air inside this bottle. And air is matter in its hottest form."

"But it's not hot here," Al said.

"For air, it's hot," the old man replied. "Air is matter in the gas form. If we make this air cooler, it will change. First it will go into the liquid form of matter. Then it will go into the solid form."

The old man put a cap on the huge bottle.

"But it's not hot here," Al said. "And . . ."

Before Al could continue, he noticed that he and the old man were in space again. Ahead of them was a large planet that had huge rings around it. The old man was holding the bottle.

C Number your paper from 1 through 24.

Story Items

1. Where did Al and the old man go after they left the sun?
2. What was inside the bottle that the old man was holding?
3. In which form of matter is the air around you?
4. If you make air cold enough, what form of matter does it turn into first?
5. If you make air still colder, what form of matter does it turn into?
6. Name a planet that has huge rings around it.

Skill Items

Use the words in the box to write complete sentences.

familiar	anxious	experience	miserable
galaxy	blizzard	surprised	fierce
midnight	visibility	level	demand

7. ____ was ____ in the ____ ____.
8. At ____, he saw a ____ ____.

Review Items

9. Which planet has more clouds around it, Earth or Mars?
10. Which planet is larger?
11. Which planet is hotter?
12. Why is that planet hotter?
13. How long does it take light to travel from the sun to Earth?
    - 8 hours
    - 8 seconds
    - 8 minutes
14. How long does it take sound to travel one mile?

15. It is quiet inside a jet plane that is going 900 miles per hour because the plane is moving faster than ______.
16. How many forms of matter are there?
17. How many miles does light travel in one second?
18. Name **2** cities in Colorado.
19. Name one city in Utah.

20. When you teach an animal a simple trick, when do you reward the animal?
21. When don't you reward the animal?
22. Let's say that you want to teach an animal a very hard trick. Can the animal do the trick at first?
23. What will happen if the animal doesn't receive any rewards until it does the trick?
24. So when you're teaching the animal a hard trick, what do you reward the animal for doing?

106

A

1

1. iron
2. control
3. molecule
4. billion
5. crystals
6. relax

B

Al Visits Saturn and Pluto

The old man and Al were approaching the planet Saturn. The old man was carrying a bottle of air.

The old man said, "Saturn is very far from the sun. So this planet is very cold. We'll go to the side of the planet that is not facing the sun. There it is over 200 degrees below zero."

The old man held up the bottle. "Watch," he said. "The air inside this bottle will now become the same temperature as the surface of Saturn."

A puddle started to form in the bottom of the bottle. The puddle was clear, like water. "What's that?" Al asked.

The old man said, "Part of the air has turned into a liquid. Air is made up of different gases. One of those gases is now a liquid."

Al said, "Would that liquid turn into a solid if it got colder?"

"Yes," the old man said. "If we took this liquid to the planet Pluto, the liquid would turn into a solid."

"Can we go there?" Al asked.

The old man smiled, and suddenly Al noticed that he and the old man were flying toward a small planet. "That's Pluto," the old man said. "It is much farther from the sun than Saturn. From Pluto the sun doesn't give off any more light or heat than a very large star would."

Al and the old man landed on Pluto. Al watched the liquid in the bottle, which slowly began to freeze. It turned into a hard lump that looked like ice.

"Now the air is a solid," the old man said.

He opened the bottle, turned it over, and the lump of solid air fell to the surface of Pluto. Al looked at that surface. It looked just like the solid air. It was shiny and hard, like ice. "What is this stuff we're standing on?" Al asked.

The old man said, "Frozen gases. All of the gases on Pluto are frozen. They cover the surface of this planet."

"Wow!" Al said. As he studied the surface, things seemed to get darker and darker. Al suddenly realized that he was standing on a floor, not on the planet Pluto. He looked around and noticed that he was back in the old man's store.

The old man was saying, "You have learned a lot about matter. Remember everything you have seen. Remember that everything is made up of matter. And matter comes in three forms. You can change matter from one form to another form by making the matter hotter or colder."

Al said, "We saw a lot of things. I just hope I can remember everything."

The old man said, "If you want to understand matter, think about water. Water is a liquid. But what happens to the liquid when you make it cold enough?"

Al said, "It turns into ice."

"Yes," the old man said. "It turns into a solid. And what happens to water if you get it hot enough?"

Al said, "It turns into steam."

"That's right," the old man said. "That steam is water in the gas form. All matter is like water. It changes from a solid to a liquid to a gas. Even the gases in the sun will turn into solid matter if you make them cold enough."

The old man bent over so that his face was close to Al's face. "Think about what you have seen on this trip. Think about the sun. Think about Saturn. Think about Pluto. And think about matter. Remember—you must pass a test on what you have seen. If you fail the test, I will never take you on another trip."

Suddenly, the old man was gone.

Al was standing alone in the dark store. He opened the door and went outside. The bell went ding, ding. There were no cars and no other people on Anywhere Street.

As Al walked slowly down the street, he thought about what he had just seen. He looked at the sidewalk and he thought, "That sidewalk would turn into liquid if it got hot enough. And that sidewalk would turn into gas if it got even hotter."

Al turned the corner and left Anywhere Street. He looked at cars and at buildings, and he realized that everything he looked at was matter. For the first time, Al knew what matter was. And he knew what the teacher meant when she had said that all matter has three forms.

Suddenly Al realized that he was very smart. That made him feel excited. "Wow!" he said, and laughed out loud. Then he started to run home.

C Number your paper from 1 through 18.

Skill Items

Here are 3 events that happened in the story. Write **beginning, middle** or **end** for each event.

1. Al suddenly realized that he was standing on a floor, not on the planet Pluto.
2. Al looked at cars and at buildings, and he realized that everything he looked at was matter.
3. The old man said, "Saturn is very far from the sun."

Review Items

4. Name the largest planet in the solar system.
5. How long does it take Jupiter to spin around one time?

6. How many miles does light travel in one second?
7. What else travels as fast as light?

8. How many forms of matter are there?
9. When things are hard, what form of matter are they?
10. When hard matter gets hotter, which form does it change into?
11. When matter gets still hotter, which form does it change into?

12. How can you change a solid form of matter into a liquid?
13. To change a liquid form of matter into a gas, you make the liquid ______.

14. **Write the letters** of the 5 things that are matter in the solid form.

15. **Write the letters** of the 5 things that are matter in the liquid form.

16. **Write the letters** of the 3 things that are matter in the gas form.

a. rock	h. soda pop
b. glass	i. tea
c. smoke	j. ice
d. air	k. wood
e. water	l. juice
f. milk	m. steam
g. brick	

17. The sun is matter in the ______ form.
18. What form of matter is the air around you?

SPECIAL PROJECT

The story you have read tells about Saturn and Pluto. You have made a chart that shows the planets from Mercury through Jupiter. Add Saturn, Pluto and the other two planets—Uranus and Neptune—to your chart. Find out the facts about these planets and write them on the chart.

A

1

1. relax
2. popcorn
3. doorknob
4. started
5. stared
6. control

B

Al Takes A Test on Matter

When Al got home, it was supper time. Al's mother asked him where he'd been, but he was embarrassed about telling her. She wouldn't have believed that he'd gone to Saturn and Pluto.

After supper, Al played ball with his sister on the sidewalk. After they had played for about an hour, they went inside. Angela said, "There's a good movie on TV, about World War Two. Why don't we watch it?"

Al hesitated. Angela continued, "I'll fix some popcorn and we'll relax and watch the movie."

Al agreed. The movie was very good, but it lasted until nearly midnight.

When the movie was over, Al was so tired that he didn't spend any time thinking about the things he had seen on his trip with the old man.

The next morning, Al was still so tired that he couldn't think about his trip. Shortly before lunch, he became so tired that he fell asleep in school.

After school Al went back to Anywhere Street, walked up to the old man's store and opened the door. Ding, ding, went the bell. The inside of the store was very quiet and very dark. Al stood in the dark for a long time.

Suddenly the old man appeared and said, "Now you must pay for the trip by taking a test. Are you ready?"

"Yes," Al said.

"Remember," the old man said, "if you don't pass the test, I will not take you on any more trips."

Al nodded and tried to make his mind start to work.

The old man said, "Which form of matter is the hottest form? Which form of matter is the coldest form?"

Al thought, but he couldn't seem to control his mind. Finally he said, "I don't know." Al looked down for a moment. When he looked up, the old man was gone, and Al was all alone in the dark store.

Al spoke to the dark store. "I'm—I'm sorry. I don't know the answer. But . . ."

Nobody replied. Al listened, but he did not hear anything. He stared into the darkness but there was no sign of the old man. Finally, Al walked outside. Ding, ding, the bell went, and the door closed behind him. As Al started down Anywhere Street, he glanced back at the window of the store. There was no sign that said, GO ANYWHERE. SEE ANYTHING. Instead there was another sign in the window, which said, STORE FOR SALE.

"What's happening?" Al asked aloud. He walked back to the door and tried to open it, but the door was locked.

Al walked home very slowly, realizing that he would never be able to go on another trip with the old man. He started to think of the places the old man could have taken him. Al wanted to swim in the ocean with whales and go inside a

volcano and learn how plants grow. But he had not passed the test, so he had not paid for his last trip.

As Al approached his house, he started to get an idea. After dinner, Al asked his mother, "Do we have a science book that tells about matter?"

His mother said, "What would we do with a book about matter?"

Al said, "I've got to get a book that tells about matter. Do you have any idea where I can get one?"

"I don't know," his mother said. Then she added, "Wait a minute. Go to the library."

"Where's that?" Al asked.

Angela was sitting across the room from Al. She stood up and said, "Come on. I'll show you."

Al and his sister walked to the library, went inside and walked up to a woman behind a large counter. Angela said, "My brother wants a book that tells about matter. He wants a science book."

"Come with me," the woman said, and led the way to a wall of the library that was covered with books—row and rows of books. She pointed to one of the rows. "These are all science books. Any one of these books will tell you about matter."

Al took one of the books and sat down at a large table where he started reading.

Angela said, "I think I'm going home. Can you find your way back?"

"Sure," Al said without looking up from the book.

When Al had finished reading the part of the book that told about matter, everything was clear to him. He knew the answer to the old man's questions. He knew that the gas form is the hottest form of matter and that the coldest form is the solid form. He knew that air turns into a solid on Pluto.

Al put the book back on the shelf and ran from the library. He ran down street after street until he came to Anywhere Street. He ran up to the old store. The sign in the window still said, STORE FOR SALE.

Al banged on the door, "Let me in," he yelled. "Let me in and I will pay for my trip."

He stopped banging and listened. No sounds came from inside the dark store. Al started to feel anxious. Again he pounded on the door. "Give me another chance," he shouted. "I'll pass any test you want to give me."

After pounding and shouting for several minutes, Al was ready to give up. Almost without thinking, he grabbed the doorknob and turned it. The door opened and the bell went ding, ding.

C Number your paper from 1 through 23.

Review Items

1. Which has **stronger** gravity, Jupiter or Io?
2. Which is **bigger** than Earth?
3. Where can you jump 8 feet high?
4. How long does it take light to travel from the sun to Earth?
5. Why doesn't it feel like you're moving when you're speeding through space?
6. What is a cloud of stars called?
7. **Write the letter** of the thing that travels the slowest.
8. **Write the letter** of the thing that travels the fastest.

   a. sound
   b. light
   c. rocket
   d. jet plane
   e. racing car

9. In what form of matter is air on Earth?
10. In what form of matter is air on Saturn?
11. In what form of matter is air on Pluto?
12. What form of matter is steam?
13. What form of matter is ice?
14. What form of matter is water?
15. How can you change a liquid form of matter into a solid?
16. How can you change a liquid form of matter into a gas?

Let's say you're training a dog to jump up in the air and do a backward somersault. **Use the words below to finish each sentence.**

- jumping up and turning upside down
- jumping up in the air
- jumping up and leaning backward

17. At first, you would reward the dog for ____.
18. Later you would reward the dog for ____.
19. Later you would reward the dog for ____.

20. The more water the glass has, the ______ the sound it makes.

- lower
- higher

21. Write the letter of the glass that will make the lowest ring.

22. Write the letter of the glass that will make the highest ring.

A B C D E F

23. When you teach animals to work for new rewards, do you change the reward **quickly** or **slowly?**

108

A

1

1. vibrate
2. create
3. iron
4. blush
5. incredible
6. incredibly
7. temperature

B

Al Takes Another Test

Al stood inside the dark store. He said, "I want to pay for my trip."

There was no answer.

Al said, "You don't have to take me on any more trips. I just want to pay for my last trip. You took me on a trip, and I want to pay for it."

"All right," a voice said. Suddenly the old man was standing in front of Al. "I will have to give you a harder test, because you did not pay for the trip the first time."

"I'm ready," Al said. "Ask me anything about matter."

The old man said, "Here is the first question: Which is the hottest form of matter and which is the coldest form of matter?"

Al smiled and answered the question.

"That is right," the old man said without smiling. "Here is the next question: Do all things turn into gas at the same temperature?"

Al said, "Not all things turn into gas at the same temperature. Look at this room. There is air in the room and there is glass in the window. Glass is solid but the air is gas. Yet the glass and the air are the same temperature."

The old man asked what a rock would do inside the sun. Al told him. The old man asked many other questions. Al answered each question.

Finally the old man put a hand on Al's shoulder and smiled. "You have passed the test," he said. "You have paid for your trip. So I will give you another chance and take you on

another trip. Where would you like to go now?"

Al said, "I had better go home right now. But can I come back tomorrow and go on a trip with you?"

"Come back tomorrow," the old man said. "We can go anywhere and see anything. And you pay for your trip by passing a test."

Al went outside. "Ding, ding," the bell sounded. Al looked at the window of the store. The sign that said STORE FOR SALE was gone and another sign was in its place.

Al ran all the way home. Angela was sitting in the living room watching TV. She said, "Hey, they're going to have a good movie on TV. Do you want to watch it with me?"

"No thanks," Al said. "I want to get to bed. I'm tired. And I've got a lot to do tomorrow."

The next day Al surprised the class again. The teacher was giving the class a lesson on science. She said, "How do you know that air is matter? You can't see air, so how could you show that air is actually matter?"

Al raised his hand. He was the only one to raise a hand. The teacher looked surprised as she asked, "What do you think, Al?"

Al said, “Here’s one way to show that air is matter. You could take a bottle of air. You put a lid on the bottle so nothing can get in the bottle and nothing can get out of the bottle. Then you start cooling the bottle. When it gets really cold, you’ll see a puddle in the bottom of the bottle. That puddle is the air. That air was in the bottle all the time. It was in the gas form when you put it in the bottle. Now it is in liquid form.”

Al stopped talking. Everyone was quiet. The teacher and the other kids stared at Al without saying anything. They just stared. Al felt embarrassed.

Finally, one of the kids said, “Wow! Where did Al learn all of that stuff?”

Another kid said, “Who said Al isn’t smart?”

As some of the kids began to applaud, Al could feel himself blush.

After school, Al went back to Anywhere Street. He opened the door to the old man’s store. “Ding, ding,” the bell sounded. “I’m ready to go on a trip,” Al said. He didn’t see anybody inside the store, but he knew the old man was there.

The old man stepped out of the darkness, smiling. “Go anywhere. See anything. Go to the center of Earth. Swim to the bottom of an ocean. Where do you want to go?”

Al thought for a moment. When Al had studied matter in the library, he had learned that all matter is made up of tiny parts called molecules. Al knew that air molecules were different from wood molecules or glass molecules. He knew that a sugar molecule didn’t look like an iron molecule or a molecule from a rock. Al wanted to know more about molecules. So he said, “Can I see molecules?”

The old man laughed. “Molecules? Look around you, my friend. You see billions and billions of molecules. Everything you see is made up of molecules. All matter is made up of molecules.”

“But I can’t see them,” Al said. “When I look at a table, I don’t see molecules. I see wood. When I look at a window, I don’t see molecules. I see glass. I want to see molecules.”

C Number your paper from 1 through 19.

Skill Items

The crystal contained more than a billion molecules.

1. What word means **a thousand millions?**
2. What word means **the smallest parts of a material?**
3. What word names a shiny material that has flat sides and sharp edges?

Review Items

4. Write the names of the 9 planets, starting with the planet closest to the sun.
5. How many moons does Jupiter have?
6. Which planet has more moons, Saturn or Jupiter?
7. Does Io move around Jupiter **fast** or **slowly?**
8. It takes Io about ______ to go all the way around Jupiter.
9. When things are hard, what form of matter are they?
10. When hard matter gets hotter, which form does it change into?
11. When matter gets still hotter, which form does it change into?
12. Which planet is colder, Saturn or Pluto?
13. Why is that planet colder?
14. What is the hottest form of any matter?
15. What is the next-hottest form of any matter?
16. What is the coldest form of any matter?
17. Which uses up more oxygen, jumping or walking?

18. What planet is shown in the picture?
19. Which is bigger, the "eye" or Earth?

A

1

1. vibrating
2. temperature
3. carefully
4. realized

B

Al Learns About Molecules

Al had told the old man that he wanted to see molecules. The old man held out his hand. In his hand was a tiny pile of sand. The old man said, "Watch very carefully. I will put one grain of sand on the floor. We will go on a trip inside that grain of sand. Then you will be able to get a good look at molecules of sand."

The old man took a tiny grain of sand from the pile and put it on the floor. He placed the grain of sand right in front of Al's shoe.

As Al watched the grain of sand, he noticed that something strange was happening. Al realized that he was getting smaller and smaller and smaller. The old man was getting smaller, too.

Al looked up. The room had become bright. The ceiling seemed to be a mile above him. Al looked at the grain of sand in front of him. It appeared to be as big as a car.

"This way, my friend," the old man called, as he climbed to the top of the grain of sand.

Al ran toward the grain of sand. He ran past an ant, which looked as big as an elephant.

Al climbed up on the grain of sand. The grain was very rough, and it was covered with big pieces of shiny rocks.

Al asked, "Are those shiny pieces molecules?"

The old man replied, "No, no, my friend. Those shiny parts are crystals." The old man continued, "We've got to get a thousand times smaller than we are now before you can see a molecule. Here we go."

Suddenly, the grain of sand seemed to get bigger and bigger. It got so big that it seemed bigger than the biggest building Al had ever seen. It got bigger than a mountain.

Soon it was so big that Al couldn't see anything but huge crystals all around him. Some crystals looked bigger than a school building.

The crystals continued to grow until they were as big as mountains. Then Al noticed that there were large holes inside the crystals. Al was starting to float into one of the holes. The floating reminded him of the way he had felt when he had floated in outer space.

The old man said, "In a minute you will be small enough to see molecules."

Al continued to float into a hole inside one of the crystals. The hole was so large that Al couldn't see anything solid.

"Where are we?" Al asked.

The old man laughed. "We are inside the grain of sand."

"We can't be," Al said. "I don't see any sand."

The old man replied, "A grain of sand is made up of space and molecules."

The old man pointed and said, "Look—way over there."

Al looked in the direction the old man pointed. He saw something that looked like a big blob, vibrating very fast.

The old man said, "That's a molecule."

"Wow!" Al said.

The old man pointed in another direction. "Look over there and you'll see another molecule."

Al looked. “I see it,” he said. Then Al saw another molecule and another molecule. The molecules seemed to be in a row. Now Al could see another row of molecules above the first row. Every molecule was vibrating very fast.

Al said, “The molecules are all lined up in rows.”

The old man said, “These molecules are in the solid form of matter. That is why they are lined up. Remember this rule: When molecules are in the solid form, they are lined up and they stay in place.”

“That’s really interesting,” Al said, looking above the top row of vibrating molecules.

The old man continued, “These molecules are the same temperature as the room. If we make the grain of sand colder and colder, you will see a change in the molecules.”

“I don’t understand,” Al said. “These molecules are in the solid form of matter. The solid form of matter is the coldest form. So how could the molecules change if the matter gets colder? The molecules will still be in the solid form.”

The old man smiled. “I see that you are using the information you have learned. Good for you, my friend. And you are right. The molecules will remain in the solid form of matter, but watch what happens to them when the temperature gets lower than the temperature on Pluto.”

C Number your paper from 1 through 24.

Skill Items

Use the words in the box to write complete sentences.

billion	vibrating	galaxy	chilly	familiar
library	molecules	midnight	crystal	confused

1. At ___, he saw a ___ ___.
2. The ___ contained more than a ___ ___.

3. What is a person doing when the person makes an object for the first time?
4. The person who makes an object for the first time is called an ____.
5. The object the person makes is called an ____.
6. How can you change a solid form of matter into a liquid?
7. To change a liquid form of matter into a gas, you make the liquid ____.
8. **Write the letters** of the 5 things that are matter in the solid form.
9. **Write the letters** of the 4 things that are matter in the liquid form.
10. **Write the letters** of the 3 things that are matter in the gas form.

a. glass	g. rock
b. smoke	h. tea
c. brick	i. wood
d. air	j. steam
e. water	k. juice
f. milk	l. ice

11. Do all things turn into a gas at the same temperature?
12. All matter is made of ____.
13. Do sugar molecules look like air molecules?
14. Do all sugar molecules look the same?
15. Why can't you see molecules when you look at an object?
16. Most sled-dog teams have an ____ number of dogs.
    - odd
    - even
17. For the Iditarod, a sled-dog team can't have more than ____ dogs.

18. Which letter in the picture shows the wheel dogs?
19. Which letter shows the lead dogs?
20. Which letter shows the swing dogs?
21. Which letter shows where the musher is most of the time?
22. Which letter shows the tug lines?
23. Which letter shows the gang line?

24. What happens if a sled dog doesn't pass the Iditarod's health examination?

110 TEST 11

Number your paper from 1 through 36.

1. How many miles does light travel in one second?
   - 200 thousand miles
   - 186 thousand miles
   - 186 miles
2. What else travels as fast as light?
3. How long does it take light to travel from the sun to Earth?
4. How long does it take sound to travel one mile?
5. It is quiet inside a jet plane that is going 900 miles per hour because the plane is moving ____.
6. **Write the letter** of the thing that travels the slowest.
7. **Write the letter** of the thing that travels the fastest.

   a. sound
   b. light
   c. rocket
   d. racing car
   e. jet plane

8. How many forms of matter are there?
9. When things are hard, what form of matter are they?
10. When hard matter gets hotter, which form does it change into?
11. When matter gets still hotter, which form does it change into?
12. How can you change a solid form of matter into a liquid?
13. To change a liquid form of matter into a gas, you make the liquid ____.
14. **Write the letters** of the 5 things that are matter in the solid form.
15. **Write the letters** of the 4 things that are matter in the liquid form.
16. **Write the letters** of the 3 things that are matter in the gas form.

   a. rock
   b. glass
   c. smoke
   d. air
   e. water
   f. milk
   g. brick
   h. tea
   i. ice
   j. wood
   k. juice
   l. steam

17. The sun is matter in the ______ form.
18. What form of matter is the air around you?
19. In what form of matter is air on Pluto?
20. In what form of matter is air on Earth?
21. In what form of matter is air on Saturn?
22. What form of matter is steam?
23. What form of matter is ice?
24. What form of matter is water?
25. What is the hottest form of any matter?
26. What is the next-hottest form of any matter?
27. What is the coldest form of any matter?
28. Do all things turn into a gas at the same temperature?
29. What are tiny parts of matter called?
30. Do iron molecules look like sand molecules?
31. Do all iron molecules look the same?

Skill Items

For each item, write the underlined word from the sentences in the box.

> At midnight, he saw a familiar galaxy.
> The crystal contained more than a billion molecules.

32. What word means a **thousand millions?**
33. What word names a group of millions and millions of stars?
34. What word means **12 o'clock at night?**
35. What word means **the smallest parts of a material?**
36. What word refers to something that is well-known to you?

END OF TEST 11

111

A

1	2
1. prove	1. globes
2. broadly	2. incredibly
3. usual	3. observer
4. created	4. nonsense

B Al Learns More About Molecules

The molecules were getting colder. As Al watched, he noticed that they were not vibrating as fast. They stayed in rows but they were moving slower and slower and slower. The old man said, “The grain of sand is now as cold as the surface of Pluto. And it’s getting colder and colder.”

Suddenly, Al noticed that the molecules were standing still, lined up in perfect rows. The old man said, “Now the grain of sand is as cold as it can get. At this temperature, nothing moves.”

As Al and the old man floated toward one of the molecules, Al observed that the molecule was made up of many little parts that seemed to be floating in space. These parts formed three large globes. The middle globe was the biggest. There was a large ball in the center of this globe. Fourteen tiny balls moved around the ball in the center.

As Al looked at the middle globe, he noticed that the tiny balls weren’t touching the center ball, but were arranged in space around the center ball. Some tiny balls were far away from the center ball. Other tiny balls were closer to the center ball. Al said, “Those little balls in the center globe look like planets around the sun.”

“You are a very good observer,” the old man said as he pointed to the other sand molecules. “And look over there,” he continued. “All the sand molecules look exactly the same. All have three globes. Each middle globe has fourteen tiny balls.”

“This is amazing,” Al said. He counted the tiny balls around one of the other middle globes and then repeated, “This is amazing.”

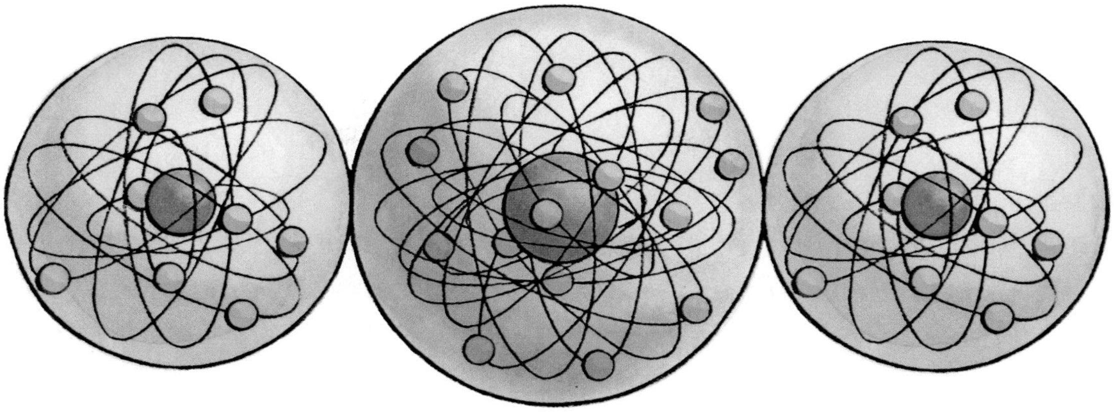

Then the old man said, "Now watch a molecule as it starts to get hotter."

The molecule started to tremble. Then it started to vibrate faster and faster and faster. The old man said, "Now the molecule is the same temperature as this room again. But watch what happens when the molecule gets so hot that the sand turns into a liquid."

The old man continued, "When the molecules are in the liquid form, they will not be in rows and they will move very, very fast."

The molecule started to vibrate fast, so fast that Al could hardly follow it with his eyes. Suddenly the molecule shot past Al and the old man and disappeared. Al noticed that the rows of molecules had disappeared. The molecules were flying this way and that way, in all directions—very fast. One of them almost hit Al and the old man.

The old man said, "The liquid form of the sand is still getting hotter." The old man continued, "In a moment that liquid will turn into a gas. You'll have to look very carefully to see the molecules."

The molecules now looked as if they were moving over a thousand miles an hour. "Wiiish." One went flying by Al like a shot. He waited and waited for another molecule to fly by, but none came by for a few minutes. Then—"wiiish"—another molecule flew by at an incredible speed.

"I don't see many molecules now," Al said.

The old man said, "When matter is in the solid form, the molecules are close together. When matter is in the liquid form, the molecules are much farther apart. But when matter is in the gas form, the molecules are farther apart than they are in the liquid form. And they move incredibly fast. They are not in rows. They fly in all directions."

"Wiiish." Another molecule flew past Al and the old man. As Al floated, he tried to make sure that he would remember the things he had seen. He remembered how the molecules looked when they were as cold as they could get. He remembered how they looked in the solid form at room temperature. He remembered how they changed when they got hot enough to go into the liquid form. And he remembered how they looked in the gas form.

Suddenly Al noticed that everything was getting darker and darker. Now Al could see that he was no longer small. He was standing inside the old man's store.

The old man said, "You wanted molecules. You got molecules. Remember everything that you have seen. Pass the test and pay for your trip. Then you can go on another trip. Go anywhere. See anything."

Al said, "Don't worry. I'll pass the test."

C Number your paper from 1 through 22.

Story Items

1. Write the letters of the 2 ways that molecules charge when they go from a solid to a liquid.
   - a. They move slower.
   - b. They move faster.
   - c. They stay in rows.
   - d. They do not stay in rows.
2. Did Al see many molecules when the sand was in the gas form?
3. In which form of matter are molecules closest together?
4. In which form of matter are molecules farthest apart?

Review Items

5. Which planet has more gravity?
6. How do you know?

For each picture, tell if the lights in the room are **on** or **off**. The solid arrows show people going into the room. The dotted arrows show people leaving the room.

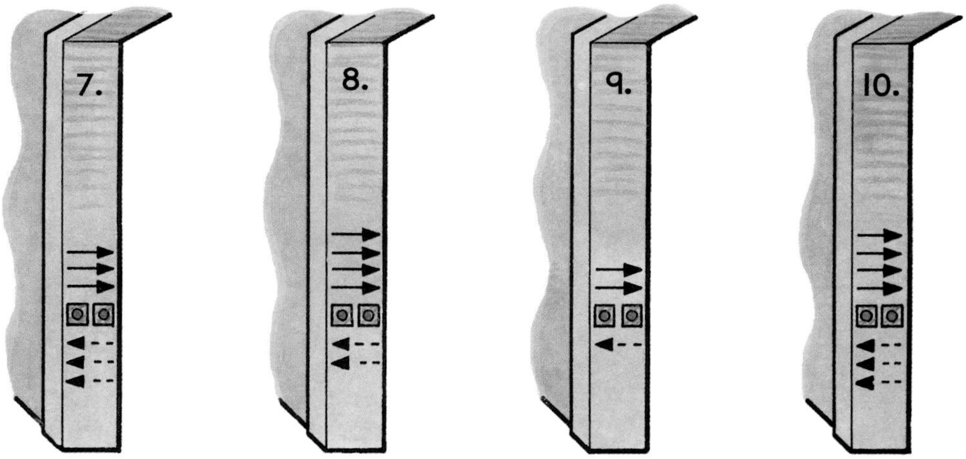

11. A person weighs 100 pounds on planet A and 300 pounds on planet G. Which planet has stronger gravity?
12. Planet M has stronger gravity than planet R. On which of those planets would you weigh more?
13. How long does it take sound to travel one mile?

14. **Write the letter** of the thing that travels the slowest.
15. **Write the letter** of the thing that travels the fastest.

a. rocket
b. jet plane
c. racing car
d. sound
e. light

16. What is the hottest form of any matter?
17. What is the next-hottest form of any matter?
18. What is the coldest form of any matter?
19. Do all things turn into a gas at the same temperature?
20. What are tiny parts of matter called?

21. How many miles does light travel in one second?
22. What else travels as fast as light?

SPECIAL PROJECT

You have read about molecules. One thing that you have learned is that molecules from different materials look different. Make a chart that shows molecules from different materials. Look up **molecules** in an encyclopedia, a science book or on the computer. Find pictures of different molecules. See if you can find pictures of water molecules and oxygen molecules.

Make pictures of some of the molecules that these books show. Label each type of molecule. You may want to make an impressive wall chart or models of some molecules.

A

1	2
1. broadly	1. however
2. prove	2. indeed
3. usual	3. concluded
4. spelling	4. demonstrated
5. studied	
6. unbearable	

B Al Takes a Test About Molecules

The next morning, Al walked to school with Angela. Al couldn't keep his secret any longer. Part of his mind told him that Angela wouldn't believe him. Another part just had to tell somebody about his experience on Anywhere Street. The air was very cold and Al could see his breath. As he breathed out and observed the little cloud, he thought to himself, "That cloud is made up of molecules."

"What did you say about molecules?" his sister asked.

Al didn't realize that he had talked out loud.

"Oh, I was just thinking about molecules," he said. By now part of him was saying, "Go ahead, tell her about Anywhere Street."

Another part responded, "No, Al. She'll think you're crazy."

Suddenly Al said, "Molecules are really interesting. Do you know that the molecules from a grain of sand all look the same?"

"Yeah," his sister replied. "We studied molecules in school."

"But did you know that all sand molecules are made up of three globes? The middle globe is the biggest. And it has fourteen tiny balls that float around a ball in the center."

His sister looked at him and made a sour face. "How do you know that?"

"You're not going to believe this," Al said. "But I saw those molecules."

"Where?" his sister asked.

For a moment Al couldn't bring himself to tell her where he had seen them. But then he took a deep breath and said, "I went inside a grain of sand."

"Oh, I see," his sister said smiling. "You went inside a grain of sand. It must have been one big grain."

"I'm not kidding," Al said. He tried to sound serious, but he couldn't seem to look Angela in the eyes. He knew how crazy he must have sounded. "I got so small that I went inside a little tiny grain of sand."

"I see," his sister said. "You went inside a grain of sand and counted the number of balls that are in the molecules. And while you were doing that, I rode a horse to the moon and back."

"I'm serious, Angela," Al insisted. "I'm telling you what happened. It really, really happened."

"Get out of here," she said, and started to walk ahead of Al. He caught up and grabbed her arm. "Now, listen to me. I want to tell you what happened." He felt angry now, and he didn't have any trouble looking her in the eyes—straight in the eyes.

Al explained about the old man and about the trip inside the grain of sand. Then Al said, "I can prove it. I can tell you about things that I wouldn't know about if I hadn't gone inside a grain of sand."

"What can you tell me?" his sister asked.

"I can tell you how the molecules move." Al and his sister were standing near an empty lot. Al picked up a stick and drew three rows of dots in the dirt. He explained, "That's how the molecules are lined up in solid matter. They're all in rows and they keep their place. But they vibrate at room temperature." Al held the end of the stick against one of the molecules that he had drawn in the dirt and said, "When the matter turns into a liquid, the molecules start moving around like this." Al drew a fast line across the dirt with the end of the stick. "They start flying in all directions."

He drew lines from another molecule in a different direction. "And when the liquid turns into a gas, the molecules move even faster, much faster. And they're very far apart. Sometimes more than a minute would pass before I'd see one. Then suddenly one would flash past me."

"Well, I'll say this," Angela said after Al had finished. "You sure know a lot about molecules. I'll give you that much. But that doesn't prove that you were inside a grain of sand."

Al stared at his sister for a moment. Then he turned away and shook his head. He knew that he wouldn't believe her if she told him she'd been inside a grain of sand. So he didn't say anything more about his trip.

Al and Angela went to school. Al did well in school. He worked hard in reading and arithmetic. The class had a spelling test, and Al missed only one word. One of the words that he got right was **molecule.** Only three other kids got that word right.

After school Al went back to Anywhere Street. As usual, there were no people or cars on the street. Al opened the door to the store, and the bell went ding, ding.

Inside the dark and quiet store, a voice said, "Are you ready to pay for your trip to the molecules?"

Al said, "Yes, I'm ready."

The old man bent over so that his face was close to Al's. The old man said, "Here is the first question: How can we make molecules stand still?"

Al said, "Make the matter as cold as it can get. When matter gets cold enough, the molecules stop moving."

The old man looked at Al. He smiled broadly and then asked, "How can you make the molecules go very, very fast?"

Al explained.

"You have passed the test," the old man said. "You are a good thinker."

The old man straightened up and waved his hand. "Now where do you want to go? Remember—go anywhere. See anything."

Al asked, "Could I take my sister with me on the next trip? She's smart and she'd really love to go on these trips."

The old man smiled. He said, "Bring her with you. But remember—she'll have to pass a test on what she sees."

"She'll pass the test," Al said.

Al ran from the store. The bell went ding, ding. Al could hardly wait to tell Angela.

C Number your paper from 1 through 17.

Review Items

1. How can you make the molecules in a liquid move slower?
   - Heat them.
   - Cool them.
2. How can you make the molecules in a liquid move faster?
3. In which form of matter do molecules move fastest?
4. In which form of matter do molecules move slowest?
5. In which form of matter are molecules lined up in rows?
6. In which form of matter are molecules farthest apart?
7. In which form of matter are molecules closest together?
8. When sand molecules are as cold as they can get, how much do they move?
9. Do they move **more** or **less** at room temperature?
10. Write the letters of the **2** ways that molecules change when they go from a solid to a liquid.
    a. They stay in rows.
    b. They do not stay in rows.
    c. They move faster.
    d. They move slower.

11. What are clouds made of?
12. What kind of cloud does the picture show?
13. What happens to a drop of water at **B?**

Use these words to answer items 14–16:

- **swing dogs**
- **wheel dogs**
- **lead dogs**

14. These dogs are very smart, and other dogs obey them.
15. These dogs are very good followers, and they are smart.
16. These dogs are responsible for freeing the sled when it gets stuck.

17. Why can't you see molecules when you look at an object?

113

A

1

1. tentacles
2. unbearable
3. squid
4. wriggled
5. nonsense

B Angela Meets the Old Man

After supper Al said to Angela, "Let's go for a walk. I want to tell you something." Al didn't want his mother to hear what he was going to tell Angela. The air outside felt very cold. As they walked along, Al said, "I asked the old man if I could take you with me on one of the trips. He said it was okay. So after school tomorrow, you come to the store with me and we can go anywhere you want to go and we can see anything in the whole solar system."

"Al, stop this nonsense," Angela said. "You had your joke about the molecules. Now stop kidding around."

"Angela, I'm not kidding. I'm as serious as I can be. Come on, just go to the store with me."

"Do you really expect me to believe that there's an old man that can take people inside a grain of sand?"

"That's right," Al insisted. "And that's not all. He can take us to the stars. He can take us inside the sun or to the bottom of the ocean. He can take us anywhere."

"I'm not going to listen to any more of this nonsense," Angela said.

Al grabbed his sister by the shoulders and faced her. The light from a streetlight was shining on her face. "Please," Al said. "Please go with me, just one time. It's not a joke. You don't have to believe me. Go with me to the store tomorrow. Would you do that much?"

She sighed and pushed Al away. "All right," she said. "I don't know why, but I'll do it."

Al said, "You won't be sorry. You'll see."

The next day seemed to drag for Al. His mind kept making up pictures of how Angela would respond when she found out that Al had been telling the truth. He could almost see her face. Her mouth would fall open and her eyes would become wide. Then she would say, "Wow, you were telling me the truth." Al's mind must have created that picture of Angela's face twenty times during the school day.

After school, Al and his sister walked down street after street. Finally, Angela stopped and said, "There is no Anywhere Street."

"No, honest," Al said. "We'll be there in a couple of blocks."

Angela sighed and started walking again. At last they came to the corner of Anywhere Street. Al pointed to the street sign. "See?" he said. "What did I tell you?"

"Well, you were telling the truth about one thing," she said.

"Right," Al said. "And look down the street. Do you see any cars or any people?"

"Wow," his sister said. "That's amazing." Then she added, "But that doesn't mean I believe you about the old man."

They walked to the store. Al pointed to the sign in the window. "See?" he said. "What did I tell you?"

"Wow," she said. Then she shook her head. "This is too much."

Al opened the door. The bell sounded. "This is Angela," Al said into the darkness. "She wants to go on a trip with me."

Silence.

Angela said, "Oh, I get it. I'm supposed to think that you're talking to somebody. There's no old man in here. There's just a dark . . ."

"Go anywhere, see anything," the old man said loudly, and seemed to pop out of the darkness.

Al looked at his sister's face in the dim light. It was just like the picture that he had imagined. Her mouth was open and her eyes were wide. She didn't say anything as she took several steps backward, toward the door.

"Go to the stars," the old man said in a booming voice. "Or travel with kangaroos across Australia. See the moons of Jupiter or swim with whales. Where do you want to go?"

Angela's expression had not changed. She stared at the old man. The old man pointed his finger at her. "Tell me where you want to go and we'll go there."

Angela spoke very softly as she said, "I—I just came here with Al. I don't want to go anywhere."

"Of course you want to go somewhere, perhaps inside a volcano."

"No," she said softly. "I just want to go home." She moved closer to the door.

"Come on," Al said. "Tell him something you'd like to learn about, and he'll show it to you."

Suddenly Angela's expression changed. "This has gone far enough," she said. "I just want to get out of here."

"Oh, you would like to be far away from here?" the old man asked.

"Very far away," Angela said. "I don't know what kind of joke this is, but I'm going to get . . ."

Suddenly the store became brighter and the walls seemed to melt and change into other forms. Al looked around and realized that he and his sister were standing in the middle of a hot field. Next to them was a jungle. Cries of birds came from the jungle, and the sun beat down on them. The old man was sitting on a large rock a few meters away, fanning himself with a large leaf. Angela's expression was once more like the one that Al had imagined.

"You wanted to get far away," the old man said. "You are far away. You are in Africa."

The heat from the sun was almost unbearable. Al took off his jacket and opened his shirt, but his sister just stood there, slowly turning around with wide eyes and open mouth.

The old man said to Angela, "Is there anything special that you would like to see here?"

She slowly shook her head no.

The old man said, "Well, I would like to see an elephant."

As soon as the words came from the old man's mouth, a great elephant charged from the jungle, holding its trunk high in the air. It was charging toward Al and Angela. Angela mumbled something and then started to run away very fast.

C Number your paper from 1 through 22.

Skill Items

The poem they created was nonsense.

1. What word means **no sense at all?**
2. What word means **made?**

Review Items

3. Write the names of the 9 planets, starting with the planet closest to the sun.
4. In which form of matter is air on Saturn?
5. In which form of matter is air on Pluto?
6. In which form of matter is air on Earth?
7. In which form of matter do molecules move fastest?
8. In which form of matter do molecules move slowest?
9. In which form of matter are molecules lined up in rows?
10. How many miles does light travel in one second?
11. What else travels as fast as light?
12. During the Iditarod, how do mushers get water for their dogs?
13. What do mushers usually use to make beds for their dogs?
14. What's the name of the first woman to win the Iditarod?
15. In what year did she win it?
16. During the Iditarod, is the snow deeper **on the trail** or **off the trail?**
17. Why?
18. The rules of the Iditarod state that every musher must rest for ______ hours at one checkpoint and must rest for ______ hours at two other checkpoints.
19. This rule was put in to protect the ______.
    - dogs
    - race officials
    - mushers
20. In what year was the first Iditarod?
21. During the first running of the Iditarod, how many dogs died during the race?
22. During more recent years, how many dogs die during each race?

114

A

1	2
1. wriggled	1. tentacles
2. anxiously	2. exclaimed
3. watermelon	3. disk
4. lumpy	4. shocked
5. grapefruit	5. grown
6. dimmer	

B

Angela and Al Learn About Water Pressure

As the huge elephant ran after Angela, Al ran over to the old man. "Stop that," he demanded. "Don't scare my sister like that."

The old man smiled.

"I mean it," Al said. "Get rid of that elephant."

"What elephant?" the old man asked.

Angela was standing about thirty meters from Al and the old man. She was slowly turning around. The elephant was not in sight.

"It's okay, Angela," Al said. Slowly Angela walked back toward Al, glancing over her shoulder every few steps. She still had a shocked expression on her face. "It just disappeared," she said softly. "That elephant just disappeared." Then she asked, "Can we get out of here?"

"Certainly," the old man replied. "But you'll have to tell me where you want to go and what you want to see."

Angela didn't say anything. She just shook her head.

Al said, "I've got an idea. Let's go to the bottom of the ocean. We could see all kinds of interesting things down there."

Angela said, "No. I don't think that . . . "

The jungle and the sky seemed to melt into a deep green. "What's happening?" Angela asked anxiously.

Al and the others were no longer standing on ground. They were floating through the green water of an ocean.

"We'll drown," Angela said. "We're underwater."

"Don't worry, my friend," the old man said. "You are with me on a very special trip. You'll be able to breathe and to talk. The water pressure will not bother you. But you will be able to see things that most people only read about."

Al could see the sun above the surface of the water. It was a light green disk. Below them, the green water turned to blue and deep purple. A school of red fish was swimming next to Al and the others. The old man said, "I will show you water pressure."

"It's impossible to see pressure," Al said. "It's just an invisible force, like the wind."

"Come with me to the bottom of this ocean and I will show you pressure." The old man pointed down. "We are only about 30 feet deep now. The bottom of the ocean below us is 200 feet from the surface, so we have a long way to go."

Al and Angela followed the old man, deeper and deeper. Occasionally, Al looked up at the sun. It became dimmer and dimmer as the water changed from green to dark blue. Now Al swam past strange lumpy rocks.

The old man said, "Those rocks are covered with coral." The old man continued, "Coral is made of millions and millions of small sea animals. When the animals die, their shells stay on the rock. After hundreds and hundreds of years, you cannot see the rock anymore because it is covered with a thick layer of coral."

When they reached the bottom, the old man said, "Now I will show you pressure." He took out a balloon and blew it up until it was about as big as an apple. The old man said, "This balloon will change as we move up toward the surface. You watch it and see how it changes. While you're watching it, remember this rule: The deeper something is, the more pressure there is on that thing." The old man repeated the rule.

"I don't understand why the pressure is greater when you're deeper," Al said.

The old man pointed up. He said, "The pressure is greater because the water above you weighs more. The weight of all that water pushes against you. So if you are very deep, there is a lot of weight pushing against you."

Al said, "I get it. And if you're not as deep, there isn't as much weight pushing down on you."

"Correct," the old man said. Then he began to swim up toward the surface. "Watch what happens to the balloon," he said.

Angela pointed to the balloon and said, "It's getting bigger." Now the balloon was as big as a grapefruit.

The old man said, "Can you tell me why it is getting bigger?"

"I think so," Angela replied. "When we go up, the water above us doesn't weigh as much. So the water doesn't push against the balloon as hard."

"A very smart young lady," the old man said as he continued toward the surface. Now the balloon had grown to the size of a watermelon.

The old man stopped 30 feet below the surface. "If we go any higher, the balloon will burst. Tell me why."

Al answered, "Because there will be less pressure and the balloon will keep getting bigger until it breaks."

The old man moved up about three feet and "BLOOM, bubble, bubble," the balloon burst and sent a huge blob of bubbles to the surface. The old man held the broken balloon and said, "You have just seen pressure."

"That's amazing," Angela said.

The old man said, "There is more to the ocean than pressure. So let's go back down and see some of the other wonders of the ocean. But before we do, I want you to think about what you have just seen. I want you to remember how the balloon changed. And I want you to understand why it changed." The old man stopped talking.

Al thought very hard. He remembered the rule: The deeper something is, the more pressure there is on that thing. He remembered how the balloon got bigger and bigger when there was

less pressure on it. After a few moments, Al said, "I'll remember everything."

"Me too," his sister said.

"Good," the old man said. "Now let's go back down and see some of the wonders of the sea."

Al was ready to see them. Angela said, "That sounds great."

C Number your paper from 1 through 22.

Story Items

1. There's a fish at each letter. Write the letter of the fish with the **greatest pressure** on it.
2. Write the letter of the fish with the **least pressure** on it.

Skill Items

Write the word from the box that means the same thing as the underlined part of each sentence.

survives	section	daydreamed	concluded
however	surrounds	experience	demonstrated

3. The fence <u>goes all the way around</u> the yard.
4. He cleaned his <u>part</u> of the room.
5. They <u>showed</u> how the machine works.

Use the words in the box to write complete sentences.

usual	nonsense	insisted	molecules	created
impressive	crystal	honest	billion	

6. The ____ contained more than a ____ ____.
7. The poem they ____ was ____.

Review Items

8. If something weighed 50 pounds on Earth, would it weigh more than 50 pounds on our moon?
9. Which is larger, Earth or Jupiter?
10. If something weighed 20 pounds on Earth, would it weigh **more than 20 pounds** or **less than 20 pounds** on Jupiter?

11. Write the letter of the footprint made by the lightest animal.
12. Write the letter of the footprint made by the heaviest animal.

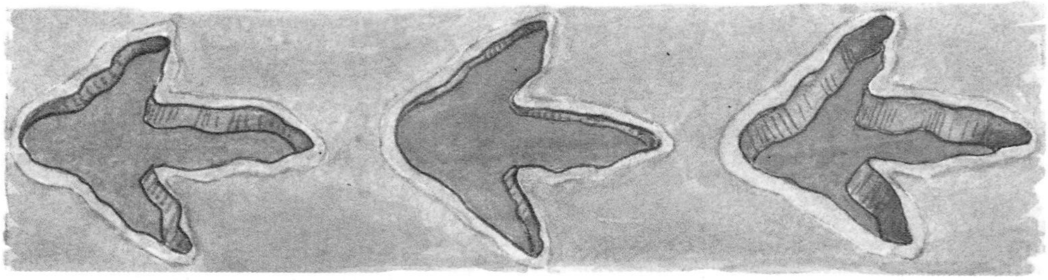

J K L

13. What color is lava when it's very hot?
14. What color is lava after it cools a little bit?
15. What color is lava after it's completely cooled?

• brown • gray • orange

Write the name of each kind of coral.

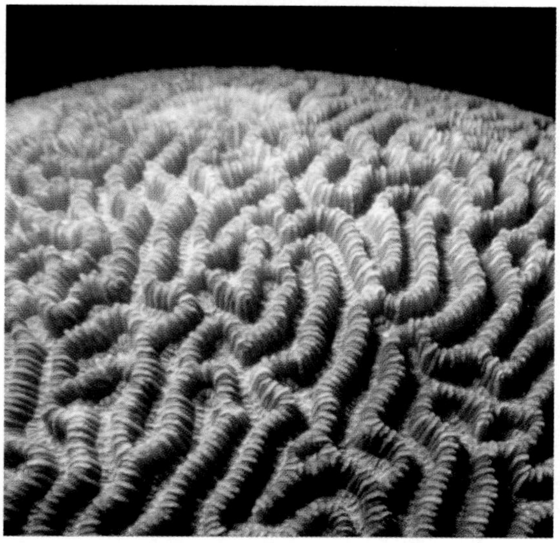

16.

17.

18.

19. An underwater hill that is covered with coral is called a coral ________.

20. Name the woman who finished the Iditarod sixteen times.
21. How many times did she **enter** the Iditarod?
22. How many times did she finish in first place?

115

A

1	2
1. transparent	1. exclaimed
2. addressed	2. indeed
3. expensive	3. squirting
4. triceps	4. headfirst
5. muscle	

B

Al and Angela See Strange Sea Animals

The old man said, "We're going to go deeper in the water again and observe some of the animals that live in the ocean. Before we go down, I want you to tell me what will happen to this balloon."

Suddenly a very large balloon appeared in the old man's hand. It was the size of a watermelon.

Angela said, "The balloon will get smaller and smaller."

"Correct," the old man said. "But can you tell me why?"

"I can," Al said. "As we go deeper, the water above us will weigh more and more. The weight of that water will press against the balloon and make it smaller and smaller."

The old man smiled broadly and said, "You learn well from the things you have seen."

Al smiled back at the old man, feeling very smart.

Then Al and Angela followed the old man down. The balloon that the old man held did just what Angela had said it would do. The water turned from light blue to dark blue as they went down deeper and deeper. When they were 200 feet deep, the balloon was about the size of an apple.

Suddenly the old man let go of the balloon. It went up toward the surface. As it went up, it got bigger and bigger and bigger.

The old man said, "Follow me and we'll go to a place where the ocean is very deep."

Down they went. The water was very dark now—deep purple. Al could no longer see the sun above him.

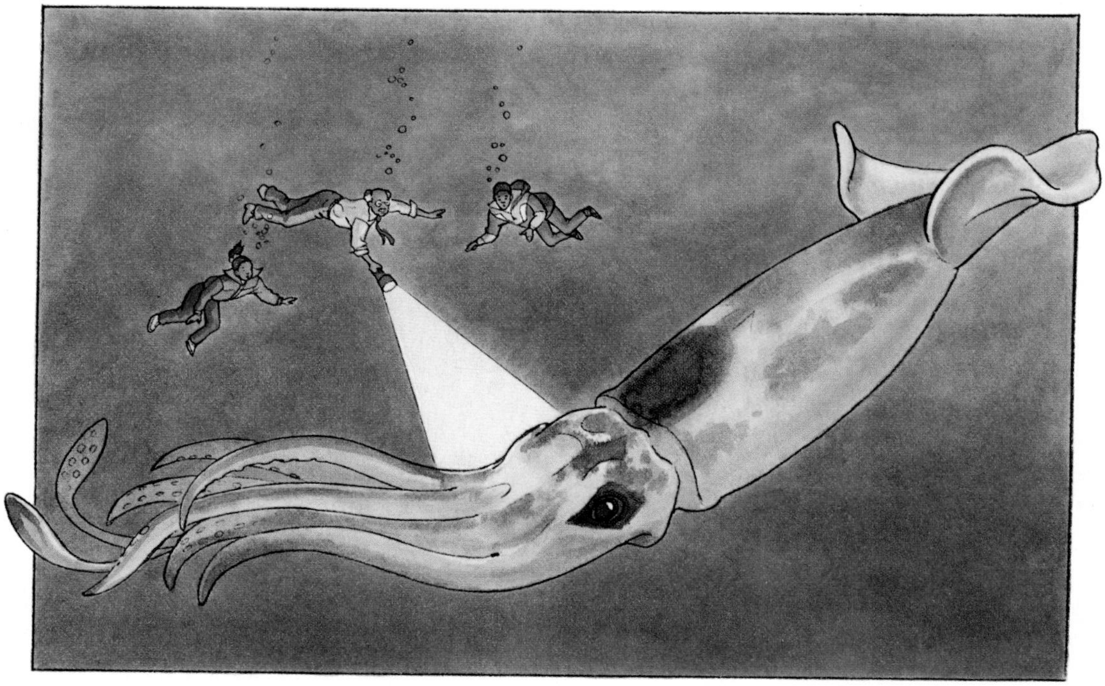

The old man held up a giant flashlight and turned it on. Then he said, "We are now 300 feet below the surface. The pressure down here is amazing. But there are animals that live down here. Let me show you one of them." The old man directed the beam of the giant flashlight to one side. For a moment Al could not believe what he saw in the beam of light. It was an incredible monster that had a tube on one end and many arms on the other end.

Al jumped back when he saw the monster. "What is that?" he asked.

The old man replied, "That is a giant squid. These squid will grow to the size of a big tree. The one you are looking at now is about fifty feet long."

"Fifty feet!" Al exclaimed. "That's longer than our house."

"Correct," the old man said.

Al was about to ask what that huge squid ate when suddenly a dark form moved into the flashlight beam. It was another animal, even bigger than the squid.

"A whale!" Angela exclaimed.

"Correct again," the old man replied.

"Is that a killer whale?" Al asked.

"No," the old man said. "This whale is called a blue whale. It is much longer than a killer whale."

"Wow!" Al exclaimed. "Will that whale eat the squid?"

"No," the old man replied. "Watch what the squid does."

Suddenly, the squid moved very fast. It moved headfirst, with its

arms ★ trailing its body. The old man said, "The squid moves by squirting out water, the same way a jet plane moves by pushing out air."

In an instant the squid caught up to the huge whale. In another instant, the squid's long arms reached out and began to wrap around the whale. The whale was bigger than the squid, but the squid had a good hold on the whale.

The old man said, "The arms of the squid are called tentacles." The old man continued, "The squid can hang on because its tentacles have little cups that stick to the surface of the whale."

Al watched the two giants fighting. The whale turned this way and that way. Then the whale shot up toward the surface of the water. The whale came down again and dove down, down, down. The squid was still hanging on.

Angela asked, "Will that giant squid kill the whale?"

"I don't think so," the old man said. "If that whale weren't so big,

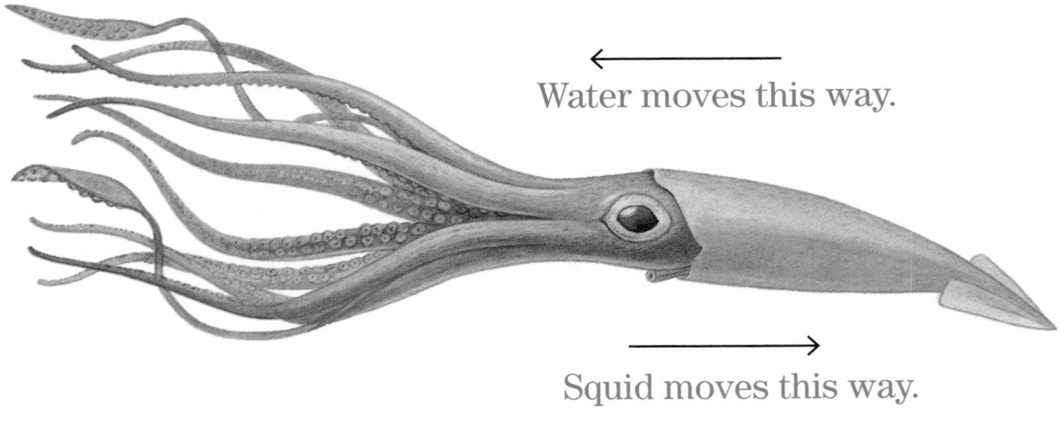

the squid would probably be able to kill it. But I think the whale will get away."

Suddenly the whale wriggled and turned. Then it shot up toward the surface again. It soon disappeared in the deep blue above Al and the others. In less than half a minute, it returned to the deep water. The squid was no longer hanging on, but Al could see rows of marks on the surface of the whale. These marks hadn't been there before. They must have been made by the cups of the squid's tentacles.

The whale slowly swam next to Al and the others. It was like a huge ship, so big that Al could hardly believe its size. Angela said, "It's hard to believe that there are animals so big."

"Indeed," the old man agreed. "You are looking at the largest animal in the world. It weighs more than ten elephants."

Suddenly the whale stopped, then dove very deep and very fast. Angela said, "I think that whale is afraid of something."

"Look up there and you'll see the animals the whale fears most," the old man said.

Al looked up. He could see something swimming in the dark water. Al said, "I see them. I see four or five big fish. They look black and white."

"They're not fish," the old man said. "They are killer whales. They're not as big as other whales, but they hunt bigger whales and they kill them. No whale can get away from them."

The killer whales suddenly dove down after the blue whale. They moved very fast. They swam past Al, Angela and the old man. Al could see the sharp teeth of one killer whale as it swam by. The old man said, "The mouth of that killer whale is so big that Angela could sit inside it."

"No thanks," Angela said. "I don't think I want to get near those fish."

"They are not fish," the old man said. "All whales are warm-blooded animals, just like a dog or a pig or a cat. Fish are cold-blooded."

The killer whales were swimming closer and closer toward the blue whale.

C Number your paper from 1 through 21.

Story Items

1. What animal did the giant squid attack?
2. Did the squid kill that animal?
3. What kind of animals scared the blue whale?
4. Why was the blue whale afraid of those animals?
5. At the beginning of today's story, the old man blew up a balloon. That balloon was the size of a ___.
6. What happened to the balloon as the old man went deeper and deeper?
7. Why did that happen?
8. How many feet deep did the old man take Al and Angela?
9. What color was the water down there?
   - light blue
   - dark purple
   - green
10. Al and Angela saw an animal that looked like a giant tube with many arms. Name that animal.
11. About how long was the animal?
12. What are the animal's arms called?
13. The animal's arms stick to things because they are covered with ___.

Review Items

14. Name **3** things an Iditarod musher does at checkpoints.
15. Why are checkpoints called checkpoints?
16. How does food get to the checkpoints?
17. About how far apart are the checkpoints?
18. About how many checkpoints are there between Anchorage and Nome?

Here's how big a balloon is at 5 feet below the surface.

R

Here's the same balloon when it is **deeper** or **not as deep.**

19. Write the letter of each balloon that is deeper than the balloon **R.**
20. Write the letter of the balloon that is deepest.
21. Write the letter of the balloon that is closest to the surface.

A B C D E

116

A

1

1. intelligent
2. imagination
3. universe
4. balanced
5. presented
6. biceps

2

1. expensive
2. greeted
3. package
4. transparent

3

1. couch
2. addressed
3. scratched
4. applauded

B

Al and Angela Go to the Bottom of the Ocean

Al, Angela and the old man swam after the blue whale. The four killer whales caught up to the blue whale, but just as they were about to sink their huge teeth into the blue whale, the old man made a very funny sound. It was something like a beep, but very high. Suddenly all the killer whales turned around and swam away from the blue whale.

The old man said, "That sound is part of the language killer whales use. That sound is a warning signal that tells them to swim away fast."

Angela asked, "Do killer whales understand language?"

"Yes," the old man replied. "They use a kind of language."

Al watched the killer whales swim out of their sight.

Then the old man said, "We're going to go deeper into the ocean."

Down and down they went, until the water was black. The old man said, "The ocean is over six miles deep in the deepest places. We are going to go down to one of the very deepest places."

At last the old man pointed his flashlight down. Al could see the bottom of the ocean. There were no plants on the bottom.

The old man said, "Plants don't grow this deep in the ocean because there is no sunlight down here."

Suddenly a fish swam by. But it wasn't like any fish that Al had ever seen before. It was very small, and the lights on its side were shining. Then another fish came by—a fat

one with great big teeth and a light coming out of its head.

Al noticed that some other fish were transparent. He could actually see right through them. Suddenly a fish with huge eyes swam into view.

Angela said, “Wow! If I hadn't seen those fish, I never would have believed they were real.”

When Al looked around, he was standing next to Angela and the old man in the store.

Angela asked, “What happened?”

Al said, “The trip is over.”

The old man said, “Yes, but you must pay for your trip by passing a test on what you saw.”

Suddenly, the old man disappeared.

Al opened the door. Ding, ding, the bell went. As they walked outside, Angela's expression was blank. She was staring straight ahead. After they had walked

halfway to the corner of Anywhere Street she said, "Did we really go to the bottom of the ocean? Did it really happen?"

"I don't know," Al said. "Funny things happen when the old man takes you on a trip."

Angela shook her head.

When Al and Angela arrived at home, their mother greeted them. She said, "The strangest thing just happened. The bell rang but when I opened the door, nobody was there. But this package was in front of the door." She held out a flat package that was about the size of a book. She continued, "The package is addressed to both of you."

Then she handed the package to Angela. Angela quickly tore off the wrapping paper. Inside was a large book. The title was *The Sea.* On the cover was a picture of a giant blue whale fighting with a giant squid.

A little card was sticking out of the book. On the card these words were written: "This book will help you go anywhere and see anything."

Al's mother looked puzzled. She said, "Somebody sent you that expensive book. But who would do that?"

"I don't know," Al said.

Al and Angela went into the living room and sat next to each other on the couch as they looked through the book. It showed pictures of the things they had seen in the ocean.

They saw pictures of strange fish with lights on their sides, and they saw killer whales. There were even pictures that showed a balloon getting bigger as it rose from the bottom of the ocean.

For over an hour, Angela and Al looked through the book. Then Al said, "Would you mind if I took the book to school with me tomorrow?"

Angela replied, "Just don't lose it."

"Don't worry," Al said.

The next day in school, Al asked his science teacher if he could show the book to the other kids in his class. He said, "I think that some of these pictures will help them understand the sea better."

His teacher replied, "Sure. Show some pictures to the class and explain them."

Al hadn't planned on explaining the pictures, and he felt anxious. He said, "I've got a book here that shows some pictures of things in the ocean."

Homer said very loudly, "What's Al doing with a real book?"

Everybody laughed—except Al and the teacher.

The teacher said, "Al has been doing very well in science lately. So let's listen to what he has to say."

Al showed the cover of the book and started to explain. He told about giant squids and blue whales. He told what the blue whale would do to escape from the squid. When he told that the whale would swim very fast to the surface and then dive very quickly, Homer said, "That's impossible. If you go to the surface too fast, you could get the bends and die. So the whale couldn't just zoom up to the surface from 300 feet deep."

"You're wrong, Homer," Al said. "Humans die if they go up too fast, but whales don't. I know."

Before Homer could object, the teacher said, "Al is right. Whales can do that. The great changes in pressure do not seem to bother the whale."

Homer made a sour face, scratched his ear and mumbled something to himself.

Al went through the part of the book that told about the animals that live in the deepest part of the ocean. After he explained the last picture, he concluded by saying, "Some of the animals that live down there are the most amazing things you've ever seen."

The class applauded. Al's face got hot, and the teacher said, "That was an excellent talk, Al. You told about those things as if you had actually seen them."

Al's face got hotter.

C Number your paper from 1 through 22.

Skill Items

The squid wriggled its tentacles.

1. What word names a sea animal?
2. What word means **squirmed around in all directions?**
3. What word refers to arms that are like huge snakes?

Here are 3 events that happened in the story. Write **beginning, middle** or **end** for each event.

4. Here's what somebody said: "That sound is part of the language killer whales use."
5. After Al and Angela left the store, Angela asked, "Did we really go to the bottom of the ocean?"
6. Al showed the book to his class and started to explain.

Review Items

7. In what state is the Iditarod sled-dog race?
8. In which city does it begin?
9. In which city does it end?

10. The Iditarod is about _____ miles from start to finish.
    - 500
    - 1600
    - 1100
11. In most years, the race takes about _____.
    - a week
    - 10 days
    - 2 weeks

12. The person who drives a sled-dog team is called a _____.
13. The drivers of the sled-dog teams command the dogs by using their _____.
    - reins
    - voices
    - steering wheels

14. There's a fish at each letter. Write the letter of the fish with the **greatest pressure** on it.
15. Write the letter of the fish with the **least pressure** on it.

16. Name the largest animal in the world.
17. That animal weighs more than ____ elephants.
18. What's the name of a smaller whale that is black and white?

19. Are whales fish?
20. Are whales **warm-blooded** or **cold-blooded?**
21. What are a squid's arms called?
22. A squid's arms stick to things because they are covered with ____.

SPECIAL PROJECT

Al and Angela saw incredible animals that live at the bottom of the ocean. You may be able to find pictures of these animals in the encyclopedia or on a CD-ROM. They may have color pictures of the fish that Al and Angela saw. Also look for pictures of fish that live in the deepest parts of the ocean.

A

1	2
1. balanced	1. intelligent
2. flaming	2. triceps
3. silently	3. nowhere
4. presented	4. spoonful
5. muscles	5. biceps
	6. unimportant

B

A Test About the Ocean

After school, Angela met Al outside. "Come on," she said. "Let's get going." She walked so fast on the way to Anywhere Street that Al had trouble keeping up with her. Al was a little out of breath by the time they reached the store with the familiar sign in the window.

"Ding, ding."

For a moment, Al and Angela stood silently in the dark store. Then the old man stepped from the darkness. Very loudly he announced, "You may go anywhere and see anything if you pass your test." Without hesitating, he continued. "Angela, here is your first question: How does a squid make itself move?"

Angela cleared her throat and said, "Well, a squid takes in water. Then it blows it out very fast. The water shoots out the back and the squid moves forward—headfirst."

"Correct," the old man said, and continued without pausing. "Next question, Al. How deep is the deepest part of the ocean?"

"Over six miles deep," Al replied without hesitating.

"Next question, Angela. What's the largest animal in the world?"

"Blue whale," she answered.

"Next question, Al. How big is the blue whale?"

Al responded, "The blue whale weighs more than ten elephants and it is much longer than a killer whale."

Without smiling the old man presented the next question, and others—many others. But Al and Angela answered all of them correctly. Then suddenly, the old man held out his hands and smiled broadly. "You are indeed intelligent students," he said. "Very intelligent. You have passed your test, so where do you want to go and what do you want to see?"

"I want to see the stars," Angela said.

"You want a star, you have a star," the old man said.

Suddenly Al noticed that there was a hole in the ceiling of the store. Through the hole, Al could see the sun shining brightly.

"That is a star," the old man announced.

"But that's just the sun," Angela said.

"Correct, but the sun is a star."

Angela said, "I didn't want to see that star. I see it all the time. I wanted to see the other stars."

"We will visit some of them. But first, let's take a closer look at the sun, so that you have an idea of what it is and how big it is. Look carefully at it."

Suddenly, the sun seemed to grow larger and larger. Al and Angela were no longer in the store. They were now floating through space, close to the surface of the sun. The surface was not flat. It was made up of flaming gases. One of those flames shot up past Al and the others.

"That's incredible," Al said.

"Yes," the old man agreed. "That flame that just shot up is twelve times bigger than Earth."

Angela added, "And that flame is nowhere near as big as the sun."

"Correct," the old man said. "Earth is like a tiny dot next to the sun. If we went through the middle of the sun and came out the other side, we would travel one hundred times as far as we would travel going through the middle of Earth."

Al asked, "Do you mean that the sun is a hundred times wider than Earth?"

"Correct," the old man replied.

"Fantastic," Angela exclaimed.

The old man said, "Remember how big the sun is because we're going to look at some other stars."

Everything turned dark for a moment. Then Al noticed that he was approaching another star. It looked small.

The old man said, "We are now very far from Earth. It would take us over five thousand years to get back to Earth if we traveled at the speed of light."

Then the old man pointed to the star and continued, "That star is very old and very small. At one time that star was as big as our sun. But now it is almost burned out. It is only eight miles through the middle. That's much smaller than Earth. Earth is eight thousand miles through the middle."

Angela said, "I had no idea that stars could be so small."

The old man said, "But the most interesting thing about this old star is not how small it is but how much it weighs. It weighs almost as much as it did when it was as large as our sun."

"That's impossible," Al said. "It's not even as big as a moon. It's a tiny little thing."

The old man said, "I will show you how much the matter from this star weighs." The old man suddenly zoomed down to the surface of the star and came back holding a spoonful of bright glowing matter. "Here is one spoonful of matter from the star," he said.

A giant balance scale appeared in the sky. The old man said, "I will put this spoonful of matter on one side of the balance scale. Then we'll see how much weight must go on the other side to make the scale balance."

The old man placed the spoonful of matter on one side of the scale. That side went down.

"Angela," the old man said. "Name something that is heavy. I will put it on the other side of the scale and we will see if the scale will balance."

"A big rock," Angela said. A rock appeared on the other side of the scale, but the scale did not move. The side with the spoonful of matter on it stayed down.

"A rock is not heavy enough," the old man said.

"Try a big truck," Al said, and a big truck appeared on the scale. The scale did not move.

"Five more trucks," Angela said. They appeared, but the scale did not move.

"A small mountain," Al said. The trucks disappeared and a mountain appeared. Al waited for the scale to move, but it didn't. Al could not believe it. On one side of the scale was a spoonful of matter. On the other side was a mountain—not a hill, but a mountain. And still the side with the spoonful of matter stayed down.

"A huge mountain," Angela said. One appeared. It was so huge that Al could hardly see the top of it. Slowly, the scale balanced.

"Incredible," Angela said. "One spoonful of matter weighs as much as a huge mountain."

"Yes," the old man said.

C Number your paper from 1 through 21.

Skill Items

Use the words in the box to write complete sentences.

expensive	wriggled	shocked	created
tentacles	nonsense	addressed	universe

1. The poem they ____ was ____.
2. The squid ____ its ____.

Review Items

3. Name the animal in the picture.
4. Which arrow shows the way the animal squirts water out?
5. Which arrow shows the way the animal will move?

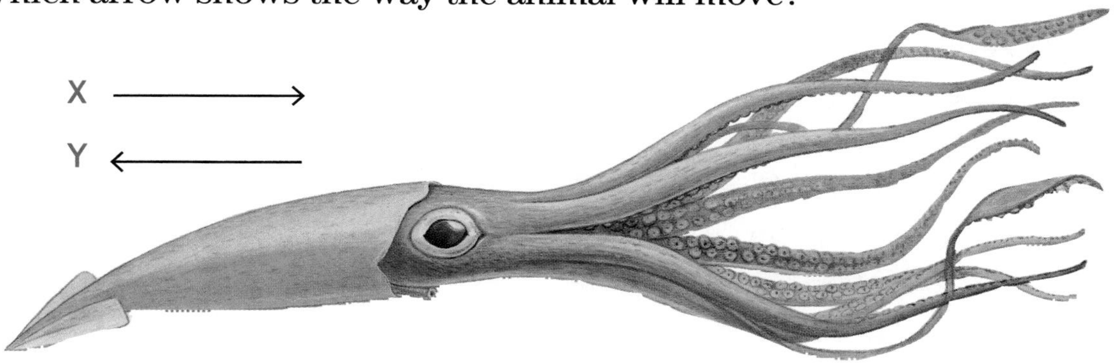

6. How long does it take sound to travel one mile?
7. Do plants grow on the bottom of the deepest part of the ocean?
8. Tell why.
9. Do all things turn into a gas at the same temperature?
10. What are tiny parts of matter called?
11. Do wood molecules look like air molecules?
12. Do all air molecules look the same?
13. Where would a balloon be bigger—at 100 feet below the surface of the ocean or at 40 feet below the surface?

14. What is animal N?
15. What is animal O?

16. The arrow on the map goes from San Francisco to ____.
17. Which ocean does the arrow cross?

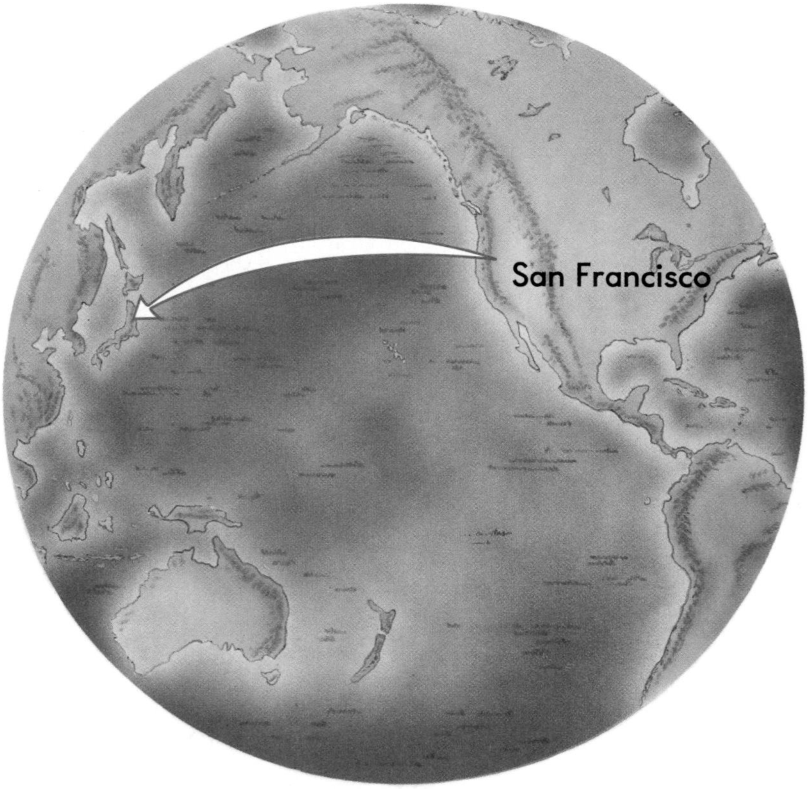

18. During the Iditarod, how much food does each dog need every day?
    - 2 pounds
    - 3 pounds
    - 1 pound
19. Each sled in the Iditarod must have room to hold ____.
    - an injured dog
    - another musher
    - a spare sled

20. Write the letter of the fish with the **least pressure** on it.
21. Write the letter of the fish with the **greatest pressure** on it.

118

A

1	2	3
1. pinwheel	1. decorated	1. Milky Way
2. snowflake	2. brightest	2. unimportant
3. nowhere	3. prettiest	3. imagination
4. headfirst	4. zoomed	4. universe

B Angela and Al See Our Galaxy

Al, Angela and the old man were looking at a star that was much, much smaller than the sun. The old man had just shown how much a spoonful of matter from that star weighs.

The old man said, "There are millions of very old stars like this one. They are very small. But there are also very large stars."

"Like our sun," Al said.

"No," the old man said. "Very large."

Suddenly Al noticed that he was moving very fast. He was passing up many stars. Then he seemed to stop. In front of him were two stars. One looked like a tiny speck next to the other.

Angela asked, "Is that small star another tiny star?"

"No," the old man replied. "The very tiny star is the same size as our sun."

Al compared the size of the two stars. The star that was as big as the sun looked hundreds of times smaller than the other star. Al was trying to imagine just how big that huge star was. But his mind couldn't get used to the idea that the tiny star was the size of the sun.

The old man pointed to the huge star. He said, "If that star were in the center of our solar system, it would be so big that Mercury would be inside the star."

"Incredible," Angela exclaimed.

The old man continued, "But Mercury would not be the only planet inside the star. Venus, Earth, Mars and even Jupiter would be inside the star." The old man continued, "That star is so huge that it would take light over 45 minutes to travel from one side of the star to the other side."

Al shook his head. He still couldn't imagine anything so big.

"That's the biggest thing I can imagine," Al said.

"Big?" the old man said. "That star is nothing but a speck compared to a galaxy."

Before Al could say anything, he noticed that he and the others were again speeding through space. They were moving toward a star. But as they zoomed closer and closer, Al observed that it was not a star. It was a cloud of stars. The cloud became larger and larger, until it seemed to fill the whole sky. It was incredible. Some of the stars were shining with all the colors of the rainbow. And the galaxy was shaped like a giant pinwheel. It was the brightest, biggest, most beautiful thing that Al had ever seen in his life. There were so many stars in the galaxy that Al couldn't even begin to count them.

Al and Angela didn't say anything for a long time. They simply looked at the incredible sight. At last Al said, "How many stars are in that galaxy? Are there more than a million?"

"Oh, yes," the old man replied. "Think of a thousand million. That's a billion. Then think of a hundred billion. One hundred billion. That's how many stars are in this galaxy."

Al tried to think of a billion and then think of a hundred billion, but the number was too big for his imagination.

The old man said, "It takes light 100 thousand years to travel from one side of that galaxy to the other side."

Al asked, "Are there other galaxies like this one?"

The old man replied, "There are millions of galaxies in the universe, but the one you're looking at is the biggest and prettiest one we know about." Then the old man asked, "Does it look familiar to you?"

"No," Al and Angela said.

"Look carefully," the old man said. "One of the stars is flashing very brightly so that you can see it."

"I see it," Angela said, pointing to one side of the galaxy.

Suddenly Al realized that he was moving toward that star. Al and the others were going through the galaxy now. There were stars all around them.

The old man pointed to the star that had been flashing. "That star is very, very special," the old man said.

"What's so special about it?" Angela asked. "It's just a little star."

The old man said, "The galaxy we're going through is called the Milky Way. And there is a star inside the Milky Way that is called the sun. That star you are moving toward is the sun. Now you know why it is special."

Al looked at the billions of stars in the Milky Way and noticed how small and unimportant the sun looked. The old man said, "Our sun is small when you think about the size of the universe. Just think—there are stars that are almost eight hundred times bigger than our sun. And there are galaxies that have billions and billions of stars."

Al tried to think about the size of the things he had seen. The sun had flames that were twelve times bigger than Earth. But there were stars that were hundreds of times bigger than the sun. And there were galaxies hundreds and hundreds and hundreds and hundreds and hundreds . . .

"What?" Al said out loud. He was startled for a moment when he realized that he was no longer floating through space. He was standing in the dark store.

The old man said, "Before you leave, I want you to take one more look at the Milky Way. Look up."

Suddenly Al realized that there was no ceiling in the store and that he could see a sky above him, covered with a cloud of stars. The old man explained, "That's how the Milky Way looks from Earth on a summer night. You are looking at it from the side, but it is still beautiful."

Al stared at the sky for a few minutes. Then the sky seemed to fade. Al and Angela were standing alone in the dark store. From somewhere a voice announced, "Pass a test on what you've seen and you can go anywhere and see anything."

"Ding, ding."

The air was cold outside the store. The sky was cloudy and a few snowflakes were starting to fall. Al said, "When I close my eyes, I can still see how the Milky Way looked when we were close to it. I'll never forget that sight as long as I live."

"Me neither," Angela said.

C Number your paper from 1 through 22.

Skill Items

Write the word from the box that means the same thing as the underlined part of each sentence.

receive	survive	whether	trembled
injured	appeared	erupt	selected

1. Most plants cannot live without sunshine.
2. She chose a very long book to read.
3. She was hurt when she fell.

Review Items

4. Which has **more** gravity, Jupiter or Io?
5. Which is **smaller** than Earth?
6. Where can you jump 8 feet high?

7. How many miles does light travel in one second?
8. What else travels as fast as light?

9. How long does it take light to travel from the sun to Earth?
10. How can you change a solid form of matter into a liquid?
11. To change a liquid form of matter into a gas, you make the liquid _____.
12. In which form of matter are molecules farthest apart?
13. In which form of matter are molecules closest together?
14. Earth is _____ through the middle.
    - 8 miles
    - 8 thousand miles
    - 8 hundred miles
15. Where would a balloon be bigger—at 100 feet below the surface of the ocean or at 200 feet below the surface?
16. How many mushers start the Iditarod at the same time?
17. How much time passes before the next musher starts?

18. Name the animal in the picture.

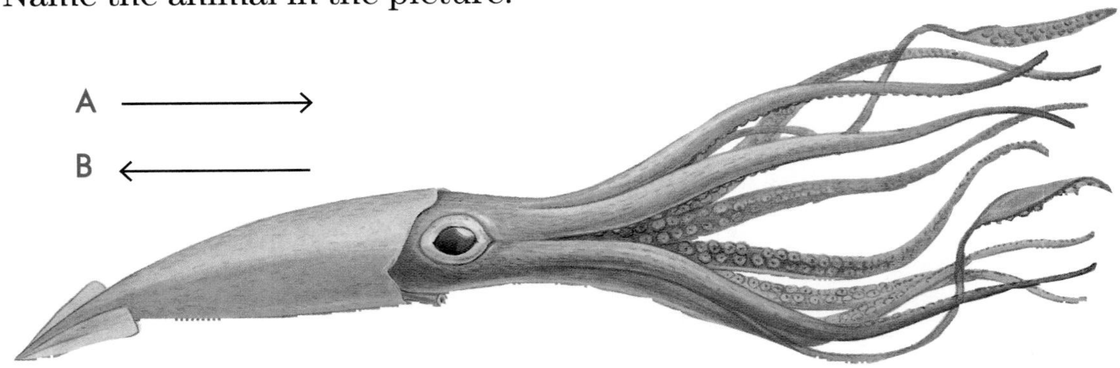

19. Which arrow shows the way the animal squirts water out?

20. Which arrow shows the way the animal will move?

21. The arrow on the map goes from San Francisco to ______.

22. Which ocean does the arrow cross?

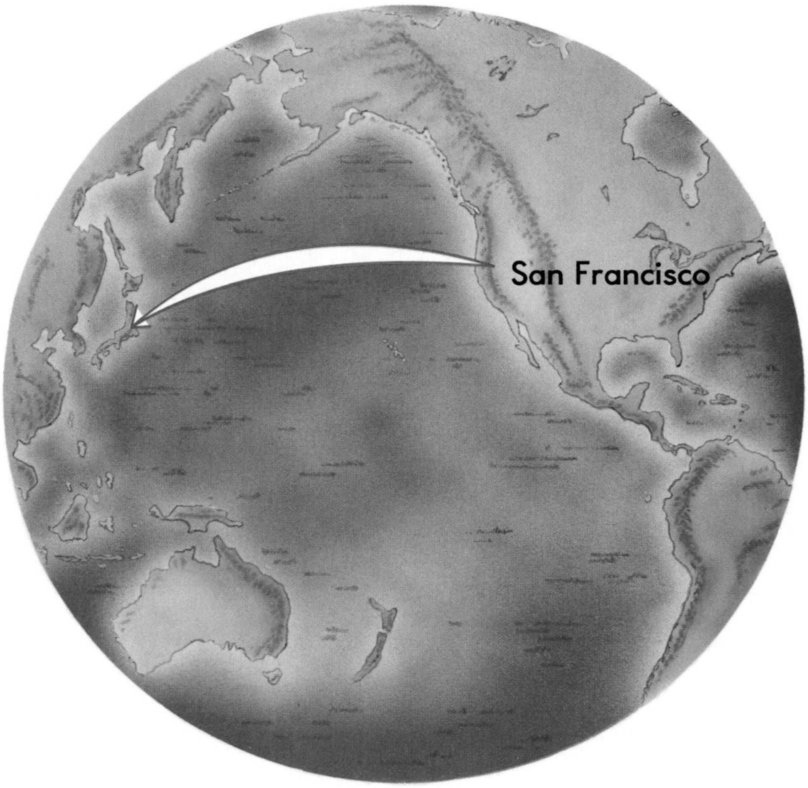

A

1
1. protect
2. thicker
3. fired
4. choose
5. difference
6. decorated

B

Angela and Al Learn About Muscles

The stores were decorated for Christmas. Displays in the windows showed many wonderful presents. But Al tried not to look at them as he walked to school. He didn't have any money, and he didn't know how he was going to buy presents. He paused in front of one store and felt very sad for a moment as he thought about how nice it would be to give his mother a real Christmas gift, something she really wanted, like a toaster. But then he told himself not to think about it. "Come on," Angela said, "or we'll be late for school."

Al's mind felt heavy in school that day. It was too filled with facts and thoughts about the things the old man had shown him. His mind was so filled with information that he didn't feel as if he was ready to learn more. In fact, he said, "Oh, no," to himself when his teacher announced that on Monday the class would have a test on the human body.

Al didn't know much about the human body, and he really didn't want to learn about it. And, he kept thinking about Christmas.

After school, he walked with Angela to Anywhere Street. They walked down the street until they came to the store with the familiar sign in the window. As soon as they entered, the old man stepped out of the darkness. "Pay for your trip by passing a test," he said in a serious voice. He fired questions at Al and Angela but they knew the answers. They told him how big the large flames from the sun were. They told him how much a spoonful of matter from the very old star weighed.

They told him how big the huge star was and how many stars are in the Milky Way.

Then without smiling, the old man said, “I will choose the trip this time. It is an incredible trip.”

“Where are we going?” Angela asked.

“Inside the human body.”

“The human body?” Al asked. “That doesn’t sound very interesting.”

“Let’s see how interesting it is,” the old man said. As soon as he had spoken those words, then something appeared in the room and the room became light. The form that had appeared looked exactly like a man, but Al could see that it wasn’t actually a living person. The man had large muscles and was wearing only swimming trunks.

“He looks very strong,” Angela said.

“Correct,” the old man replied. “And the first thing we will do is look more carefully at those muscles.”

The old man continued, “The body has many parts and every part has a job to do.”

The old man walked up to the model of the man and pointed to one of his arms. “That is how an arm looks to you. But you cannot see all of the parts in the arm because they are under the skin.”

Then the arm of the man seemed to change. The skin disappeared and Al could see all the muscles in the arm.

The old man pointed to the muscle on the front of the upper arm. He said, “The name of this muscle is the biceps.” Then the old man pointed to the muscle on the back of the upper arm and said, “This muscle is the triceps.”

The old man said, “If you know the ★ rule about how muscles work, you can figure out which job each muscle does. When a muscle works, it pulls and gets shorter.” The old man continued, “Watch the man lift a weight. See which muscle is getting shorter and thicker. That’s the muscle that is working to lift the weight.”

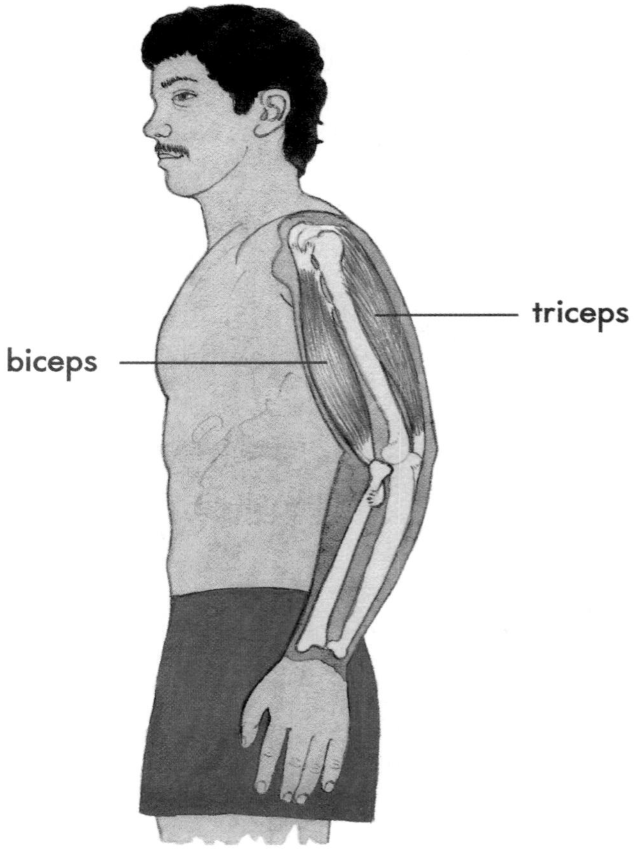

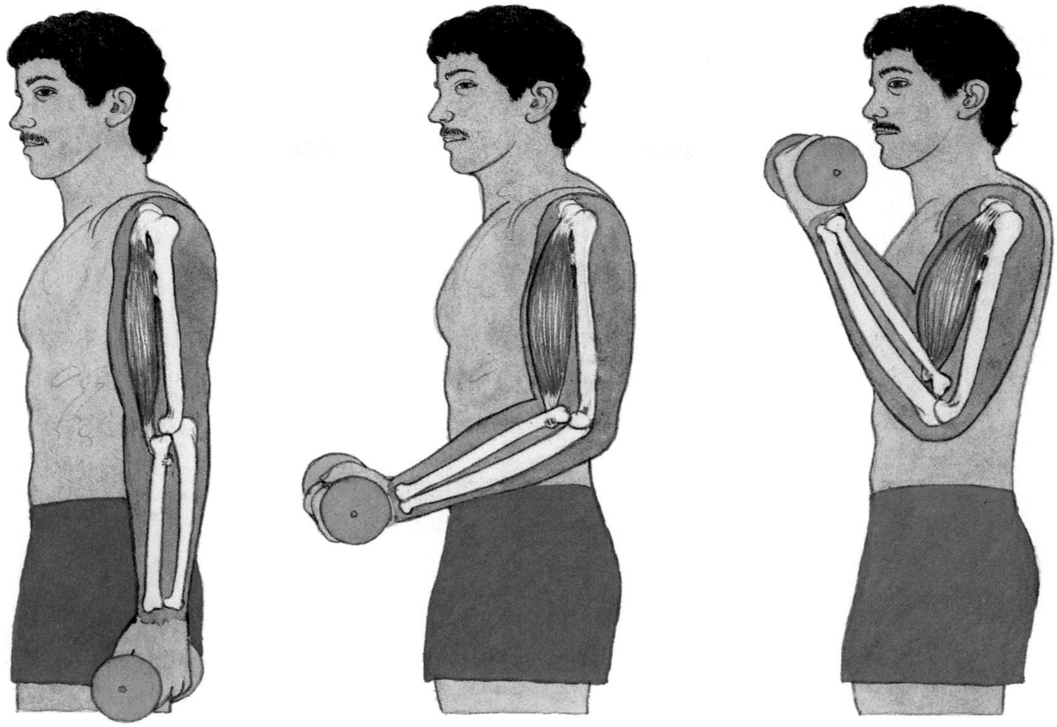

Suddenly, a weight appeared in the man's hand. Then the arm started to bend and lift the weight.

The muscle on the front of the arm got shorter and thicker as the weight moved up.

"Which muscle works to bend the arm?" the old man asked.

Together Al and Angela said, "The biceps."

"Correct," the old man said. "Now the arm will straighten. Watch which muscle straightens the arm."

The arm pushed the weight overhead. As the weight moved overhead, the muscle on the back of the arm became thicker and shorter.

The old man said, "Tell me the name of the muscle that straightens the arm."

"The triceps," Al and Angela answered together.

"How do you know that the triceps straightens the arm?" the old man asked.

Before Al could respond, Angela said, "Because it gets shorter and thicker when the arm straightens."

"Remember the rule," the old man said. "Muscles do only one thing when they work. Muscles pull. And when they pull, they get shorter and thicker. The muscle that is working is the muscle that is getting shorter and thicker."

Suddenly the skin disappeared from the rest of the man's body. Al could see every muscle. He could see muscles in the chest, muscles in the legs and muscles of the neck.

"Wow!" Angela exclaimed. "I never knew there were so many muscles in the body."

"Yes," the old man said. "And every muscle has one job. Every muscle helps the man move one part of his body one way. Watch the man move. See if you can figure out which muscle is working."

The man's leg started to bend back. Angela pointed to the muscle on the back of the upper leg. "There's a muscle getting shorter and thicker."

The old man said, "That's right. The only muscle that can bend the man's leg is the muscle on the back of the upper leg. It pulls and gets shorter to bend the leg back."

Now the man's head started to move back and Al could see that the muscles at the back of the neck were getting shorter and thicker. He pointed to them and told the old man that they were the muscles that moved the head back.

As the man's head started to move forward, Al could see the muscles in the front of the neck getting shorter and thicker. They were moving the head forward.

Angela observed, "The muscles work in pairs. One muscle moves a part of the body one way. The muscle on the other side of the part moves that part the other way."

"Correct," the old man replied. "And if one of those muscles is cut, the part cannot move. Watch what happens when the muscle in the back of the upper leg is cut." The man's leg started to bend back. Suddenly, it stopped and came forward. The old man explained, "The muscle in the back of the upper leg is cut now, so the man cannot bend the leg back. There is only one muscle that can do that job, and that muscle is not working."

"That's amazing," Angela said.

C Number your paper from 1 through 21.

Story Items

1. The only muscle that can move your head **forward** is the muscle on the ______ of your neck.
   - front
   - back
2. The only muscle that can move your head **backward** is the muscle on the ______ of your neck.
   - front
   - back

Skill Items

Write the word or words from the box that mean the same thing as the underlined part of each sentence.

a scary	large	intelligent	a transparent
balanced	a fantastic	unimportant	

3. I have a very smart dog.
4. The speech was not important.
5. She told an amazing story.

The triceps muscle is bigger than the biceps muscle.

6. What word names the muscle on the front of the upper arm?
7. What word names the muscle on the back and side of the upper arm?
8. What do we call a part of your body that is attached to bones and moves bones?

Review Items

9. The sun is matter in the ______ form.
10. What form of matter is the air around you?
11. Name the largest animal in the world.
12. That animal weighs more than ______ elephants.
13. What's the name of a smaller whale that is black and white?
14. Al and Angela went to a huge star. Name the planets that would be inside that star if it was in the center of our solar system.
15. Name the galaxy that Al and Angela saw.

Here's how big a balloon is at 50 meters below the surface of the ocean.

Here's the same balloon when it is **deeper** or **not as deep.**

16. Write the letter of each balloon that is deeper than balloon **J.**
17. Write the letter of the balloon that is closest to the surface.
18. Write the letter of the balloon that is deepest.

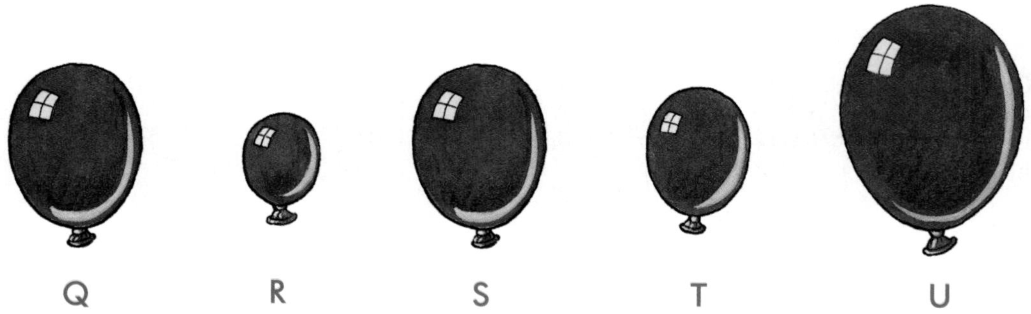

19. The rules for the Iditarod require each musher to have certain things. Write the letters of those things.
    a. booties
    b. snowshoes
    c. extra dogs
    d. firewood
    e. a good sleeping bag
    f. extra shoes
    g. enough food for a week
    h. enough food for a day
    i. an ax
    j. a tent
20. When Iditarod mushers are on the trail, how much help can they get from someone else?
21. Why can't you see molecules when you look at an object?

Number your paper from 1 through 30.

1. In which form of matter are molecules lined up in rows?
2. In which form of matter do molecules move slowest?
3. In which form of matter do molecules move fastest?
4. In which form of matter are molecules closest together?
5. In which form of matter are molecules farthest apart?
6. Are whales fish?
7. Are whales **warm-blooded** or **cold-blooded?**
8. What is animal A?
9. What is animal B?
10. What is animal C?

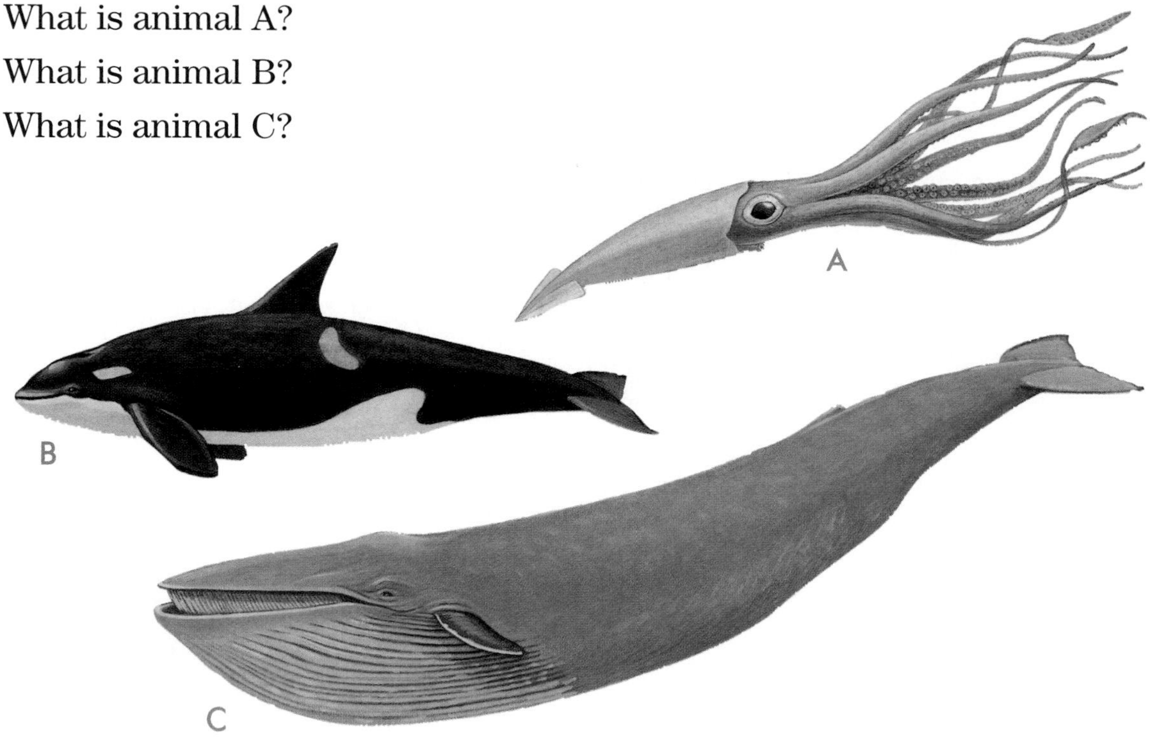

11. Name the galaxy that we live in.
12. Name the muscle on the **back** of the upper arm.
13. Name the muscle on the **front** of the upper arm.
14. How many jobs does each muscle have?
15. Name the arm muscle that gets shorter when you bend your arm.
16. Name the arm muscle that gets shorter when you straighten your arm.

17. When you straighten your arm, one of the muscles gets longer as the other one gets shorter. Name the muscle that gets longer.

Here's how big a balloon is at 30 feet below the surface of the ocean.

Here's the same balloon when it is **deeper** or **not as deep.**

18. Write the letter of each balloon that is deeper than balloon **M.**
19. Write the letter of the balloon that is deepest.
20. Write the letter of the balloon that is closest to the surface.

21. Write the letter of the fish with the greatest pressure on it.
22. Write the letter of the fish with the least pressure on it.

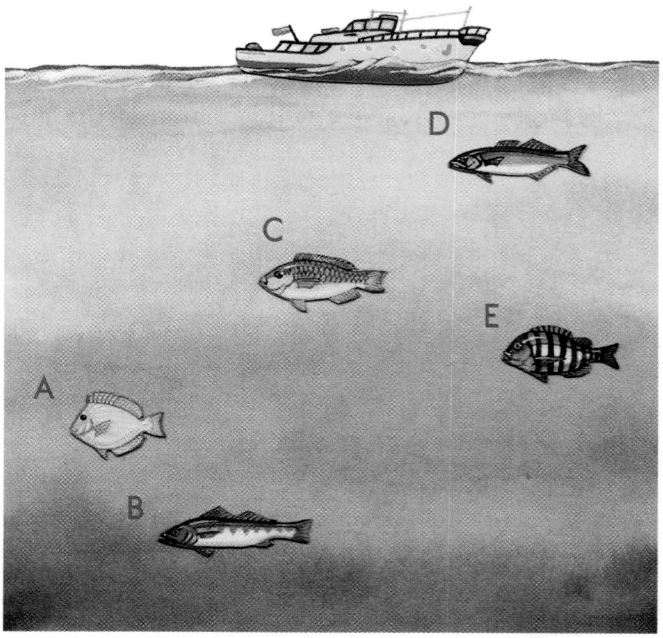

Skill Items

For each item, write the underlined word or words from the sentences in the box.

> The poem they created was nonsense.
> The squid wriggled its tentacles.
> The triceps muscle is bigger than the biceps muscle.

23. What underlining refers to arms that are like huge snakes?
24. What underlining refers to a part of your body that is attached to bones and that moves bones?
25. What underlining means **squirmed around in all directions?**
26. What underlining names the muscle on the front of the upper arm?
27. What underlining means **made?**
28. What underlining means **no sense at all?**
29. What underlining names the muscle on the back and side of the upper arm?
30. What underlining names a sea animal?

END OF TEST 12

121

A

1	2	3
1. blood vessel	1. permit	1. Halloween
2. heart	2. protect	2. ugh
3. chamber	3. difference	3. pink
4. paralyzed	4. demonstrating	4. tube
5. skull		5. injury
6. lungs		6. spinal

B Al and Angela Learn About Bones

Al and Angela were looking at a model of the human body. The model was demonstrating how the muscles worked. The old man had just shown Al and Angela what happens if one of the muscles is cut.

Now the old man pointed to the model and continued, "The muscles permit the body to move. But the muscles don't work alone. Most of them are attached to bones and the muscles move the bones."

The old man continued, "I'll show you how important the bones are. First I'll fix up the muscle in the man's leg so that it works again. And then, I'll remove the bones from the legs. Watch what happens."

The man's legs suddenly bent and the man fell over. Angela said, "He can't stand up without bones in his legs."

"Correct," the old man said.

Al added, "So the leg bones help make the legs strong."

The old man said, "Yes, some bones help make the body strong. Other bones protect parts of the body that are very important to the body." The old man waved his arm. "Look at the bones that are beneath the muscles."

Suddenly the muscles on the man's body disappeared. The man was now nothing but a skeleton. "Ugh," Angela said. "That looks creepy, like an outfit that people wear on Halloween."

"No," the old man said. "The skeleton is not creepy. It does jobs that are very important to the body. Remember, if you didn't have a skeleton, you couldn't stand up, or run, or hold things in your hand."

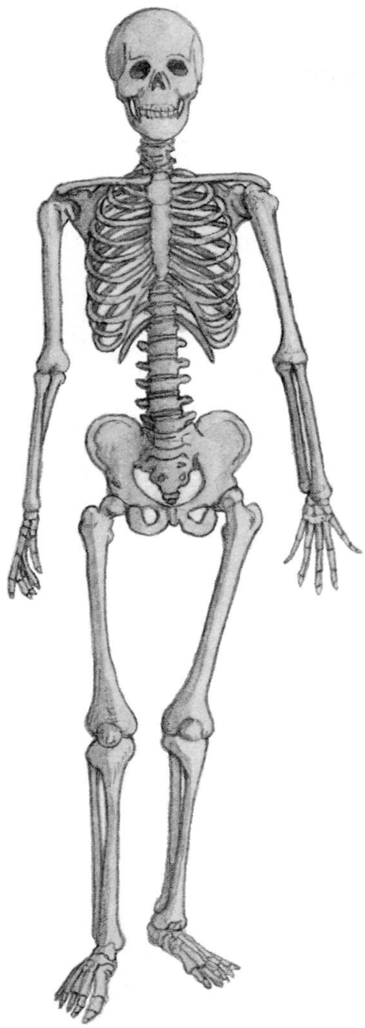

The old man walked over to the skeleton and said, “Here are some facts about the skeleton. Listen carefully. There are 206 bones in the body.” The old man continued, “Some bones are very small and some are very big.”

The old man touched the hip bone. “Here is a big bone.”

The old man touched the skull. “Here is another big bone.”

The old man pointed to the skull. “The skull bone has a special job,” he said. “Do you know what is inside the skull?”

“The brain,” Al said.

“Correct,” the old man replied. Then he said, “Watch.” The skull bone disappeared. Al could see the man’s brain. It looked very soft. The old man pointed to the back of the brain. “If something hit the brain here, the man would never see again.”

Then the old man touched a lower part of the brain. He said, “And if something hit the brain here, the man would never breathe again.”

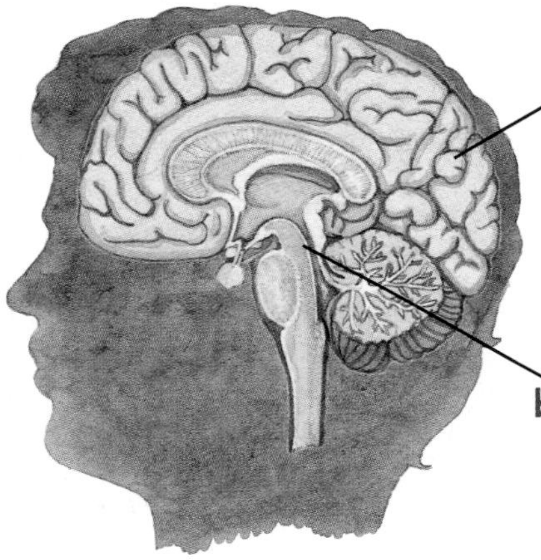

Angela said, “So the skull protects the brain. Nothing can hit the brain ★ because the skull covers the brain.”

The old man said, “Correct.” Then he pointed to the ribs and continued, “These bones protect other important parts of the body. Watch.”

A heart appeared inside the man’s chest. The heart was beating. It was much bigger than Al thought it would be.

The old man said, “Your heart is about as big as your fist. And it works all of the time. If it stops beating, you stop living. The ribs protect the heart."

Something else appeared inside the man's chest—two great big pink lungs. They looked very soft.

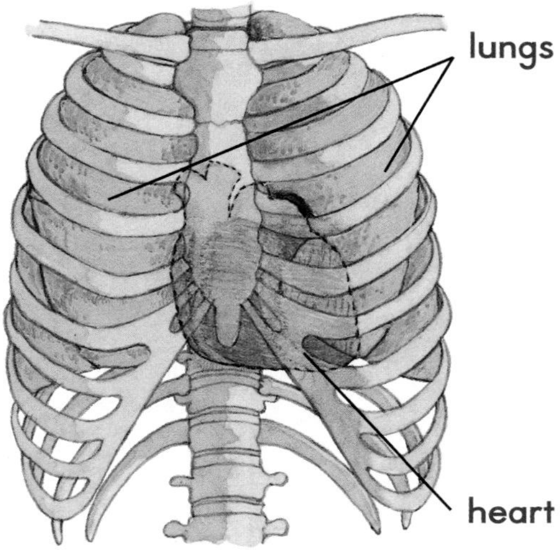

"What do the lungs do?" Angela asked.

"Lungs take in the air when you breathe," the old man said. "Look at how soft they are. If they are hurt, the man will not be able to breathe. And if he cannot breathe, he will die."

The old man said, "Remember—bones do two things. What are those two things?"

Al answered the question.

The old man said, "If you think you can remember everything you have seen, we can learn more about the body. Or would you rather stop the trip now?"

"Let's learn more," Al said. He had almost forgotten that he hadn't wanted to learn about the body.

Al said, "Seeing a real body in action is much better than reading about it in a book."

The old man smiled and bent down so that his face was very close to Al's. Very softly, the old man said, "It's much better to see a body in action unless you know how to read a book carefully." For a very long moment, the old man stood very close to Al. Then he stood up, waved his arm and said, "Let's continue on our trip. For this part, we're going to go inside the body."

The muscles appeared over the bones of the man's body. Then skin covered the muscles. The man once more looked just like a real person. The only difference about him was that he seemed very big and he seemed to be growing and growing and growing. Soon he was the size of a giant.

"Wow," Angela exclaimed.

Al said, "This is just the way I felt when I went inside a grain of sand."

When the man's body was so huge that Al couldn't see above the man's knee, everything started to become dark. Then Al noticed that he seemed to be floating. He was inside a very large tube that was filled with liquid.

The old man said, "We are now inside the body and we are no bigger than a speck compared to the body."

C Number your paper from 1 through 18.

Skill Items

Use the words in the box to write complete sentences.

balanced	muscle	wriggled	biceps	presented
tentacles	elbow	triceps	fantastic	

1. The squid ______ its ______ .
2. The ______ ______ is bigger than the ______ muscle.

Review Items

3. Name the muscle on the **front** of the upper arm.
4. Name the muscle on the **back** of the upper arm.
5. Name the muscle that works when you **straighten** your arm.
6. Name the muscle that works when you **bend** your arm.
7. How many jobs does each muscle have?
8. Name the arm muscle that gets shorter when you bend your arm.
9. Name the arm muscle that gets shorter when you straighten your arm.
10. When you're training an animal, what do you do each time the animal does the trick?
11. What do you do if the animal does not do the trick?
12. Name **2** things you could give a dog to reward it.
13. When you straighten your arm, one muscle gets longer as another muscle gets shorter. Name the muscle that gets longer.
14. Are killer whales fish?
15. Tell if killer whales are **warm-blooded** or **cold-blooded.**
16. Name **3** animals that are warm-blooded.
17. Name **3** animals that are cold-blooded.
18. The ______s are the coldest places on the earth and the ______ is the hottest place on the earth.

122

A

1	2
1. cell	1. spinal cord
2. blood vessel	2. paralyzed
3. heart	3. thumb
4. chamber	4. injury
5. jerk	
6. differently	

B

Angela and Al Learn About the Heart

The old man was taking Al and Angela through a tube inside the body. The tube was filled with liquid. "What's the liquid inside this tube?" Angela asked.

"Blood," the old man replied.

"Ugh," Al said. "I don't like blood."

"Blood is very important to your body," the old man said. "And that blood moves through tubes called blood vessels. We are inside a blood vessel."

Suddenly Al noticed a great pounding sound—"Cu-boom—cu-boom—cu-boom." The sound was very loud.

"What's that sound?" Angela yelled.

The old man replied, "That's the man's heart."

The old man turned on a flashlight. Al could see the blood vessel and the dark liquid inside it.

Angela said, "That liquid is almost black, but blood is red."

The old man said, "Blood is not always red. We will follow the blood through the body. You will see what happens to it."

"Cu-boom—cu-boom." The sound of the heart was getting louder and louder. Now Al noticed that the liquid inside the tube was moving.

"The heart is like a great pump," the old man explained. "The heart pumps blood through the body night and day. When the heart pumps, the blood in the blood vessels moves."

"Cu-boom—cu-boom." The sound of the heart was so loud Al could hardly stand it.

The old man yelled, "We're going into the heart soon."

The old man's light was shining on something that looked like a strange door in the blood vessel ahead of them. The door was made of muscle. The door kept opening and then closing.

Al and the others were moving toward the door along with everything in the blood vessel. When they were directly in front of the door, Al noticed that he and the others were in a small chamber. The chamber was wider than the rest of the blood vessel. "We are in one chamber of the heart," the old man said.

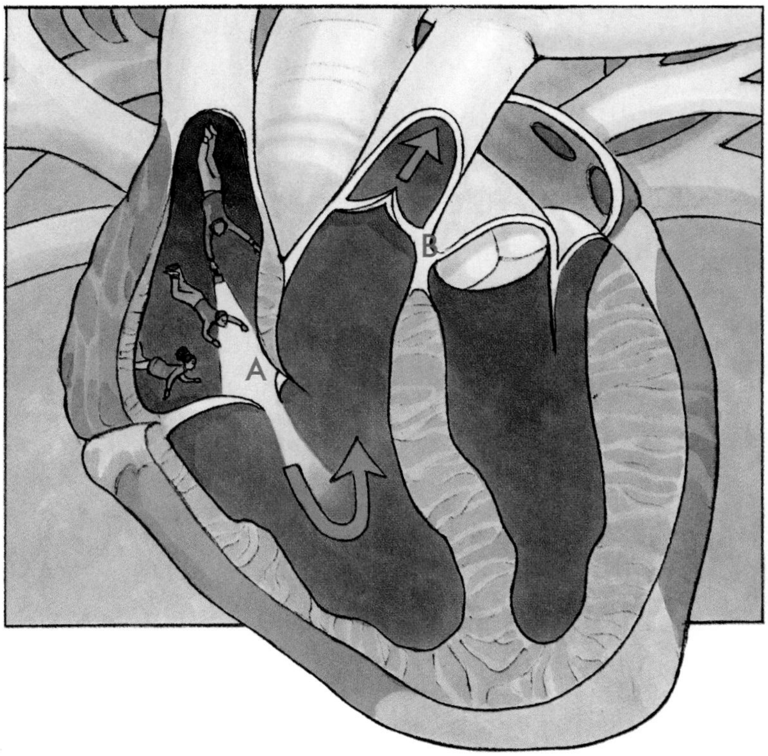

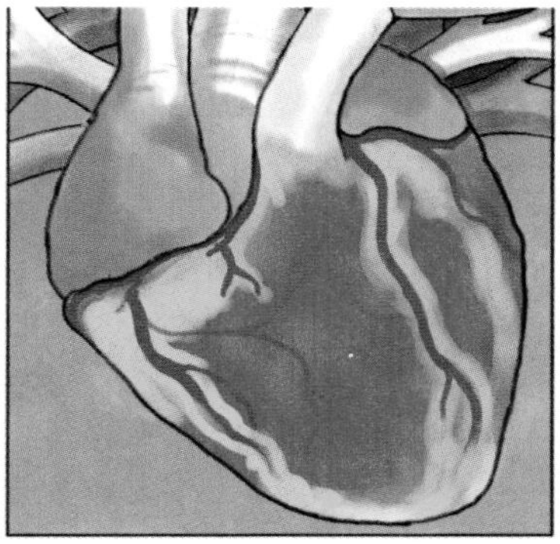

Suddenly the walls of the chamber changed shape, as if the chamber was suddenly squeezed. At the same time, the heart made a terrible cu-boom sound. Al could feel great pressure. In an instant, the door in the bottom of the chamber opened. Al and the others rushed through the door.

Al felt dizzy. He looked around and observed that he was now in a much larger chamber. Al noticed that the chamber had two doors in the ceiling—the one he had just been pushed through and another one.

The old man said, "The heart is going to pump again. This time we will shoot out of that other door."

Suddenly the walls of the large chamber seemed to be squeezed together. There was great pressure and a great cu-boom sound. At the same time, the second door in the ceiling opened. Al and the others shot up through the door and into a tube.

When they slowed down, the old man said, "You can hear two sounds in the heart. The first is the little sound, cu. The other is the big sound, boom. Each time you hear the little sound, blood goes from the first chamber into the second chamber. Each time you hear the boom sound, the blood goes from the second chamber and leaves the heart."

Angela said, "Let's see if I understand. The blood makes the little sound when it leaves the little chamber, and makes the big sound when it leaves the big chamber."

"Correct," the old man said.

Al noticed that he and the others were in a tube like the one that they had been in before they entered the heart. But the liquid in this tube moved differently. Each time the heart made the boom sound, everything in the tube moved forward with a great jerk. Then it stopped until the heart boomed again.

"The heart is pushing blood into this tube," the old man said. "Each time new blood is pushed into the tube, all the other blood in the tube must move forward to make room for the new blood."

"This is a rough ride," Al said. "Where does this tube go now?"

The old man said, "To the lungs."

Angela said, "Why does this blood vessel go to the lungs?"

The old man said, "The body is burning all the time. That's why it's warm. Remember that—the body is burning all the time. But things can't burn without oxygen."

"What's oxygen?" Al asked.

The old man explained, "Oxygen is part of the air you breathe. The body needs this oxygen if the body is to keep working. The blood in this blood vessel has no more oxygen in it. That is why this blood is black, not red." The old man continued, "The only way this blood can get oxygen is to go to the lungs."

Angela said, "I just hope I can remember all this. The blood is black because it doesn't have oxygen. So it must go from the heart to the lungs and get oxygen."

The old man said, "And you will have no trouble seeing when the oxygen gets into the blood."

Al noticed that the blood vessel was getting smaller and smaller. It was becoming so small that Al could hardly squeeze through it. Also, the walls of the blood vessel were getting very thin and transparent.

In the narrow blood vessel, Al could see that the blood was filled with little parts. Some of them were like disks. All the disks were black. Then suddenly he could see the disks change. They were changing color and becoming bright, bright red.

"This is amazing," he shouted to Angela.

The old man said, "The red blood is now full of oxygen. It picked up the oxygen from the lungs. Could you tell when the oxygen entered the blood?"

Al said, "When the oxygen entered the blood, the blood became bright red."

"Correct," the old man said.

C Number your paper from 1 through 20.

Skill Items

Here are 3 events that happened in the story. Write **beginning, middle** or **end** for each event.

1. When they were directly in front of the door, Al noticed that he and the others were in a small chamber.
2. "Blood is very important to your body," the old man said.
3. The walls of the blood vessel were getting very thin and transparent.

Review Items

4. Most muscles are attached to ______.
5. What **2** body parts do the ribs protect?
6. How many bones are in the human body?
7. How many miles does light travel in one second?
8. Write the **2** things that bones do.
    - make the body move
    - make the body strong
    - protect body parts
    - get short and thicker
9. Name the bone on the top of the head.
10. What does that bone protect?
11. What would happen if someone hit the **back** of your brain?
12. What would happen if someone hit the **lower part** of your brain?
13. Your heart is about as big as your ______.
14. What might happen if something hurt your lungs?

15. The only muscle that can move your head **backward** is the muscle on the ____ of your neck.
16. The only muscle that can move your head **forward** is the muscle on the ____ of your neck.

17. Which letter shows the biceps?
18. Which letter shows the triceps?
19. Which letter shows the muscle that straightens the arm?
20. Which letter shows the muscle that bends the arm?

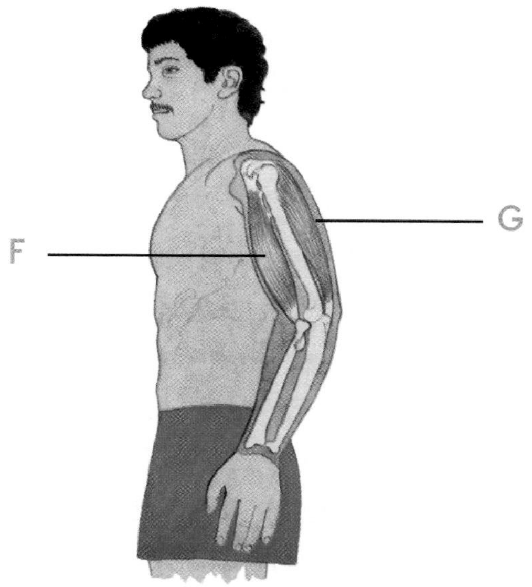

A

1	2
1. cerebrum	1. mixed
2. magnifying	2. joining
3. image	3. leads
4. boat-shaped	4. branched
5. thumb	
6. cell	

B

Al and Angela Follow Blood Through the Body

Al and Angela were inside a blood vessel filled with oxygen blood. They had gone through two chambers of the heart. They had gone to the lungs where the blood changed color. Now Angela observed, "The blood vessel is getting bigger." Al noticed that many smaller blood vessels were joining the vessel they were in.

The old man said, "We are leaving the lungs now."

"Where are we going?" Angela asked.

"Back to the heart," the old man said.

"Oh, no!" Angela said. "Not again. Why does the blood have to go back to the heart?"

The old man said, "The blood in this vessel has fresh oxygen, but it must get to the parts of the body that need oxygen. So the heart has to pump this blood to the arms, legs, head and other parts of the body."

They were getting closer to the heart, and Al could hear it going "cu-boom." The old man said, "This time we're going to go through two new chambers. The second chamber pumps very hard because it must start the blood moving to all parts of the body."

They approached a chamber. When they were inside the chamber, the walls of the chamber squeezed together. Everything shot through the door in the floor and they were squeezed into a second chamber. They were in that chamber for only a moment when

"BOOOOOMMMMM." The walls of the chamber came together and a door in the chamber opened.

"Whooooosh." Everything in the chamber went flying up into another blood vessel. It felt as if they were moving four hundred miles an hour.

After they had slowed down, Angela said, "Wow! I'm dizzy."

"Me too," Al said.

Angela said, "And I'm all mixed up. First we came into the heart. Then we went out of the heart. Then we came back to the heart."

The old man said, "Just remember this: The blood needs oxygen. Black blood comes to the heart, and the heart pumps the blood to the lungs. That's where the blood gets fresh oxygen and turns bright red. Now the fresh blood goes back to the heart so that it can be pumped to all the parts of the body that need fresh oxygen."

Everything in the blood vessel moved along in jerks. Every time the heart pounded, the blood jerked ahead. Then it would stop. Then the heart would pound again, and everything would jerk ahead.

Angela asked, "Are we going to keep jerking along like this until we reach a part of the body that needs oxygen?"

"Correct," the old man replied. "We are going to a muscle in the hand, and we will continue to jerk along until we get there."

The old man continued, "The blood vessel we are in goes along the inside of the wrist. If you want to feel that, hold your hand so that your palm is facing up."

"Then feel along your wrist on the side where your thumb is. You will feel a tube that is pounding each time the heart pounds. That is the tube that we are in."

Angela had trouble finding the blood vessel in her wrist, so the old man helped her.

The old man said, "After we reach the muscles in the man's hand, we will go back in a blood vessel that does not jerk along."

Al noticed that the blood vessel they were in was getting very small. Every now and then the blood vessel branched. And every time the blood vessel branched, it got smaller.

The old man said, "We are now in a muscle. That muscle is in the man's hand."

The blood vessel was now as small as the blood vessels in the lungs, and it was transparent. Al could see rows and rows of boat-shaped forms outside the blood vessel. "What are those things?" he asked.

"Muscle cells," the old man said. The old man continued, "Muscles are made up of tiny cells. And each cell needs oxygen as it works. Right now, the oxygen is leaving the blood and going into the muscles."

Angela said, "The blood is changing color. It's getting darker and darker."

The old man said, "The blood has done its job. Now it must go back to the heart and back to the lungs so that it can get fresh oxygen."

The old man pointed to a blue blood vessel on the inside of Angela's wrist. "That's like the one we will go back in. It's blue because it's filled with dark blood."

Angela put her fingers on that blue blood vessel. She observed, "It doesn't pound when the heart beats."

"Correct," the old man said. "Remember, the blood vessels that pound go from the heart to different parts of the body. The blood vessels that do not pound are not going from the heart. They are going back to the heart."

"And the vessels that are returning blood to the heart are blue," Al said. "I'll bet that's because they're filled with dark blood."

"Correct," the old man said.

The old man continued, "If the blood vessel is blue, it is filled with dark blood and it is going back to the heart so the heart can pump the dark blood to the lungs."

Angela said, "Tell me if I've got this straight. Blood vessels that go from the heart pound every time the heart beats. Blood vessels that are taking dark blood back to the heart do not pound and they are blue. The blood around us is dark so we are now in a tiny blue blood vessel that leads back to the heart."

"Right," the old man said. "You are really thinking now."

Then the old man continued, "If you wish, we can take that trip around the body one more time. We'll first go back to the heart, then to the lungs . . ."

"No," Angela said. "I remember how it works. I don't want to go through the heart again."

"All right," the old man said, "Let's stay in the man's hand and look at another part of the body."

In an instant, Al and the others were no longer inside a blood vessel. They were floating next to something that looked like a huge white rope that stretched as far as Al could see. The rope had many branches coming from it.

C Number your paper from 1 through 20.

Skill Items

Write the word from the box that means the same thing as the underlined part of each sentence.

managed	chilly	assigned	received
curious	surrounded	demanded	level

1. Bill got a present in the mail.
2. The baby insisted on more food.
3. The street they live on is flat.

Review Items

4. How many jobs does each muscle have?
5. How many bones are in the human body?
6. Write the **2** things that bones do.
   - get shorter and thicker
   - make the body move
   - make the body strong
   - protect body parts
7. Your heart is about as big as your ____.
8. What might happen if something hurt your lungs?
9. Things can't burn without ____.
10. In the lungs, the color of blood changes from ____ to ____.

11. What color is blood that does not have oxygen?
12. What color is blood that has fresh oxygen?

13. Write the letter of the storm clouds.
14. Write the letter of the clouds that have frozen drops of water.
15. Write the letter of the clouds that may stay in the sky for days at a time.

A

B

C

16. When you teach an animal a simple trick, when do you reward the animal?
17. When don't you reward the animal?

18. Let's say that you want to teach an animal a very hard trick. Can the animal do the trick at first?
19. What will happen if the animal doesn't receive any rewards until it does the trick?
20. So when you're teaching the animal a hard trick, what do you reward the animal for doing?

A

1	2
1. forearm	1. pulse
2. shoelace	2. nerve
3. trickles	3. shocks
4. hollow	4. stings

B Angela and Al Learn About Nerves

Al studied the white, branching rope for a few moments, trying to figure out what it was. He knew that it was part of the man's hand, but he couldn't imagine what it was. It wasn't a blood vessel; it wasn't a muscle; and it wasn't a bone. At last he asked, "What is that thing that looks like a rope?"

The old man said, "This is a nerve in the man's hand. There are nerves like this one in every part of the body."

Al looked at the long white rope. Then he asked, "What do nerves do?"

The old man said, "A nerve is like an electric wire. It carries messages. This nerve goes from the hand to the man's brain. It carries messages from the hand."

The old man continued, "Hold onto the nerve. You will see what kind of messages they are."

Al and Angela touched the nerve. They could feel little pulses that felt like tiny electric shocks. Pulse, pulse, pulse, the nerve went. The pulses weren't strong enough to hurt. They felt like little trickles of electricity.

The old man said, "You are feeling the messages that are coming from the man's hand right now. Watch what happens when the man starts to tie his shoe."

Suddenly, the pulses started to go faster and faster.

The old man said, "The man is feeling things. He is feeling the shoelace. He is feeling how his fingers move. And everything that he feels sends a message to the brain."

The old man continued, "Those fast pulses are messages about everything the hand feels."

The old man said, "I'm going to cut the nerve that leads from his hand. No messages will go past the place that is cut. Watch."

Al watched the old man cut the nerve. Suddenly Al could not feel any more pulses in the nerve.

The old man said, "You can follow that nerve all the way to the man's brain and you will find that it does not carry any messages now. The nerve cannot carry messages from the hand because it is no longer connected to the hand."

Angela and Al moved along the nerve, up the man's forearm. The nerve was not pulsing. They returned to where the old man was. The old man said, "Remember, if this nerve is cut, the brain doesn't get any messages from the hand. The brain doesn't know what the hand is feeling. So the man could hit his hand with a hammer and he would not feel a thing because the message from his hand can't get to the brain."

The old man snapped his fingers. Once again Al could feel the pulses coming through the nerve. "The nerve is no longer cut," the old man said. "So the man can feel things in his hand again."

The old man said, "This nerve goes from the hand to the brain. It tells the brain what the hand feels." The old man pointed ★ to another nerve. "This nerve goes the other way," he said. "It carries messages from the brain to the hand. These messages tell the hand what to do. If the man tells his hand to make a fist, the message comes through that nerve."

The old man told Al, "Grab both nerves."

Al could feel pulses in both nerves. The old man said, "The nerve that goes from the hand is telling the brain what the hand is feeling. The message from the brain is telling the hand how to move to tie the shoe."

Al said, "What would happen if you cut the nerve that goes to the man's hand?"

The old man said, "Good question. Let's cut that nerve and find out."

The old man cut the nerve. The pulses going to the hand stopped. But the nerve from the hand continued to pulse.

The old man said, "Watch what happens when a bee stings the man's finger." The nerve leading from the man's hand began to pulse very rapidly. But there was no pulsing in the nerve that went to the man's hand. The old man explained, "The man can feel the pain in his hand, but he can't do anything about it. He can't move that hand. That hand is paralyzed. That means the hand cannot move, no matter how hard the man tells himself that he wants to move it."

Angela said, "Let me make sure that I have everything straight. The nerves that go from the hand to the brain tell the brain everything that the hand feels. The nerves that go from the brain to the hand tell the hand how to move. And the hand can't move without the message from the brain."

"Correct," the old man said. "There is an easy way to show how the nerves work. Close your eyes, Angela."

Angela closed her eyes. Then the old man said, "Hold your hand up in the air. Hold it up as far as it can go."

Angela kept her eyes closed and held up her hand. The old man said, "How did your muscles know what to do? Do your muscles have ears?"

Angela smiled. "No," she said. "I told my muscles what to do."

"Correct," the old man said and continued. "Nerves took the message from your brain and told your arm what to do. But how do you know that your hand is over your head? You can't see your hand because your eyes are closed. So how do you know that your hand isn't in your pocket?"

Angela said, "Well, I can feel my hand. I can feel that it's over my head."

The old man said, "You can feel your hand because your brain is getting messages from your hand. You know that your hand is over your head because your hand is sending messages to your brain."

Angela opened her eyes. "Wow!" she said. "The body is really something."

C Number your paper from 1 through 20.

Story Items

1. The nerves that tell the brain what the hand feels go from the ____ to the ____.
2. The nerves that tell the hand how to move go from the ____ to the ____.
3. The nerves that tell the foot how to move go from the ____ to the ____.
4. The nerves that tell the brain what the foot feels go from the ____ to the ____.

Skill Items

The injury to his spinal cord paralyzed him.

5. What word means that a part of the body can't move?
6. What word means **a serious hurt?**
7. What **2** words name the bundle of nerves inside the backbone?

Review Items

8. Things can't burn without ____.
9. In the lungs, the color of blood changes from ____ to ____.
10. How many chambers does the heart have?
11. How many chambers did Al and Angela go through **before** they went to the lungs?
12. How many chambers did they go through **after** they went to the lungs?
13. Where does black blood go after it leaves the heart?
14. Then the blood goes back to the ____.
15. Then the blood goes to the ____.
16. Why does oxygen blood have to go back to the heart after it leaves the lungs?
17. When oxygen leaves the blood, the color of the blood changes from ____ to ____.

Here's how big a balloon
is at 20 meters below
the surface of the ocean.

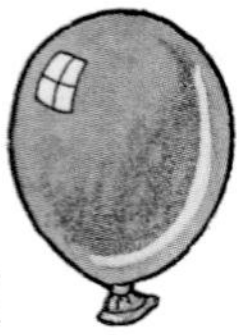

X

Here's the same balloon when it is **deeper** or **not as deep.**

18. Write the letter of each balloon that is not as deep as balloon **X.**
19. Write the letter of the balloon that is closest to the surface.
20. Write the letter of the balloon that is deepest.

A B C D E

A

1

1. retina
2. spiral
3. shovel
4. collect

2

1. backbone
2. bundle
3. masses
4. image

3

1. cerebrum
2. blind
3. hollow
4. magnifying

B

Making Pictures With a Magnifying Glass

You can make pictures in a dark room by using a magnifying glass. Picture A shows a magnifying glass that is near a flower. The picture of the flower is on the dark wall. The picture is upside down.

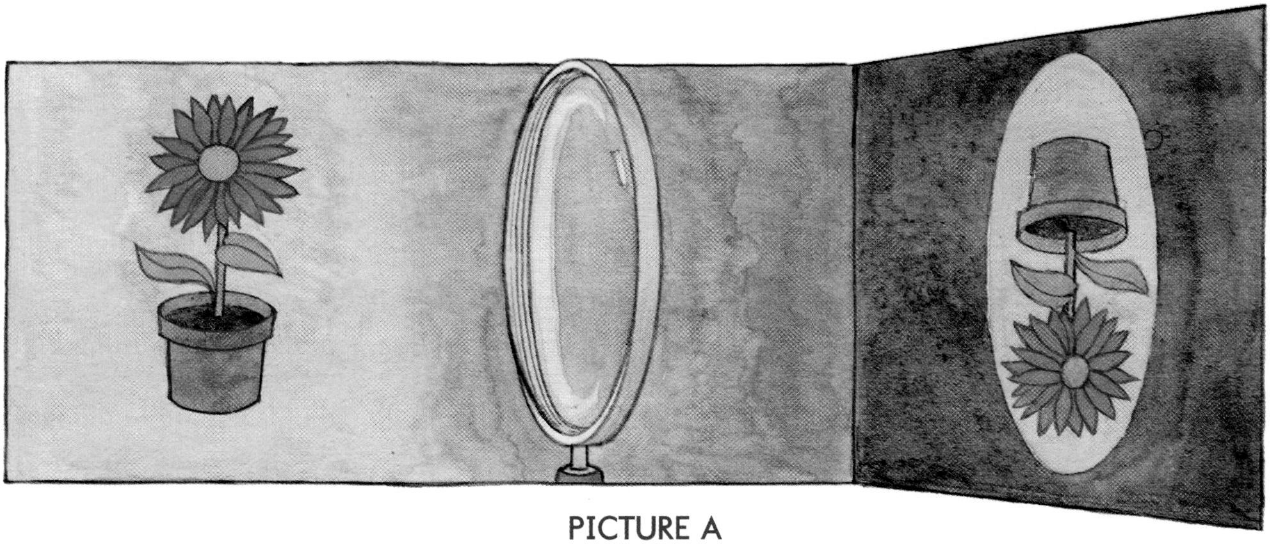

PICTURE A

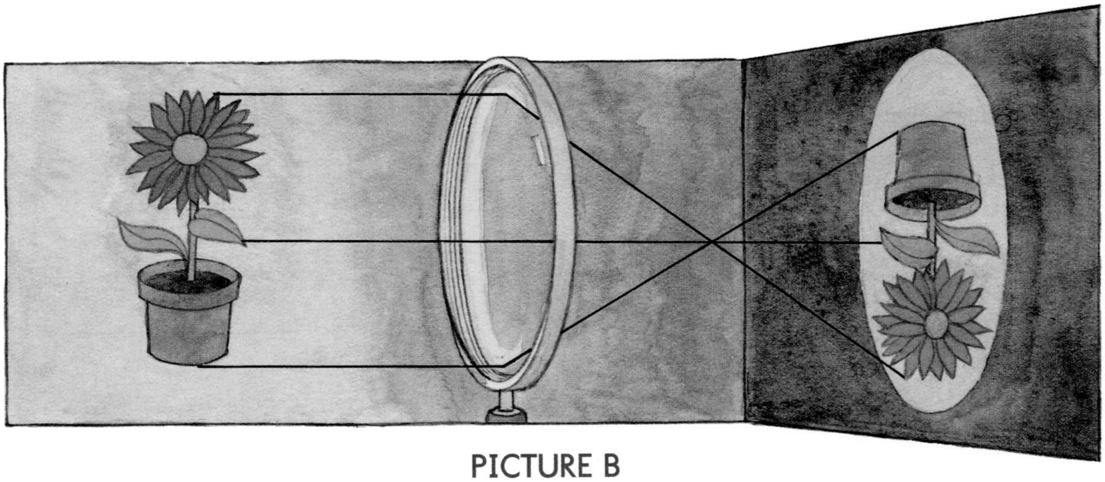

PICTURE B

Picture B shows how the picture got on the wall. The light that enters the magnifying glass bends. When it hits the wall, the light from the top of the flower is on the bottom of the picture. The light from the bottom of the flower pot is on the top of the picture.

The human eye works just like a magnifying glass in a dark room. The light enters a hole in the front of the eye. The light bends, and the picture is on the back of the eye. Notice that the picture is upside down. This is the image the person sees.

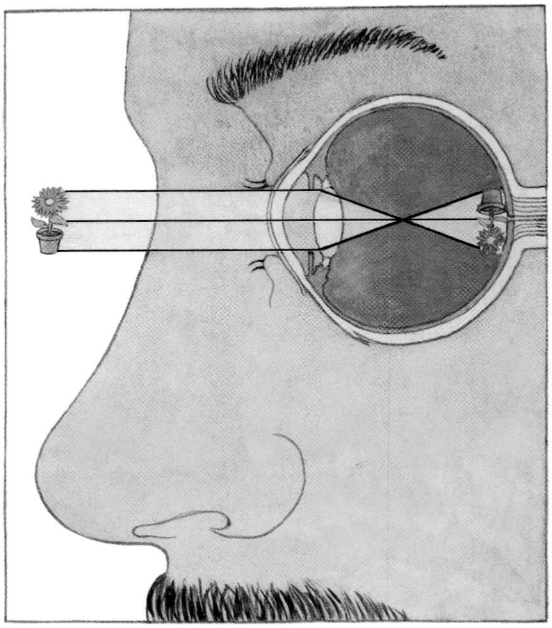

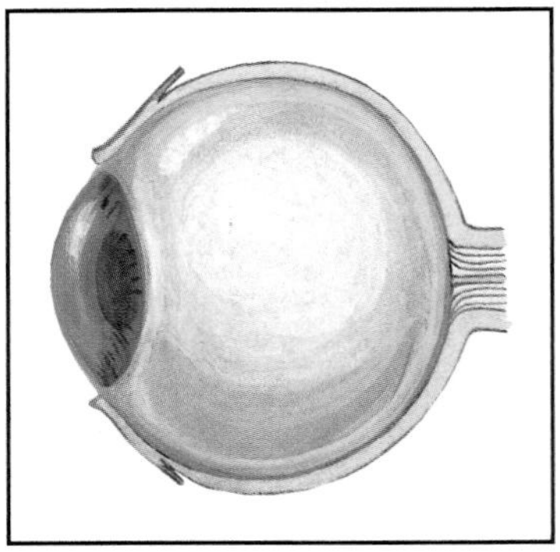

PICTURE C

C

Al and Angela Learn About the Brain

Al, Angela and the old man were in the human body looking at nerves. The old man was saying, "Remember—every part of the body must have two kinds of nerves."

Angela said, "One kind of nerve sends the messages to the brain and the other kind of nerve sends messages from the brain to the body."

"Correct," the old man replied. "Now let's follow this nerve and see how it gets to the brain. We are moving up the arm toward the shoulder."

As they moved along, Al noticed that other nerves joined the nerve they were following and that the nerve they were following became thicker and thicker.

The old man said, "We are at the shoulder now and we are moving toward the spinal cord."

"What's the spinal cord?" Angela asked.

The old man said, "Do you know where your backbone is?"

Angela said, "Sure. It goes up and down the middle of my back."

The old man touched his backbone. Then he said, "The nerves that go to the brain go up through the backbone. There is a great bundle of nerves that goes right through the middle of the backbone. The nerves form a great cord, or rope. That cord is called the spinal cord."

"Wow!" Angela exclaimed. Then she repeated "spinal cord" to herself four times.

Al could now see the backbone directly ahead of them. It was made up of little bones, one bone on top of the other. The nerve that they were following went right into the backbone along with some nerves from other parts of the body. Some of these nerves were thick and some were thin.

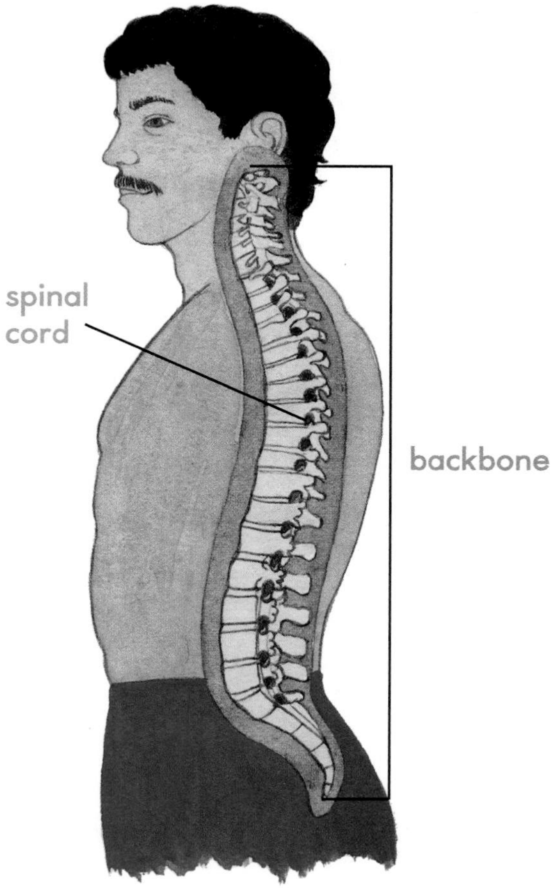

Angela said, "There must be hundreds of nerves in the body."

"Correct," the old man said. "Just remember—every part of the body must have two types of nerves. And all those nerves go through the spinal cord."

Al, Angela and the old man continued to follow the nerve into the backbone. Al could now see that each bone in the backbone was hollow.

A very thick bundle of nerves was running up and down through the middle of the hollow bones. There were so many nerves that Al could hardly keep track of the nerve they had been following.

Al could feel all kinds of messages in the nerves.

The old man said, "When we reach the top of the spinal cord, we'll go into the brain. We don't have very far to go, because we entered the spinal cord at the man's shoulder."

As Al looked down the spinal cord, he could see that some bundles of nerves entered down at the bottom of the man's backbone. Just then the old man said, "We are getting ready to enter the brain."

Al looked at the great masses of nerves at the top of the spinal cord. "Wow!" he said. "Look at all the nerves that go to the brain."

"No," the old man said. "Remember—many of these nerves are coming from the brain."

"I keep forgetting," Al said.

Now Angela, Al and the old man moved into the brain. Millions of small nerves went this way and that way. Some of these nerves were very short. As Al moved through this mass of nerves, he could feel that they were pulsing all the time. Some of the pulses were strong, and some were weak.

The old man said, "We are in the section of the brain that controls things you don't have to think about. You don't have to tell yourself to sweat when your body gets hot. You don't have to tell your heart to pound hard when you're running and your body needs more oxygen. You don't have to tell your body to breathe when you're asleep. All of the things that you don't think about take place in this part of the brain."

As Al, Angela and the old man kept moving up through the brain, Al noticed that the brain was starting to look different. There were even more nerves than there were in the lower part of the brain. The old man said, "Now we are going into the part of the brain that does the thinking. This part is called the cerebrum. When you tell your hand to make a fist, this is the part of the brain that is working. When you think about something that you see, this is the part that does the thinking. When you think about what somebody says to you, you are using this part."

Angela asked, "What did you say this part of the brain is called?"

Al told her.

"Correct," the old man said. "The thinking part of the brain is the cerebrum."

Angela and Al looked at the nerves that tangled this way and that way through the cerebrum. "Wow!" Angela exclaimed.

D Number your paper from 1 through 24.

Skill Items

Write the word from the box that means the same thing as the underlined part of each sentence.

applauded	concluded	warm	selecting	comfortable
chilly	observing	incredible	appearing	

1. They were watching the baby birds.
2. Her hands were sort of cold.
3. The parents clapped at the end of the play.

Use the words in the box to write complete sentences.

spinal cord	biceps	speck	injury	indeed
muscle	knee	paralyzed	triceps	heart

4. The ____ ____ is bigger than the ____ muscle.
5. The ____ to his ____ ____ him.

Review Items

6. Which has **more** gravity, Jupiter or Io?
7. Which is **smaller** than Earth?
8. Where can you jump 8 feet high?

9. How long does it take light to travel from the sun to Earth?
10. Muscles are made up of tiny ___.
11. Blood vessels that are blue are filled with ___.
    - red blood
    - dark blood
12. Muscle cells need ___ to work.
13. The nerves that tell the brain what the foot feels go from the ___ to the ___.
14. The nerves that tell the foot how to move go from the ___ to the ___.
15. If you cut the nerve going from your brain to your arm, you could not ___ your arm.
16. If you cut the nerve going from your arm to your brain, you could not ___ your arm.
17. Write the letter of the blood vessels that pound every time the heart beats.
18. Write the letter of the blood vessels that do not pound.
19. Write the letter of the blood vessels that are blue.
    a. blood vessels that lead from the heart
    b. blood vessels that lead to the heart
20. Which letter on the map shows Alaska?
21. Which letter shows Canada?
22. Which letter shows the main part of the United States?
23. Which **2** letters show where Eskimos live?

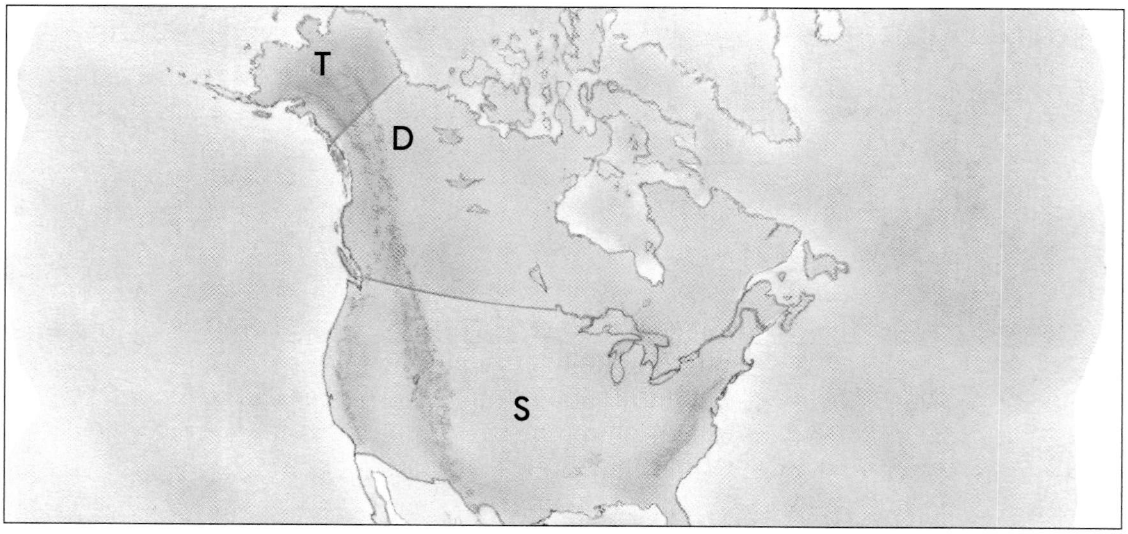

24. How warm is it during winter in Alaska?

A

1	2
1. horizon	1. bedroom
2. lens	2. eyeball
3. pupil	3. mailman
4. retina	4. maybe
5. tying	5. forearm
6. backbone	6. shoelace
7. single	

B

How the Eye Works

The eye works just like a magnifying glass. The eye bends the light. The light forms a picture on the back of the eyeball. That's the image the person sees.

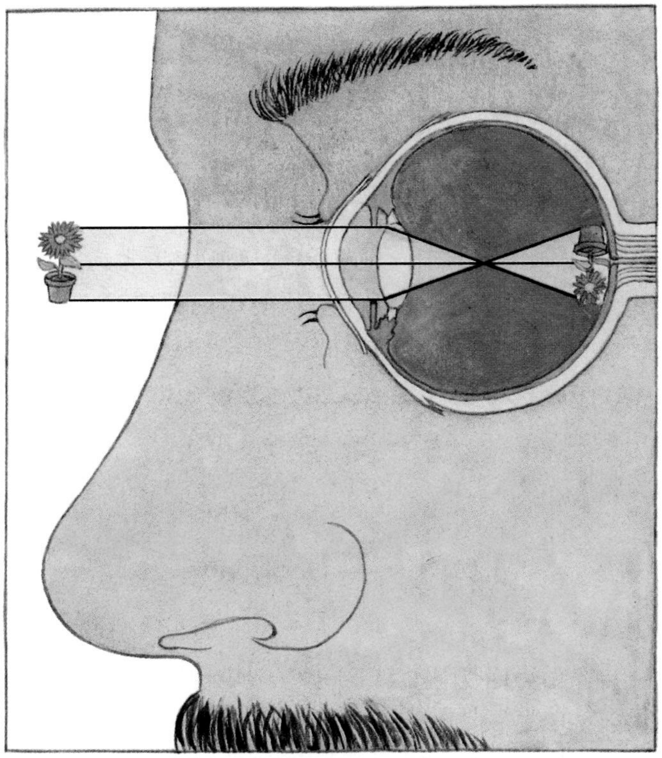

PICTURE 1

If you look at the eye from the front, you can see the hole that light enters. It's called the pupil. The pupil looks like a round black disk in the middle of the eye.

Remember, the pupil is a hole. It's black because the inside of the eyeball is dark. Behind the pupil is a lens. That's the part that bends the light.

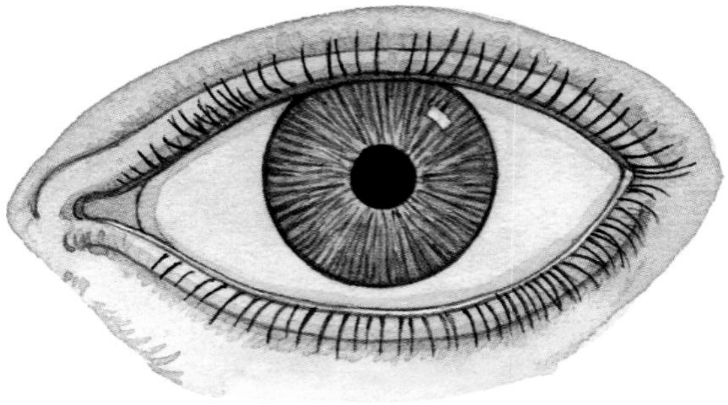

PICTURE 2

C Angela and Al Learn About the Eye

"Wow!" Al said as he observed the thinking part of the human brain. There were millions and millions of nerves inside the cerebrum.

The old man said, "Observe what the brain does when the man does different things. The man is sitting in his bedroom. He just finished tying his shoe. The man just woke up, so he is still a little sleepy. Watch what happens to his brain when a lion walks into his bedroom."

Suddenly the nerves behind Al started to pulse rapidly. An instant later, every nerve in the brain seemed to be pulsing. Nerves were firing all around Al.

Angela said, "This man's brain is going wild."

The old man snapped his fingers and said, "The lion is gone now." The pulsing in the brain started to slow down again.

"Here's what happened," the old man said. "The man looked at the lion. When the brain realized what he was looking at, part of the brain started to work very hard. The man became frightened. So every part of his brain tried to work at the same time. Then the lion disappeared and the man's brain started to slow down. The man started to wonder how a lion got into his bedroom. He started thinking that maybe he was just having a bad dream."

"Poor man," Al said. Then he laughed. "That was a dirty trick to play on him."

The old man said, "Yes, it was. But it really showed us how his brain works."

Angela, Al and the old man moved to the left side of the brain. Al could now see a great thick bundle of nerves leading to the back of the brain. "What is that?" he asked.

The old man explained, "Those are the nerves that come from his left eye. Each eye has a great bundle of nerves that goes to the brain. The pulses from those nerves go to the back of the brain."

The old man continued, "Right now the man is looking out the window. He is watching the mailman walk down the street and his brain is paying attention to the mailman."

The old man said, "If you want to see the things the man is looking at, just follow this bundle of nerves to the eye."

Angela, Al and the old man moved along the big nerve to the eye. Then they went inside the big nerve. When they came ★ out, they were inside the eye. It was a great round chamber that seemed bigger than a big building.

On the other side of the chamber was a big round window. Light was coming through the window. The rest of the chamber was very dark.

The old man said, "We are inside the eyeball, near the back of it. You can't see this part of the eye when

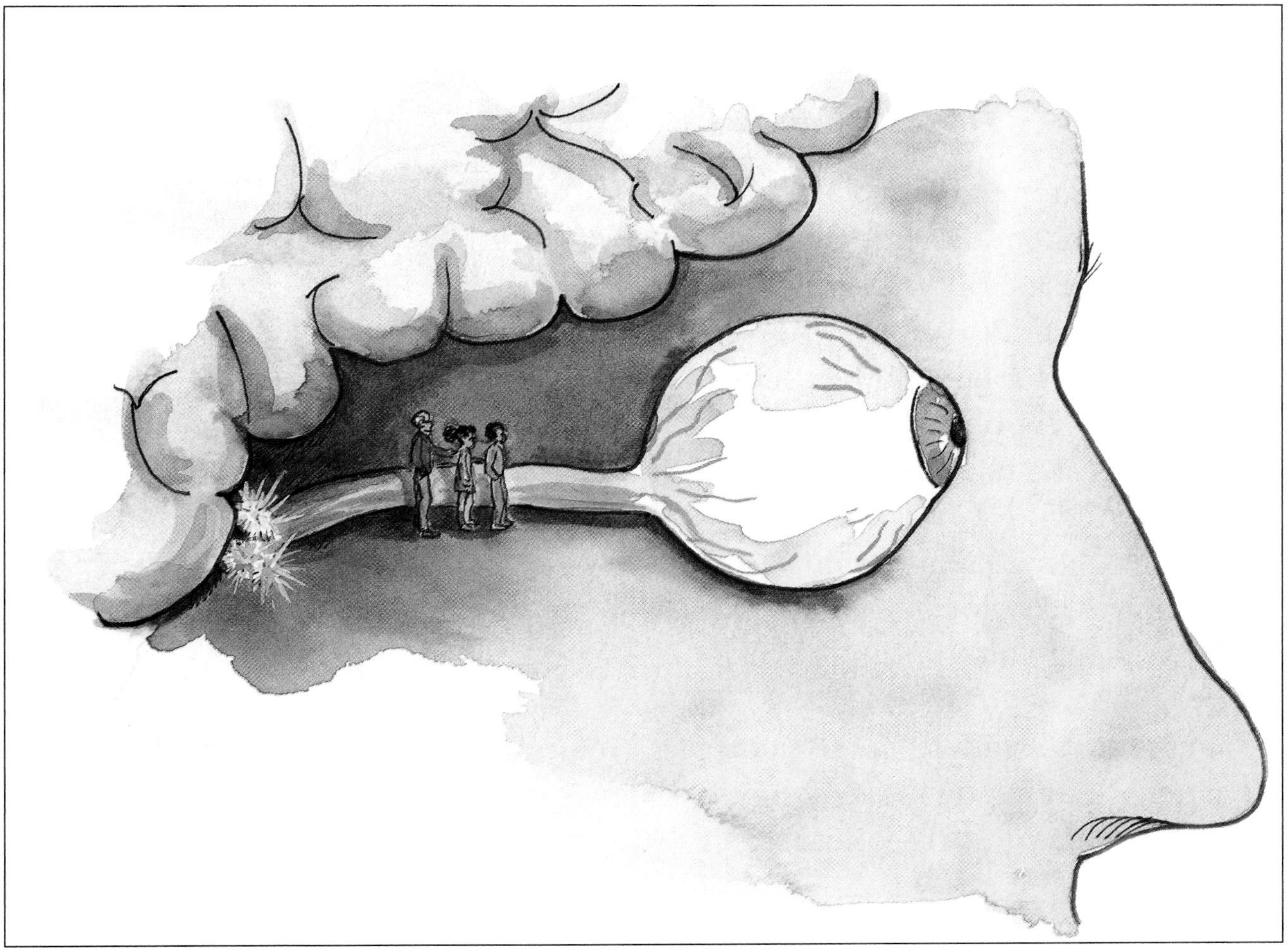

you look at somebody. You can see only the front of the eye." The old man pointed to the round window on the front of the eyeball. "That is the part that lets light into the eye."

Then the old man said, "Turn around. Look at the back of the eyeball. It is called the retina. On the retina you will see what the man is looking at."

As the old man talked, Al turned around and looked at the retina. At first he could not believe what he saw. There was a great big picture on the back of the eyeball. The picture went from the top of the eyeball to the bottom of the eyeball. And it went from one side all the way to the other side. Al studied the picture. He could see things in the picture and he could see the colors. He could see a mailman walking, a tree, a sidewalk and a little dog. He could see houses. But everything he saw was upside down.

Angela was looking at the picture too. She said, "I don't believe it. This is like being at a movie with everything upside down."

"Correct," the old man said. "And everything is in color."

"Wow!" Angela said. "I still don't believe it."

The old man said, "In a moment the man will look down to see if his shoes are tied. Watch the picture."

Suddenly, the picture changed. Al could see two shoes in the picture. He could also see part of the man's legs. One of the shoes was not tied. The shoe started to get bigger and bigger.

The old man said, "The man is bending down now. He's getting closer to his shoes. That's why they look bigger."

The man's hands came into the picture. They started to tie the shoe.

Al said, "This is amazing. We can observe everything the man sees by looking at the man's retina."

Angela added, "And each picture goes to the brain through a huge nerve."

"You are both correct," the old man said.

D Number your paper from 1 through 23.

Use some of these words to answer items 1 and 2.

lens	retina	eyeball	pupil	black	nerve

1. What is the name of the hole at the front of the eye?
2. What color is that part?
3. What's strange about the images that are formed in your eye?
4. Which letter shows where the pupil is?

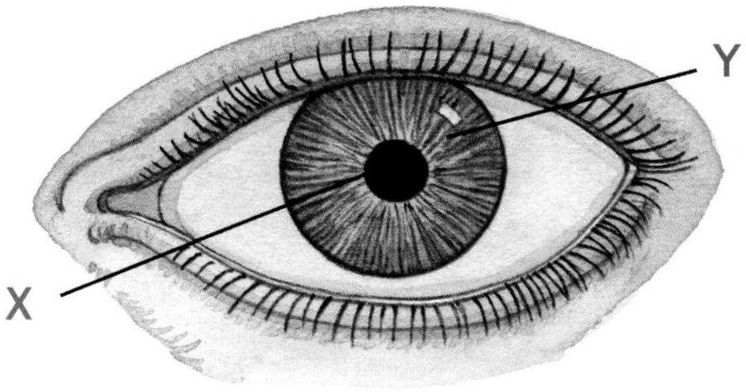

5. What's part A?
6. What's part B?
7. Write the letter of the part that bends the light.
8. Write the letter of the part that shows a picture of what the eye sees.

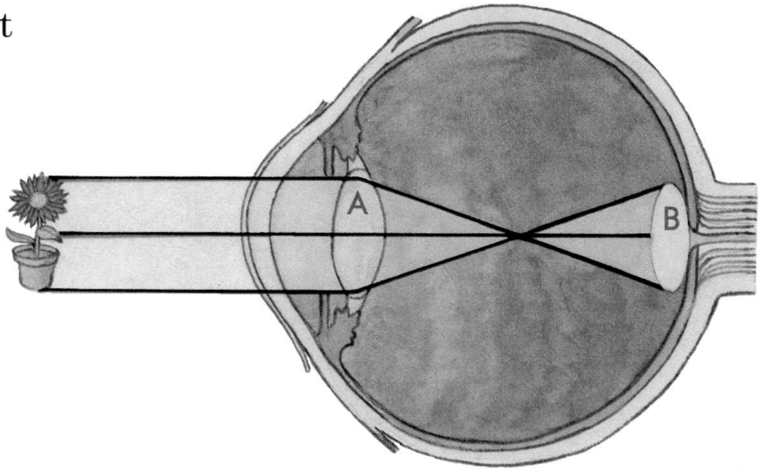

Review Items

9. How many miles does light travel in one second?
10. What else travels as fast as light?
11. How long does it take sound to travel one mile?
12. When would the nerves in your toe pulse faster—when you're asleep or when you hurt your toe?
13. The nerves that tell the brain what the leg feels go from the ____ to the ____.
14. The nerves that tell the leg how to move go from the ____ to the ____.
15. If you make a picture of a tree using a magnifying glass, the top of the tree will be at the ____ of the picture.
16. Which letter on the map shows Alaska
17. Which letter shows Canada?
18. Which letter shows the main part of the United States?
19. Which **2** letters show where Eskimos live?

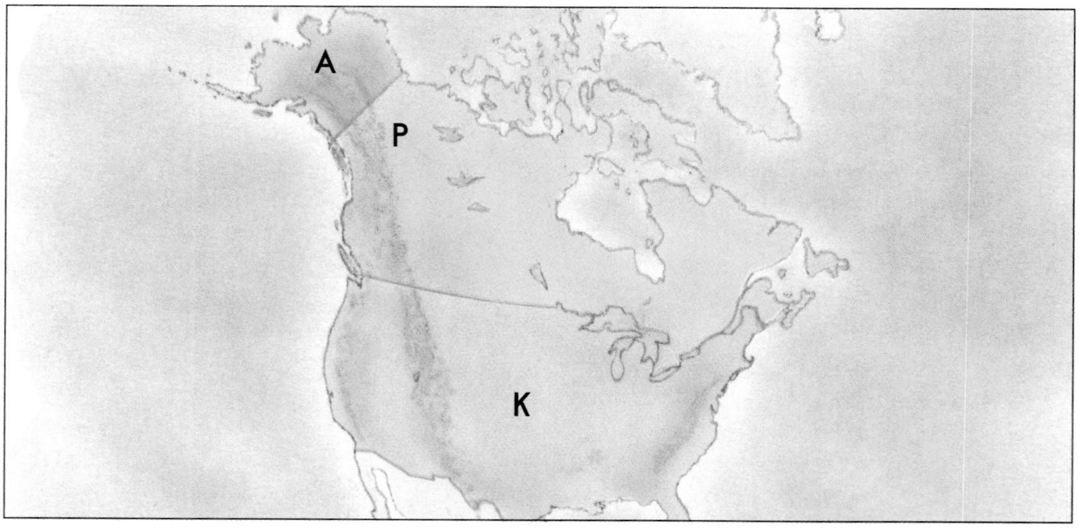

20. How warm is it during winter in Alaska?
21. If you move up too fast from very deep water, you may get the ____.
22. What forms in your blood as you go up too fast?
23. When you go up very fast, is there **more pressure** or **less pressure** on your body?

A

1

1. collects
2. horizon
3. discussed
4. single
5. blind
6. spiral
7. explained

B Al and Angela Learn About the Ear

Angela, Al and the old man were inside a man's eye. By looking at the image on the retina, they could see a picture of everything the man saw.

Angela said, "I don't understand how the picture from the eye gets into that nerve that goes to the brain."

"I will explain," the old man said, pointing to the retina. "The retina can feel light. There are thousands of nerves in the retina. Each nerve can feel if light hits it. All the nerves that feel light send a message. These messages go down that big bundle of nerves to the back of the brain."

Al thought for a moment. Then he said, "What if that big nerve from the eye to the brain was cut? Would the man be able to see anything?"

The old man said, "The man would be blind in that eye if the nerve was cut."

The old man pointed to the window in the front of the eye. He said, "Right behind the pupil is a very important part of the eye. Do you know the name of that part?"

Angela said, "I remember that. That's the lens. The lens bends the light that comes into the eye."

Al said, "Bends the light? What do you mean?"

Angela said, "Look at the picture on the back of the eye. That picture is upside down. How did it get upside down?"

Al said, "I don't know."

Angela explained, "The lens in the eye bent the light so that it would form a picture on the retina.

After the light is bent, the picture is upside down."

Al and Angela watched the pictures on the retina for a few minutes. During this time, Al kept thinking about where he had been. He had thought that a trip inside the body would be boring.

Suddenly the old man said, "Let's go to the ear." Slowly Angela, Al and the old man went back down the nerve from the eye and back into the brain. They moved to the side of the brain, where they came to a strange chamber that was shaped like a spiral. They entered at the small end of the chamber. And then they started to follow it as it spiraled around and around, becoming larger and larger.

"Is this what the inside of my ear looks like?" Angela asked.

"Yes," the old man said. "When you look at a person's ear, you see only the outside part of the ear. The part you see works like a funnel. It collects the sound and directs it into the inner ear. That's where we are now. But you can't see the inner ear from the outside."

The old man explained, "We're way inside the ear, at the place it joins the brain."

Rows of hairs lined the inside of the chamber. The old man pointed to a hair. He said, "There is a nerve that goes to the brain from every hair in the ear. And when the hair vibrates, the nerve pulses. The more the hair vibrates, the harder the nerve pulses."

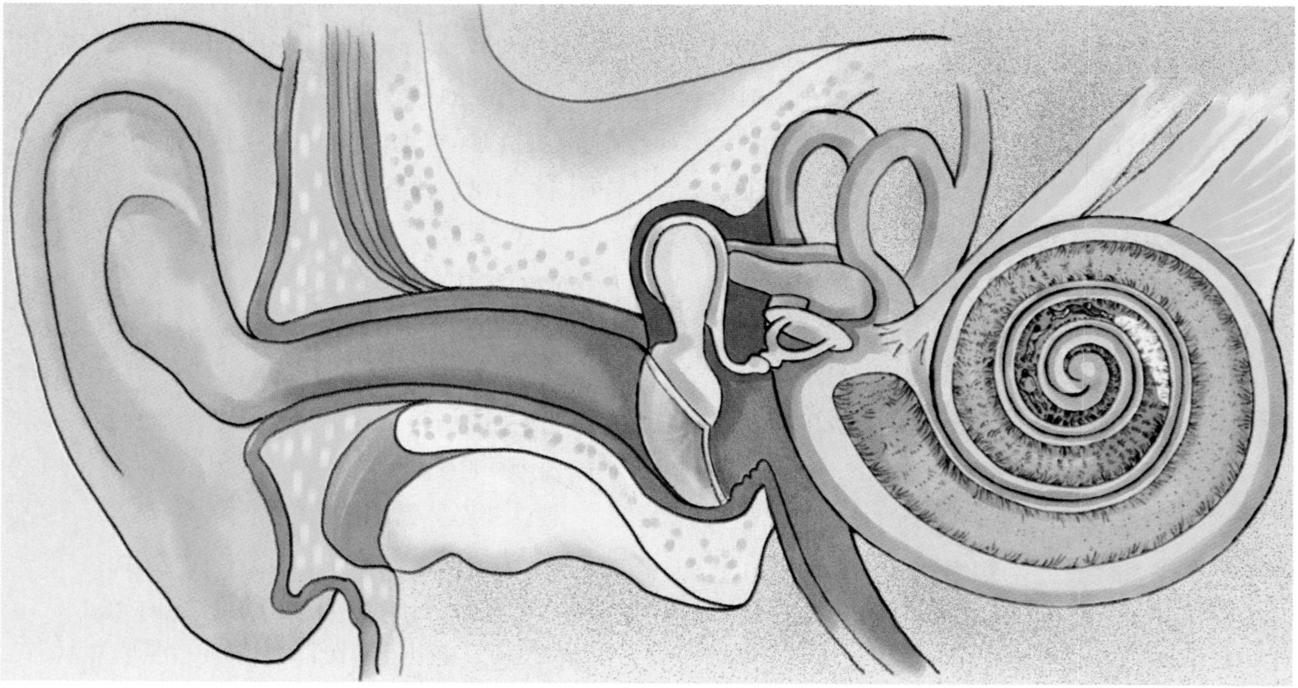

"Wow!" Angela exclaimed. "Look at all the hairs inside this ear. And every hair can make a nerve pulse."

Al, Angela and the old man went down and around the spiral. The chamber got bigger and bigger as they moved through it.

The old man said, "In a moment the man will hear a church bell. It is a very big bell and it makes a very deep sound."

Al wasn't sure what to expect. Then suddenly—"BONNNNNG, BONNNNNNG"—the chamber seemed to tremble. The sound was very, very loud.

Al looked around at the hairs inside the chamber. "Look," he said, and pointed to the largest part of the chamber. Every hair in that part of the chamber was vibrating. But no hairs in the other parts of the chamber were vibrating.

"Some of those hairs aren't working," Al said. "When the bell sounded, only some of them vibrated."

The bell sounded again. "BONNNNG, BONNNNG." Again, the hairs in only one part of the chamber vibrated.

"Al is right," Angela said. "Only the hairs in one part of this chamber are working."

The old man said, "Watch what happens when the man listens to a different bell. In a moment he will hear a telephone ring. Watch."

Al watched. "Rrrrrring . . . Rrrrring . . . Rrrrring."

As soon as the telephone started to ring, the hairs in the middle part of the chamber began vibrating but the hairs at the large end of the chamber did not vibrate.

Angela pointed to the vibrating hairs and said, "The hairs in that part of the ear didn't work when the church bell rang. But look at them now. They vibrate when the telephone rings."

The old man smiled and said, "I want both of you to think. The man is now going to hear a very high whistle. It is much higher than a telephone ring. Can you tell me where the hair will vibrate when the man hears the whistle?"

Al started thinking. The church bell was very deep, very low. The hairs that vibrated when this bell sounded were in the large end of the chamber. The ring of the telephone was a higher ring. The hairs that moved when the telephone rang were in the middle of the chamber. Al said to himself, "If the whistle is higher than the telephone, it would vibrate the hairs at the small end of the chamber."

Al pointed to the small end of the chamber. Angela also pointed to that part at the same time. Al said, "The hairs will move in that part of the ear."

The old man clapped his hands, smiled, and then he put his arms around Al and Angela. "You are both smart and I am proud of you."

Al smiled. Angela smiled. The old man smiled. Then, "tweeeeet." The hairs near the small end of the chamber started to vibrate. The old man said, "That's all there is to the inner ear. High sounds are picked up at the small end of the chamber. Lower sounds are picked up in the middle of the chamber. And the lowest sounds are picked up where the chamber is the largest."

Al looked at the hairs inside the ear. He didn't say anything. He just observed them and thought.

C Number your paper from 1 through 19.

Skill Items

Here are 3 events that happened in the story. Write **beginning, middle** or **end** for each event.

1. Then "tweeeeet." The hairs near the small end of the chamber started to vibrate.
2. Here's what somebody said: "The more the hair vibrates, the harder the nerve pulses."
3. By looking at the image on the retina, they could see a picture of everything the man saw.

Review Items

4. What do nerves that lead from the brain to the foot tell the foot?
5. What do nerves that lead from the foot to the brain tell the brain?
6. Which part of your **brain** works when you **think** about what you are hearing?
7. What is the name of the hole at the front of the eye?
8. What color is that part?
9. What part of the eye is just behind the hole?

10. Which picture shows where the paths of light will go after they go through the lens?

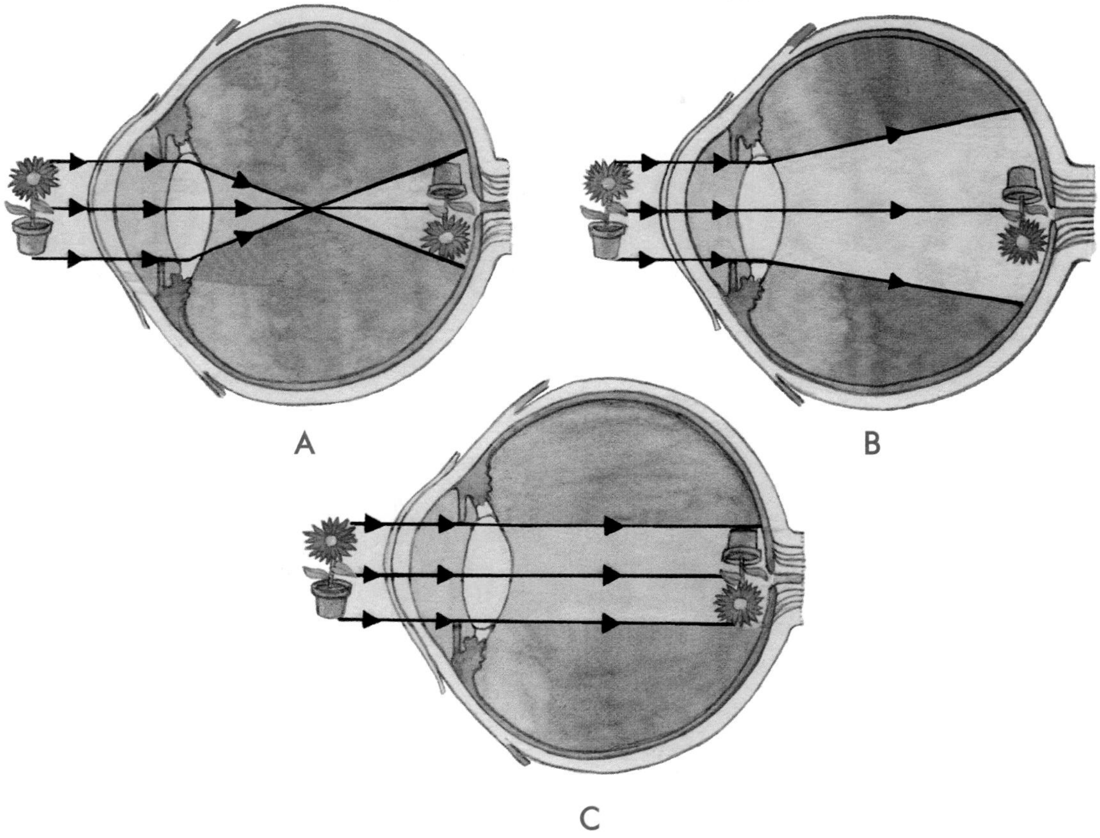

11. When you dive down 33 feet, you have ____ times the pressure on you that you have at the surface.
12. When you dive down 66 feet, you have ____ times the pressure on you that you have at the surface.

13. In what country are the states of Colorado and Utah?
14. Name the mountains you drive over to get from Colorado to Utah.
15. In which direction do you go to get from Colorado to Utah?
16. Name **2** cities in Colorado.
17. Name one city in Utah.

18. Which letter shows Colorado?

19. Which letter shows Utah?

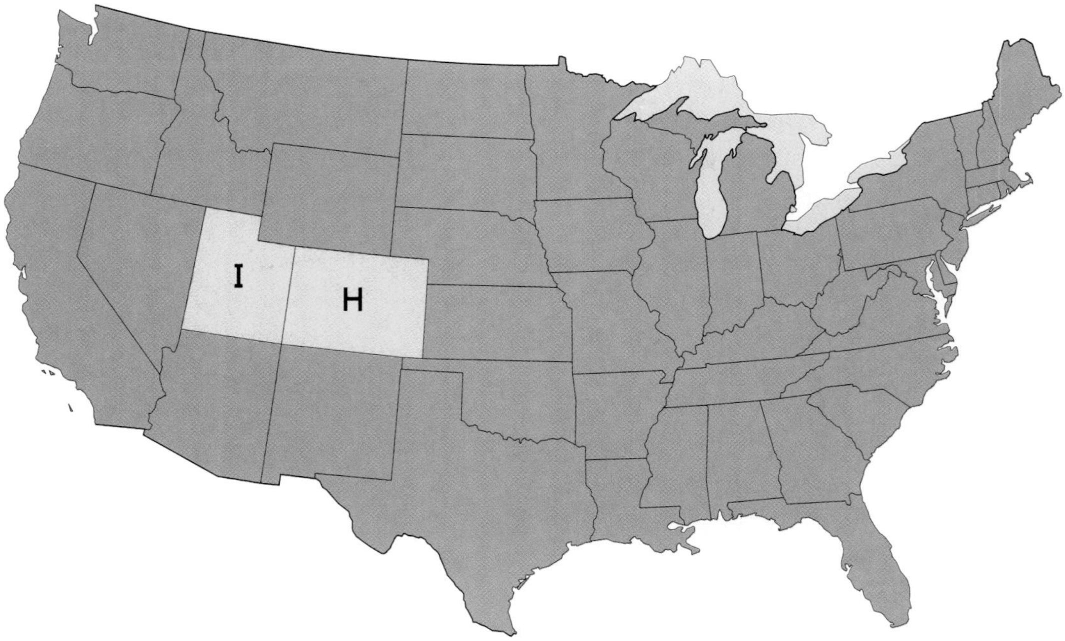

A

1

1. briskly
2. shovel
3. dressing
4. snowball
5. discussed

B Angela and Al Study for a Test

Al and Angela were inside the human body. They had just learned about the parts of the ear that vibrate when different sounds enter the ear. They had learned where the hairs are that vibrate for low sounds and for high sounds.

The old man said, "The human body is amazing, and we could continue this trip through the body for hours without seeing everything. But we have seen enough for one trip. So remember the things you have seen. Remember the muscles, the bones, the nerves, the heart, the blood, the brain, the eye and the ear. Remember everything."

The old man's voice seemed to change and Al felt as if he was moving through space. Suddenly he realized that he was once more standing inside the dark store.

The old man said, "Go anywhere. See anything. And pay for your trip by passing a test on what you see."

Angela said, "I just hope that I can remember everything we saw. We saw so much. I don't know that I can remember everything."

The old man handed a book to Angela and Al. Al moved the book close to his face so that he could read the title, *The Human Body*.

The old man said, "That book will help you study for your test. Tomorrow is Saturday, and my store will be closed. So come back Monday."

"Thank you for the book," Al said. "We'll return it on Monday."

The old man said, "Nobody brings things back to this store. If you get something, it's yours."

Suddenly the room became very quiet. Angela and Al waited for a few moments before Al said, "Let's go."

Angela and Al went outside, where it was starting to snow. A layer of snow a few inches thick was on the sidewalk. After Angela and Al had walked to the corner of Anywhere Street, Al turned around. The only footprints in the snow were his and Angela's.

The street around the corner of Anywhere Street was crowded with people, and Al could hear Christmas music.

Angela said, "Next week is Christmas. Look at all the people out shopping for presents."

As Al looked, he remembered that he didn't have any money to buy Christmas presents. He said, "I guess Christmas is fun if you have money to buy presents for people."

Angela agreed. Then she added, "Christmas makes me feel sad. I just wish . . ."

"Let's not think about that," Al said. "Let's figure out how we're going to study for that test on Monday."

"Well," Angela said, "tomorrow morning we'll get together and go through that book until we get tired."

Al and Angela didn't say much more as they walked home. The snow was falling gently. In the distance were sounds of Christmas music. The air seemed almost too warm for snow to be falling.

• • •

Al's mother said, "Before you do anything else this morning, I want you to shovel the sidewalk."

Al was in his bedroom, just finishing dressing. "Oh, Mom," he said. "That snow must be almost a yard deep."

His mother said, "Just go down and eat breakfast, then shovel that walk."

Al sighed and said, "Oh, all right."

Al ate breakfast quickly. Then he put on his jacket and his gloves. Angela was waiting for him at the door. She was wearing a warm coat and earmuffs. She said, "You shovel for a while and then I'll shovel for a while."

"Yeah," Al said. "Let's get it finished as fast as we can."

Al got the shovel and started to work. He shoveled and shoveled until his back started to hurt from bending over, and he started to sweat. Just as he straightened up and was ready to tell Angela that it was her turn to shovel, wham. Something hit him in the middle of his back. Al turned around and noticed Angela hiding behind a tree. She was holding a snowball and smiling.

As Al bent down to make a snowball, she threw another snowball. Whizzz, it flew over Al's head. Al stood up and was ready to throw his snowball when—wham. Right in the middle of his chest. "Is that all the harder you can throw?" he shouted and sent his snowball whizzing toward Angela. She ducked behind the tree and the snowball sailed by her.

Whiiizzzz. Angela threw a snowball that missed Al.

Whiiizzzz. Al threw a snowball that missed Angela.

Wham. Al hit Angela in the shoulder.

Whiiizzzz. Angela missed.

"What's going on out there?" Al's mother was standing on the front steps with her hands on her hips. "You can play with snowballs <u>after</u> you shovel the walk."

Angela shoveled until she was tired. Then she rested while Al shoveled. Soon the walk was clear of snow.

Then Angela said, "Let's study. Maybe we can throw snowballs when we're through."

They went inside where it felt very warm. Angela got the book and opened it. The first part told about muscles. The pictures looked just like things that Al and Angela had seen on their trip.

The next part of the book told about the bones. This part also showed things they had seen, like a man with no bones in his legs.

Angela read parts of the book aloud. When she came to a sentence that said, "Bones do two things," Al said, "I know what those things are." He explained them.

For over four hours, Angela and Al went through the book and talked about the things they read. They discussed the heart and the blood. They talked about the two kinds of nerves that are in the body. They discussed the brain, the eye and the ear. When they were finished with the book, it was getting dark in the room.

"Hey, Mom," Al called. "What time is it?"

"Four o'clock," she called from the other room.

Al said, "I've had enough studying for a while. Let's go outside and I'll give you a lesson in throwing snowballs."

Angela said, "How can you give lessons in something you don't know how to do?"

They went outside, where the snow was still falling. The walk that they had shoveled earlier was covered with about three inches of snow. Al ran behind a tree, made a large wet snowball, stood up and said, "Here's how to . . ." Splat. Right in his chest.

C Number your paper from 1 through 22.

Story Items

1. Why were people out shopping for presents?
2. Why did Al feel sad about Christmas?
3. How long did Al and Angela study the book the old man gave them?
4. What did they do outside after they finished studying?

Review Items

5. In what form of matter is air on Pluto?
6. In what form of matter is air on Earth?
7. In what form of matter is air on Saturn?
8. When things are hard, what form of matter are they?
9. When hard matter gets hotter, which form does it change into?
10. When matter gets still hotter, which form does it change into?

11. If you make a picture of a tree using a magnifying glass, the bottom of the tree will be at the ______ of the picture.
12. Where would a balloon be bigger—at 80 feet below the surface of the ocean or at 20 feet below the surface?

Write **big** or **small** to tell in which part of your ear chamber you would pick up each sound.

13. very high voice
14. low voice
15. high whistle
16. big church bell

17. Name the bundle of nerves that goes up and down through the middle of your backbone.
18. What's strange about the bones in the backbone?
19. What's strange about the images that are formed in your eye?
20. The retina is covered with ______.
    - hair
    - nerves
    - blood
21. Coral is made up of the ______ of tiny ______.
22. An underwater hill that is covered with coral is called a coral ______.

129

A

1	2	3
1. absolutely	1. correct	1. briskly
2. thermometer	2. throughout	2. flipped
3. suspended	3. everybody	3. erasing
4. flunk	4. nighttime	4. mistakes
5. grade	5. closest	5. nodding
		6. darkness

B

The Earth and the Sun

You've learned that the earth tilts. During our summertime, does the North Pole tilt toward the sun or away from the sun? During our wintertime, does the North Pole tilt toward the sun or away from the sun?

Look at picture 1. You can figure out which half of the earth is closest

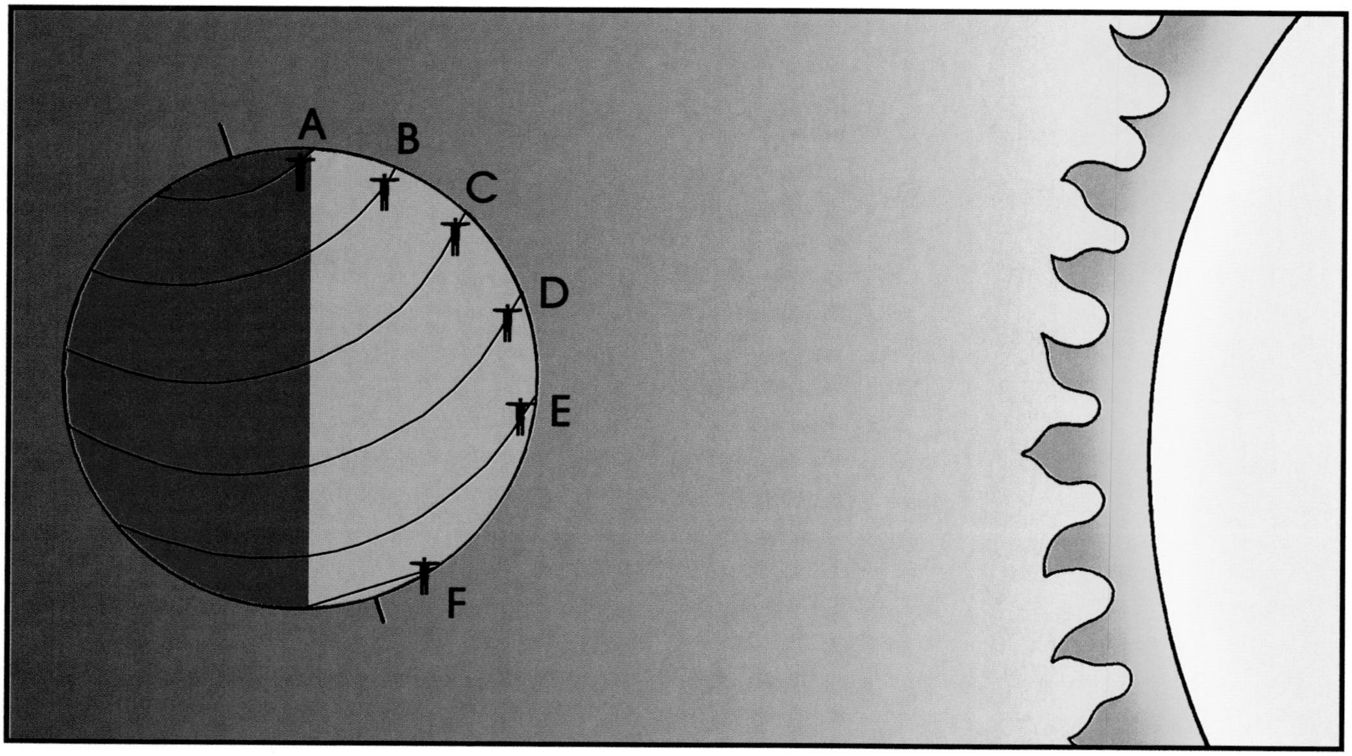

PICTURE 1

to the sun. That's the half that is bright. What season is it in picture 1?

The earth turns around one time every 24 hours. Every time the earth turns around one time, most places on the earth have night and day. But it's different at the poles. The lines on the earth show how far people in different parts of the earth move every time the sun turns around. Touch person A. In 24 hours, that person follows the line around the earth and goes all the way back to point A. Which person goes farther in 24 hours, person A or D? When the earth goes around, person A is in darkness all the time. Person D is in daylight part of the time and in darkness part of the time. Person F is in daylight all the time.

Look at picture 2. It shows the same people in the same places. But it shows our summer, not winter. During summer, person A is always in sunlight as the earth turns around. And person F is always in darkness as the earth turns around.

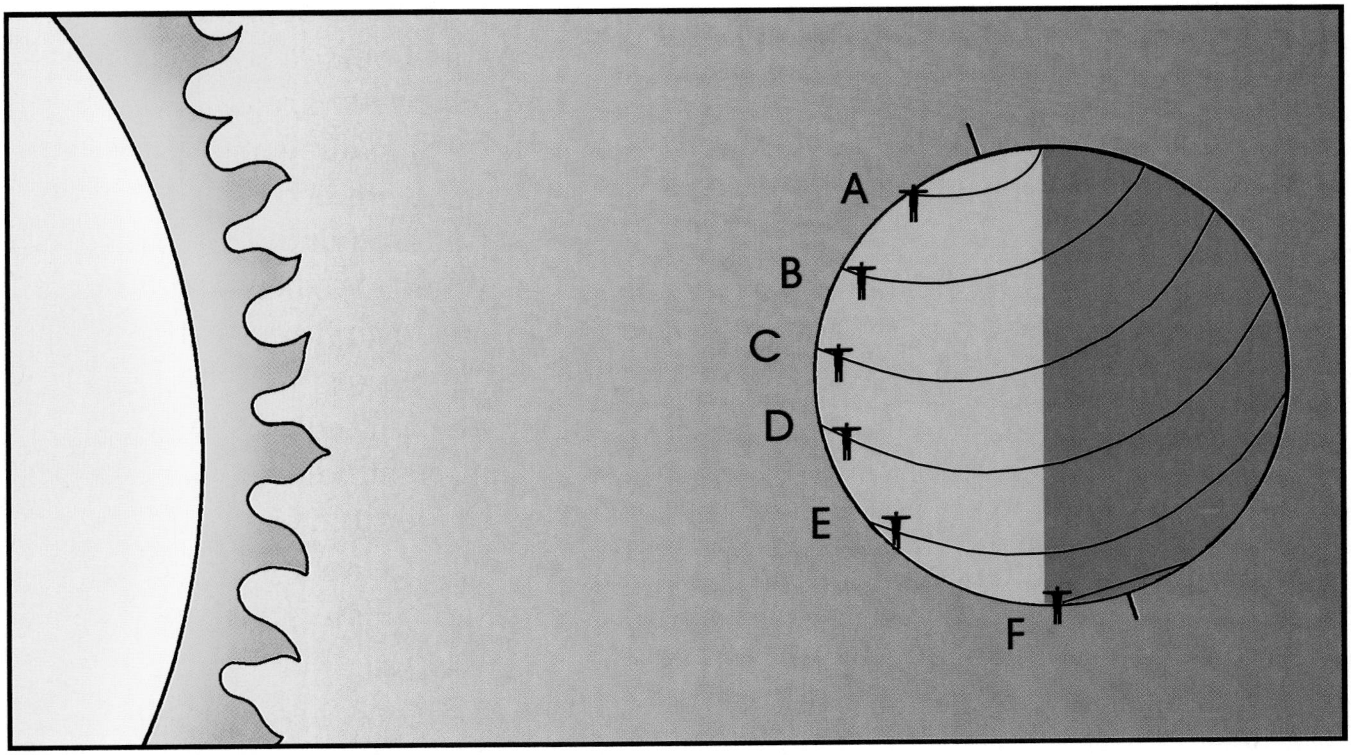

PICTURE 2

C Angela and Al Take a Test on the Human Body

"I know you have been looking forward to this Monday morning," Al's teacher said to the class. "Today we are going to have our test in science."

Some of the kids said, "Oh, no!" Al didn't say anything.

Homer asked, "Are some people going to flunk this test?"

The teacher said, "If they don't get enough correct answers, they will fail the test."

Homer turned to Al and said, "Did you hear that? You're going to flunk the test."

Some of the kids laughed.

Al said, "Oh yeah? I'll get more answers . . ."

"Both of you, stop that," the teacher said. Then she said to Homer, "I don't know what's going on between you and Al, but I don't want that kind of talk in this classroom. Al has been doing a very good job in science these past two weeks. In fact, I don't know a student who is doing better."

Some of the kids laughed and Homer looked down. The teacher passed out the test. There were forty questions on the test. Most were about the body.

Al knew the answer to every single question. He wrote down the answers and then read his test over to make sure that there were no mistakes. He took his paper up to the teacher's desk.

As he walked past Homer's desk, he noticed that Homer was still working on the fifteenth question. Homer was erasing something that he had written.

The teacher looked at Al and asked, "Did you finish the test already?"

Al responded by nodding his head yes. He went back to his desk, took out the book on the human body and started to read it again.

As he was reading about the cerebrum, he noticed that the teacher was standing next to his desk. She said, "Al, here is your test. You got everything right. I have given that test for years and I don't remember anybody getting everything right before."

The teacher told everybody their grades before school was out. Al got an A plus, the highest grade possible. Homer got a B.

Al met Angela outside school, where he told her about the test. "I got every single answer correct," he said. "Imagine that. I never thought I would be smart in school, but I am smart."

She said, "Oh, it was probably a very easy test."

"No way," he said. "It was the hardest test you'll ever see."

Then he continued, "Wait a minute. I have that test in my notebook. I'll bet you can't answer every question correctly."

They stopped while Al flipped through his notebook until he found the test. Al pulled it out and said, "I'll read the questions. You tell me the answers."

The wind blew briskly, carrying small flakes of snow. Al had trouble holding the test up so that he could read the items. He read them, and Angela answered every item correctly. After she had finished, she looked at Al and smiled. "I told you it was an easy test," she said.

He shook his head and put the test back in his notebook. Then he announced, "But you wouldn't have been able to answer the questions if you hadn't gone on the trip through the human body. And you wouldn't have gone on the trip through the human body if I hadn't made you go. So, I'm the one you can thank for knowing all those answers."

She shook her head. "Yes, you are the greatest," she said smiling. "Without you, I wouldn't know anything. You're the smartest person in the world." She began to laugh and Al could feel himself becoming angry.

Then suddenly, her expression changed and became serious. She put her arm around him and said, "I'm really glad you talked me into going on that trip. It was the most amazing thing I've ever seen."

Al looked down and smiled. He was no longer angry.

As soon as Al and Angela turned the corner at Anywhere Street, they could no longer hear the cars and the people or the sound of Christmas songs. They walked up to the store. The sign was still in the window: GO ANYWHERE. SEE ANYTHING.

As they went into the store, the bell went ding, ding. Inside, they waited.

Suddenly the old man was standing in front of them. He said, "There will be no test for you today."

Al looked at Angela. Then he looked back at the old man. Al asked, "But we're ready for the test. Why can't we take it now?"

The old man smiled. He said, "You can't take it because you have already taken it. I happen to know that both of you correctly answered all the questions on a science test. So why should I waste time giving you another test? Simply tell me where you want to go and what you want to see and we will go on another trip together."

D Number your paper from 1 through 24.

Skill Items

A single star was near the horizon.

1. What word names the line between the earth and the sky?
2. What word means **one?**

Review Items

3. What is the hottest form of any matter?
4. What is the next-hottest form of any matter?
5. What is the coldest form of any matter?
6. Do all things turn into a gas at the same temperature?
7. What are tiny parts of matter called?
8. When sand molecules are as cold as they can get, how much do they move?
9. Do they move **more** or **less** at room temperature?

10. Which letter in the picture shows the wheel dogs?
11. Which letter shows the lead dogs?
12. Which letter shows the swing dogs?
13. Which letter shows where the musher is most of the time?
14. Which letter shows the tug lines?
15. Which letter shows the gang line?

16. In which form of matter are molecules farthest apart?
17. In which form of matter are molecules closest together?
18. What would a person see if the big nerves from the eyes to the brain were cut?
19. What is each hair inside the ear connected to?
20. What kinds of sounds are picked up in the smallest part of the ear chamber—high sounds or low sounds?
21. When you open a bottle of soda pop, what happens to the pressure inside the bottle?
22. What forms in the soda pop?
23. Most sled-dog teams have an _____ number of dogs.
    - even
    - odd
24. For the Iditarod, a sled-dog team can't have more than _____ dogs.

Number your paper from 1 through 28.

1. How many bones are in the human body?
2. Name the **2** things that bones do.
3. Things can't burn without ______.
4. In the lungs, the color of blood changes from ______ to ______.
5. What color is blood that has fresh oxygen?
6. What color is blood that does not have oxygen?
7. How many chambers does the heart have?
8. How many chambers did Al and Angela go through **before** they went to the lungs?
9. How many chambers did they go through **after** they went to the lungs?
10. Where does black blood go after it leaves the heart?
11. Then the blood goes back to the ______.
12. Then the blood goes to the ______.
13. If you cut the nerve going from your brain to your hand, you could not ______ your hand.
14. If you cut the nerve going from your hand to your brain, you could not ______ your hand.
15. Name the bundle of nerves that goes up and down through the middle of your backbone.
16. What's strange about the bones in the backbone?
17. Which part of your **brain** works when you **think** about what you are seeing?
18. What's strange about the images that are formed in your eye?

Write **big** or **small** to tell in which part of your ear chamber you would pick up each sound.

19. big church bell
20. high whistle
21. low voice
22. very high voice

23. Which picture shows where the paths of light will go after they go through the lens?

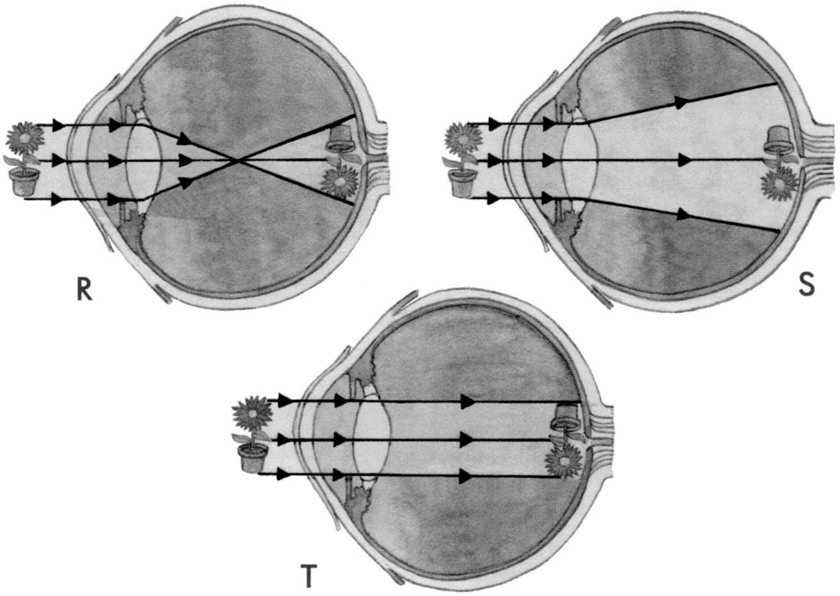

Skill Items

For each item, write the underlined word or words from the sentences in the box.

> The injury to his spinal cord paralyzed him.
> A single star was near the horizon.

24. What underlining names the bundle of nerves inside the backbone?
25. What underlining means **one?**
26. What underlining means **a serious hurt?**
27. What underlining names the line between the earth and the sky?
28. What underlining means that a part of the body can't move?

END OF TEST 13

A

1	2	3
1. attractive	1. throughout	1. lighting
2. veld	2. summertime	2. strongest
3. comment	3. everybody	3. mitten
4. troops	4. nighttime	4. suspended
5. baboon		5. thermometer
		6. absolutely

B

Winter at the North Pole

Al and Angela were in the old man's store getting ready for another trip.

Angela said, "I don't care where we go. I'll go anywhere."

"Good," the old man said. "We will go to the poles of the earth."

"What are those?" Al asked.

The old man explained.

The air suddenly became very cold. The cold was so bitter that Al could hardly breathe. He closed his eyes for a moment. When he opened them, they started to burn from the cold. Al now realized that he was wearing a great coat with a big hood, and a thick mitten on each hand. But he was still cold.

"Where are we?" Al asked.

"At the North Pole," the old man responded.

Al looked up. There were stars in the sky, but the sky was black.

Angela said, "Why is it so dark here?"

"Because it is winter at the North Pole," the old man replied. "The sun doesn't shine all winter long at the North Pole."

Al started to cough. He coughed and coughed. The more he coughed, the more the cold hurt his lungs. The old man snapped his fingers, and suddenly Al didn't feel cold anymore.

"Wow!" Al said. "That cold air really hurts."

"Correct," the old man said. "If you lived near the North Pole, you would have to be very careful during the cold weather. If you start breathing too hard, the cold air will freeze your lungs. It will also freeze the inside of your nose and the inside of your mouth."

Al said, "How cold is it here?"

The old man held up a thermometer. He turned a light on the thermometer and said, "Read it."

Al read the thermometer. The red line was at sixty below zero.

Angela said, "That is cold." She was quiet for a moment and then she said, "I still don't understand why it's dark here in the wintertime."

The old man said, "I will show you."

The old man snapped his fingers, and models of the sun and the earth appeared in front of Al and Angela. Both the earth and the sun were suspended in the air. The sun was shining brightly, lighting up everything around it. The old man pointed to the model of the earth, which was slowly turning as it hung in the air.

"You know that the earth is tilted," the old man said, pointing to the model of the earth.

"Yes," Al said. "And I can tell what season it is by looking at which way the North Pole is tilting."

The old man asked, "What season is it at the North Pole of this earth?"

"Winter," Al said.

"And how do you know that it is winter?"

Angela explained.

"Correct," the old man said and then pointed to the earth. "Can you show where we are on this model?"

"Yes," Angela said. She walked over to the model and pointed to the part where she and the others were.

The old man said, "Let's put models of us on that globe so that we can see what happens as the earth turns around." The old man snapped his fingers. Suddenly, three tiny forms appeared at the North Pole of the globe. Al looked at Angela and smiled.

"Observe the earth as it turns around," the old man said.

The model began spinning around faster and faster as Al and Angela studied it. Suddenly Angela said, "I get it. I know why it's dark here all winter."

"Explain," the old man said.

Angela said, "Half the globe is dark. The North Pole tilts away from the sun. So as long as the North Pole tilts this way, it is on the half of the earth that is dark all the time. The earth turns around and around, but the North Pole always stays on the dark side."

"A very good explanation," the old man said to Angela. Then he asked, "Can you figure out what the days and nights would be like during the summertime at the North Pole?"

Al and Angela looked at the globe. Al tried to figure out the answer but he was having trouble.

The old man said, "If you use the facts you know, you can figure out the answer. Tell me how the North Pole tilts during the summertime."

"Toward the sun," Al said.

As soon as he had spoken, the model of the earth moved so that the North Pole was tilting toward the sun. "There," the old man said. "Now you see us at the North Pole during summertime."

Al watched the earth spin around one time, two times, three times. Then he pointed to the little people who were at the North Pole. He said, "Now the North Pole is always on the half of the earth that is lit up by the sun. The earth turns around and around but the North Pole is always in the sun."

The old man added, "That means the sun shines all the time during summer at the North Pole. There is no time when the sun sets. You can see the sun all day and all night."

The old man snapped his fingers and the models of the sun and the earth disappeared. It was now so dark that Al couldn't see anything except spots in front of his eyes. He rubbed his eyes as he listened to what Angela was saying. "So it is dark at the North Pole throughout the whole winter," she said. "The sun never shines because the North Pole tilts away from the sun and is on the half of the earth that is always dark."

"That is absolutely right," the old man responded.

Then the old man said, "I want you to feel winter at the North Pole for a few minutes. Think about what it would be like to live here."

The wind howled and Al felt it blowing snow in swirls around him. He could feel how cold it was. He wondered how anything could grow here or live here. What would they eat? How would they stay warm? How would they keep from going crazy even if they could stay alive? The strongest feeling that Al had was that he wanted to get out of this terrible place.

C Number your paper from 1 through 22.

Skill Items

Use the words in the box to write complete sentences.

paralyzed	difference	horizon	injury	blood vessel
chamber	single	lungs	spinal cord	

1. The ____ to his ____ ____ him.
2. A ____ star was near the ____.

Review Items

3. The nerves that tell the brain what the hand feels go from the [redacted] to the [redacted] .
4. The nerves that tell the hand how to move go from the [redacted] to the [redacted] .

Write **big** or **small** to tell in which part of your ear chamber you would pick up each sound.

5. high whistle
6. very high voice
7. big church bell
8. low voice

9. Which letter shows the part of the earth where it is night?
10. Which letter shows the part of the earth where it is daytime?

11. Which pole is at the top of the earth?
12. Which pole is at the bottom of the earth?

13. How many miles does light travel in one second?
14. What else travels as fast as light?

15. How many suns are in the solar system?
16. How many planets are in the solar system?
17. Name the bundle of nerves that goes up and down through the middle of your backbone.
18. What's strange about the bones in the backbone?

Write which season each Earth shows.

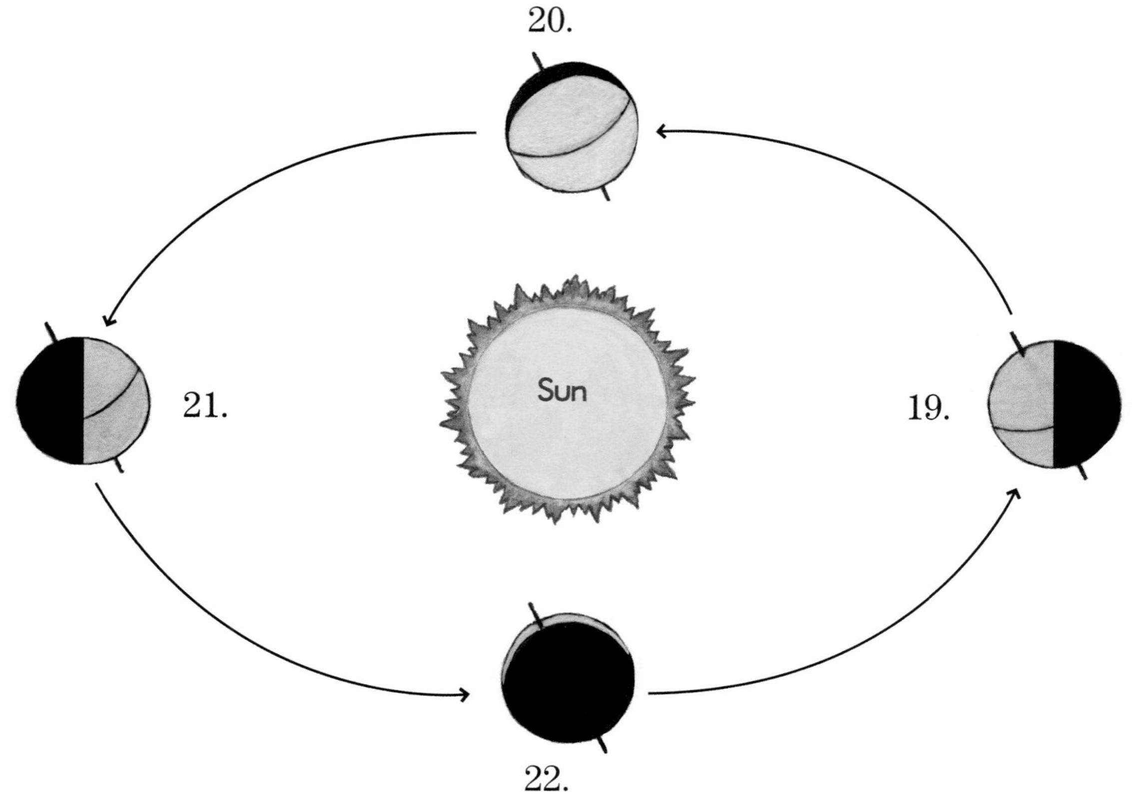

A

1	2	3
1. prevent	1. attractive	1. veld
2. regular	2. commented	2. aha
3. curvy	3. examined	3. baboon
4. camera	4. decorations	4. iris
	5. scooped	5. square

B

Angela and Al Learn About Snowflakes

After standing quietly for a couple of minutes, Al said, "Could we leave this place? There doesn't seem to be anything interesting to see here." The old man snapped his fingers. Suddenly Al no longer felt cold.

Angela laughed and said, "Yes, the only thing around us is wind and snow."

"Snow," the old man repeated. "Perhaps you would like to take a closer look at snow."

Al said, "I've seen a lot of snow. In fact, I've shoveled a lot of it."

The old man turned on a flashlight and directed the beam into a swirling mass of snow that was blowing in the wind. "Observe," he said. Suddenly, one of the snowflakes in the beam of light started to grow. Al watched it as it grew in size until it was as large as a basketball.

The snowflake was beautiful. It was very flat and it looked like a very fancy wheel with six spokes that came out from the center. Each spoke was covered with fancy decorations, and each spoke looked just like the others.

The old man said, "You are looking at an ordinary snowflake. Do you think it is attractive?"

"It's beautiful," Angela exclaimed.

The old man said, "Well, look around you at the millions and millions of snowflakes. And as you look at them, think about this fact: No two snowflakes look the same."

"That's incredible," Angela exclaimed.

The old man said, "Don't take my word for it. Pick out any snowflake you wish. I will make it big so that you can see if it's the same as the one we already have."

Angela pointed to a snowflake that landed on her mitten. "Make that snowflake big," she said.

The snowflake floated into the air and then it started to grow. Soon it was as large as the first snowflake. It was shaped like a fancy wheel with spokes. But it didn't look anything like the first snowflake.

Al and Angela looked at the two snowflakes. "Wow!" Angela said. "I never knew snowflakes were so pretty."

Al scooped up a handful of snow. "Could you make all of these snowflakes big?" he asked.

The old man snapped his fingers. The snowflakes became suspended in the air and started to grow. Soon every one of them was as big as a basketball. Hundreds of huge snowflakes surrounded Al and Angela.

Al examined them. Every snowflake had spokes, but no two snowflakes looked exactly the same.

Angela and Al looked at the snowflakes for about a minute. Finally the old man said, "Each snowflake is different, but there is something the same about all of

them. Study the snowflakes and see if you can figure out what is the same."

Al looked at the different snowflakes. Some had thin spokes that were decorated. Some had fat spokes that came to a sharp point. Some had shorter spokes, and some had longer spokes.

"They all have spokes," Al said.

"Correct," the old man replied. "Can you tell me what is the same about all the spokes?"

Al counted the spokes of a very fancy snowflake with a large center part and short spokes. "Six spokes," he said to himself. He looked at another and counted the spokes. "Six spokes," he repeated to himself.

Just then Angela said, "They all have six spokes."

"I was just going to say that," Al said. Angela looked at Al and made a face.

"Very good," the old man commented. "Now you know something about snowflakes that you didn't know before. Are you ready to learn more about the snow at the North Pole?"

"How much more is there?" Al asked. Before he completed the question, he noticed that he was starting to sink into the snow, straight down inside a hole that was forming.

The old man said, "We are now 10 feet below the surface of the snow. And we are a long way from the bottom of the snow.

The old man continued, "Let's go down another 10 feet and see what is down there." Angela, Al and the old man sank deeper into the snow. They were still not at the bottom of the snow.

Angela said, "Wow! We're down 20 feet and we're still in the snow."

"Correct," the old man said.

Al felt the sides of the hole. The snow was hard, almost like ice. He asked, "And why is the snow so hard? It's almost like ice."

The old man said, "I will show you why the snow is hard."

The old man pulled a small block of snow from the wall of the hole and handed it to Angela. The block was about as big as the blocks that children play with. Then the old man put another small block on top of the first block. Then the old man added more blocks to the pile. Angela said, "Stop. This pile is getting too heavy to hold."

"Aha," the old man said. "The pile of blocks you are holding is only three feet high. And it is getting too heavy to hold. Think how heavy the pile would be when it is 20 feet high."

The old man snapped his fingers and the pile of snow blocks disappeared.

Angela said, "I get it. Snow is heavy. It pushes down with so much pressure that it packs the snow together. That's why the snow down here is almost like ice."

"Correct," the old man said. "Let's go down to the bottom."

The hole got deeper. Angela, Al and the old man went down another 10 feet and stopped. They did the same thing again and again. Still, they had not reached the bottom of the snow.

"We are now 70 feet below the surface of the snow," the old man said. "Get ready for a surprise. We are going to see what is at the bottom of the snow."

The hole got a little deeper. Suddenly Angela, Al and the old man were no longer in the snow and ice. They were underwater.

The old man said, "There is no land at the North Pole. There is just snow and ice. The snow and ice float in water."

"No land?" Angela asked.

"That's right," the old man replied. "The North Pole is bigger than any state in the United States. But it is nothing but ice and snow floating in the ocean."

"Wow!" Angela exclaimed.

"Wow!" Al exclaimed.

C Number your paper from 1 through 26.

Review Items

1. Where does black blood go after it leaves the heart?
2. Then the blood goes back to the [redacted].
3. Then the blood goes to the [redacted].
4. When you think, what part of your brain are you using?
5. The retina is covered with [redacted].
   - blood
   - bones
   - nerves
6. What would a person see if the big nerves from the eyes to the brain were cut?
7. During what season is it dark at the North Pole?
8. How cold does it often get during that season?
   - 200 degrees below zero
   - 60 degrees below zero
   - 90 degrees below zero

9. Which letter shows the North Pole?
10. Which letter shows the South Pole?

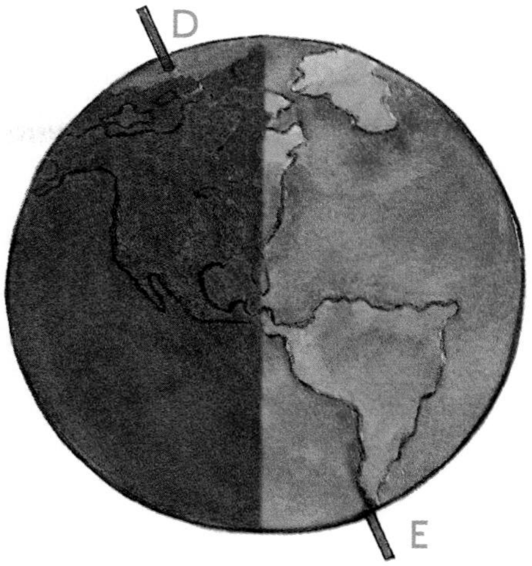

The old man made three tiny forms appear at the North Pole on the model Earth. Write **dark** or **light** for each blank.

11. When it was **winter,** those forms stayed on the ______ half of the model Earth.
12. When it was **summer,** those forms stayed on the ______ half of the model Earth.

13. What season do we have when the North Pole tilts **away from** the sun?
14. What season do we have when the North Pole tilts **toward** the sun?
15. How many suns are in the solar system?
16. How long does it take light to travel from the sun to Earth?
17. How long does it take sound to travel one mile?

18. If you're underwater 100 feet deep, the pressure is much greater than it is on land. How many times greater is it?
19. When divers are that deep, how long should they take to return to the surface of the water?
20. What may happen to the divers if they go up faster than that?

21. Name the two poles.

22. Why can't you see molecules when you look at an object?

Write which season each Earth shows.

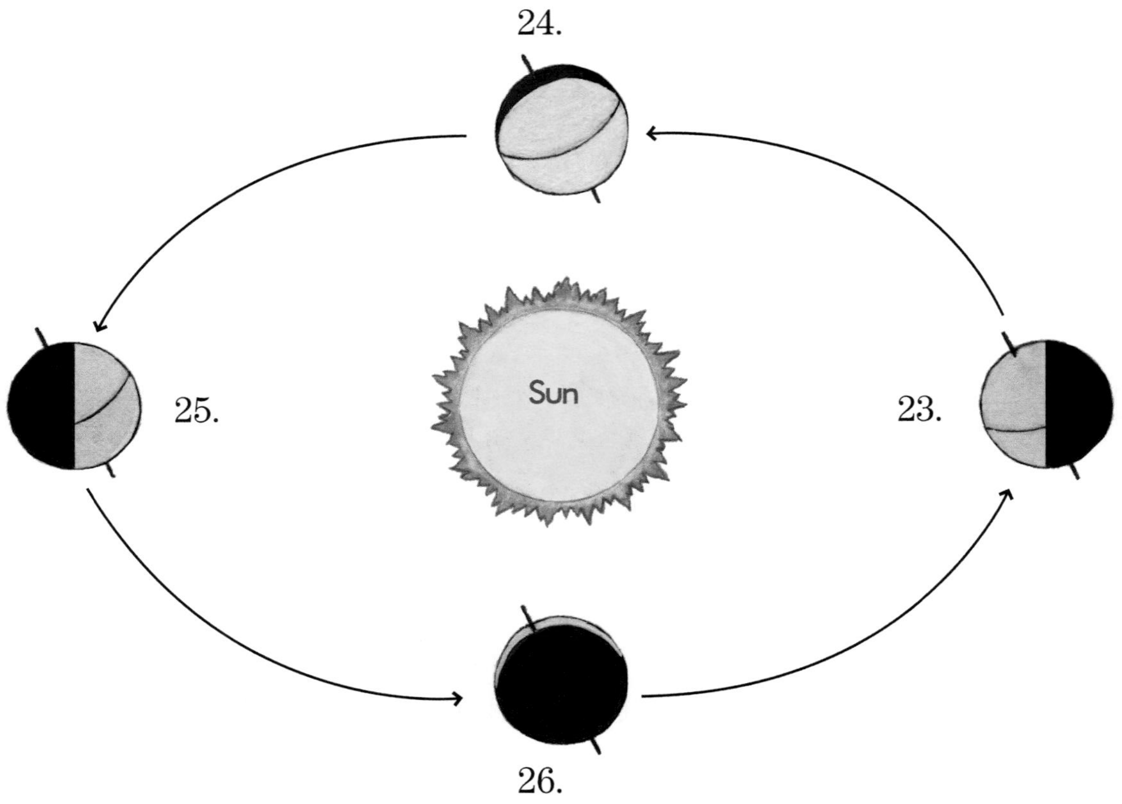

A

1	2
1. Endurance	1. titled
2. iris	2. prevents
3. square	3. camera
4. curved	4. retina

B

The Camera and the Eye

A camera may not look like an eye, but it works a lot like an eye. Here is a camera.

PICTURE 1

Here's how it looks if we cut the camera in half and look at it from the side.

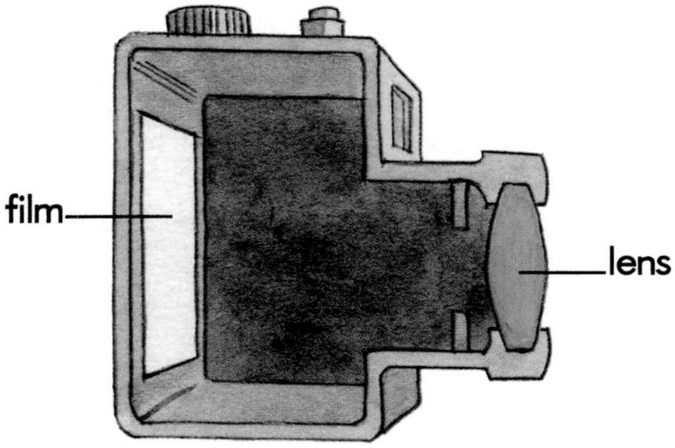

PICTURE 2

The inside of a camera is dark like the inside of the eye. There is a piece of curved glass at the front of the camera. That's the lens.

The camera lens works like the lens of an eye. The lens is transparent so that light can pass through it. The only way that light can get inside the camera is to pass through the lens. The lens bends the light. The paths of light cross after they go through the lens and then they form an image at the back of the camera. That image is upside down.

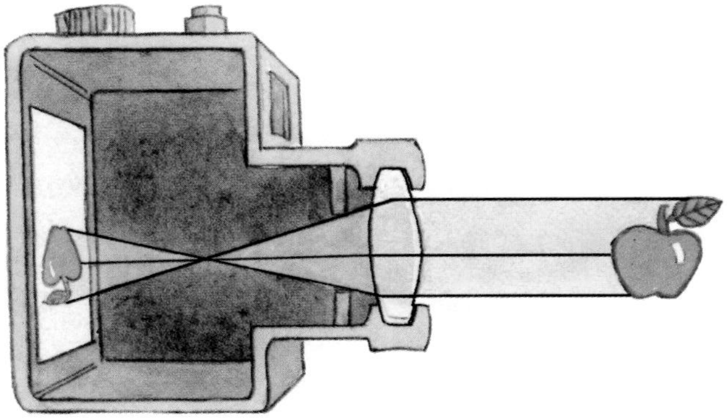

PICTURE 3

The camera doesn't have a retina to feel the light, but it has film stretched out across the back of the camera. The picture is formed on the film, and the film feels the light.

Both the camera and the eye have an iris.

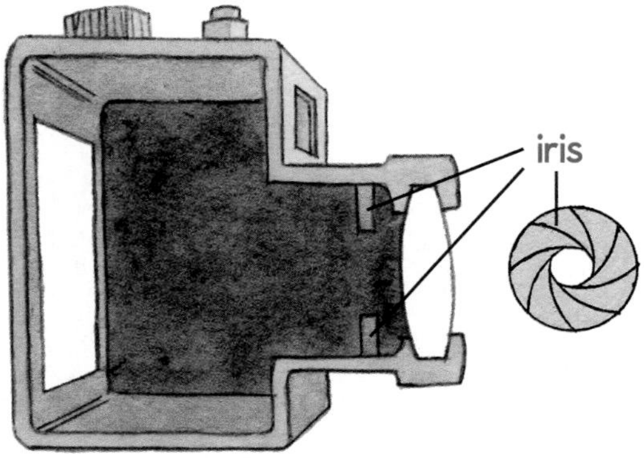

PICTURE 4

When you're taking a picture in a dark place, a larger hole lets in enough light for a good picture. The iris can open up and make a large hole like this.

PICTURE 5

When you're taking a picture in a very bright place, the iris can close down and make a very small hole like this.

PICTURE 6

The small hole doesn't let too much light reach the film.

The eye works the same way. When it's dark out, the iris makes the pupil larger. That large hole lets in a lot of light.

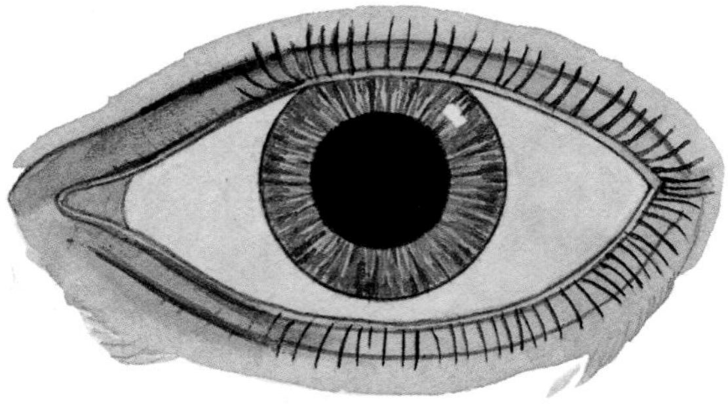

PICTURE 7

When it's bright out, the iris makes the pupil very small. The small hole prevents too much light from hitting the retina.

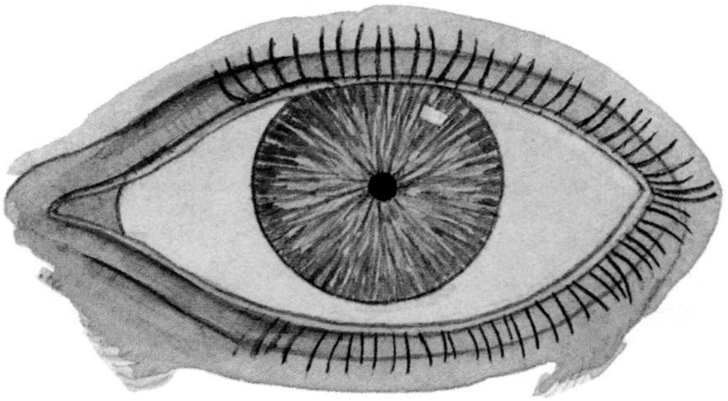

PICTURE 8

The parts of a camera are easy to remember if you remember the parts of an eye. Both the eye and the camera have a lens. Both the eye and the camera have an iris. Both have a part where the picture forms.

C A Trip to the South Pole

Al, Angela and the old man were in the dark cold water below the North Pole. They had gone down from the surface of the snow until they had reached the water.

The old man said, "We have seen one pole. Now let's go to the other pole. But before we do . . ."

Al and Angela no longer seemed to be underwater. A model of the sun and the earth appeared in front of them. The old man said, "Look at the globe and tell me what season it is at the North Pole."

Angela quickly answered.

The old man pointed to the South Pole. "When the North Pole tilts away from the sun, the South Pole tilts . . ."

"Toward the sun," Al said, pointing to it.

Angela said, "That means the South Pole is on the half of the earth that is in sunlight all the time."

"Correct," the old man said. "Look at the model of us standing on the South Pole as the earth turns around and around."

Al and Angela watched. The models of three tiny people were standing on the South Pole. As the globe turned around and around, the three tiny people remained on the half of the globe that was in the sunlight.

The old man said, "Now we will go to the South Pole. But the earth will be spinning around hundreds of times faster than it usually spins."

Suddenly, things started to get brighter and brighter. Al could see that he was standing on snow. He could see the sun. It was just above the horizon. The air was very cold.

Al quickly observed that the sun was moving. But it was not coming up and it was not setting. It was just moving in a great circle along the horizon. Soon it had gone in a full circle and was starting another circle.

The old man said, "Remember, the earth is spinning very fast. If the earth was spinning at its regular speed, it would take 24 hours for the sun to make a full circle. You just saw it make a circle in only a few seconds."

"Amazing," Angela exclaimed. "The sun just moves around and around the horizon."

"Correct," the old man said. "It makes one full circle every 24 hours."

The old man continued, "Do you want to see how deep the snow is at the South Pole?"

"Sure," Angela said. "And I know just what's going to happen. We're going to go down 70 feet. And then we'll be in the ocean, because there is no land under the South Pole."

"Let's see if you are right," the old man said.

Al and the others started sinking down and down into the packed snow—for over a mile.

And then—Al, Angela and the old man were going through rock.

Angela said, "I was wrong. There is land under the South Pole."

"Correct," the old man said. "There is no land under the North Pole, but there is a great mass of land under the South Pole."

"How big is the mass of land under the South Pole?" Angela asked.

The old man replied, "Think of a square that is one mile on each side. That's a large square."

The old man continued. "Now think of a thousand squares that big."

As Al was trying to think about a place that big, the old man continued. "Now think of five million squares that big. That's how big the land under the South Pole is."

Angela said, "Five million square miles. That's incredible."

D Number your paper from 1 through 24.

1. Name the part of the eye where pictures are formed.
2. Name what's inside the camera where pictures are formed.
3. What part of a camera bends the light that goes through it?
4. What part of an eye is like the lens of a camera?
5. What part of a camera lets just enough light into the camera?
6. What part of an eye is like the iris of a camera?
7. A camera lens bends light that goes through it because the lens is ______.
   - straight • big • curved
8. If you're taking a picture where it's very bright, you would set the iris of a camera so the hole is ______.
   - large • small
9. If you're taking a picture where there is very little light, you would set the iris so the hole is ______. large

10. Which iris is right for taking a picture in a bright place?

A B

11. Which iris sees well in a bright place?

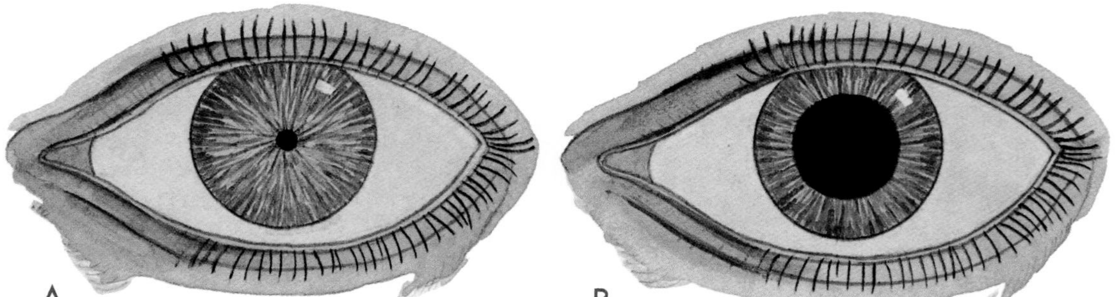

A B

12. Which iris is right for taking a picture in a dark place?

A

B

13. Which iris sees well in a dark place?

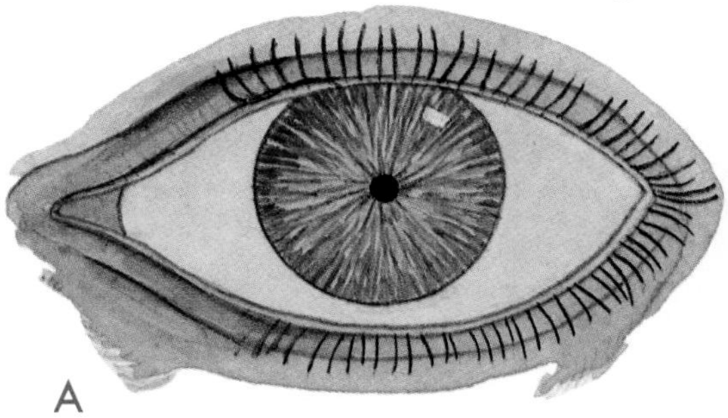

A

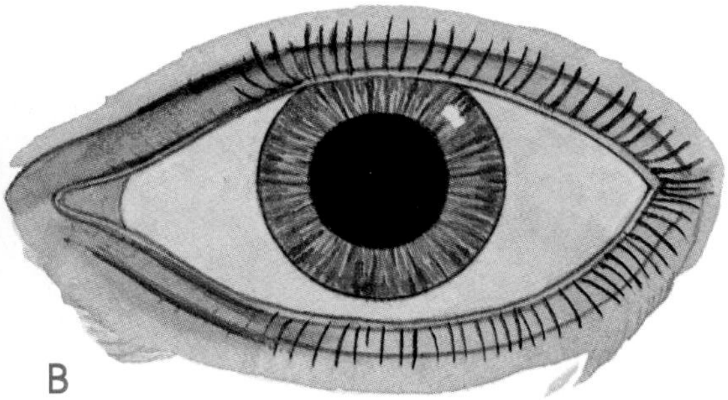

B

Skill Items

Write the word from the box that means the same thing as the underlined part of each sentence.

decorated	noon	permitted	chamber
protected	midnight	relaxed	window

14. The bell rang at 12 o'clock at night.
15. They took it easy at the beach.
16. The TV was in a special room.

Review Items

17. What is the chamber inside the ear shaped like?
18. What is the inside of the ear's chamber lined with?
19. Do any two snowflakes look **exactly** alike?
20. All snowflakes are the same because they all have ____ spokes.
21. About how deep is the snow at the North Pole?
22. What is under the snow at the North Pole?
23. How much land is under the snow at the North Pole?
24. Which would be harder, snow that is **40 feet below** the top of a pile or snow that is **20 feet below** the top of the pile?

A

1	2	3
1. gorilla	1. sweater	1. curb
2. leopard	2. camp	2. party
3. porpoise	3. snowstorm	3. Scott
4. doorbell	4. Johnson	4. titled
	5. spun	5. crept

B

A Book About the Poles

The trip to the poles was nearly over and Al was trying to remember everything he had seen. He was thinking about what was under each of the poles. He thought about how deep the snow was at the poles. He reminded himself about which pole has daylight all the time when the North Pole tilts away from the sun. His mind went over the facts that he had learned about snowflakes.

Suddenly everything started to grow dark, and Al realized that he was back in the store on Anywhere Street.

Through the darkness the old man said, "Go anywhere. See anything. Pay for your trip by passing a test on what you see."

"We'll be back tomorrow to take the test," Angela said.

"Good," the old man replied.

Then the inside of the store grew very quiet. The old man had disappeared.

"Let's go," Al said.

Angela opened the door. The bell went ding, ding. Outside, the snow was very deep and new snow was starting to fall. The snow on the sidewalk in front of the store was above Al's knees.

Angela said, "It's amazing to look at all this snow and realize that no two snowflakes are exactly the same."

Al and Angela started wading through the snow to the corner of Anywhere Street. And as soon as they went around the corner, Al could hear the sound of Christmas songs and could see people on the sidewalk. Cars in the street were moving very slowly through the snow.

One car near the curb was stuck in the snow. The driver was trying to move the car. "Wzzzzzz." The tires spun around and around, but the car did not move forward.

The driver rolled down the window and called to Al and his sister, "Can you give me a hand? I'm late and I've got to get home."

"Sure thing," Angela said.

As she and Al got behind the car, she said, "When I count to three, push hard."

Al got set. "One . . . two . . . three." Al pushed as hard as he could. The tires went "wzzzzzz." But Al's feet slipped out from under him and the car did not move.

"Let's try it again," Angela said. "One . . . two . . . three." This time Al's feet did not slip. He pushed. Angela pushed. The car tires went "wzzzzzz," and the car started to move forward.

"Wzzzzzz." Now the car was moving a little faster—three feet, six feet, nine feet. The car crept along, almost stopping. "Wzzzzzz." Push, push! Now the car started moving faster and faster as it got into the tracks that other cars had made. The driver drove to the next corner, pulled over and stopped.

"Hey," he called, and motioned to Al and Angela.

They ran over to the car. The driver handed each of them a five-dollar bill. "Thanks a lot," he said. "Today's my wife's birthday and I can't be late for the party."

"Wow!" Angela said. "Thanks a lot."

"Yeah, thanks," Al said.

The car drove away. Al was out of breath. He stood there for a moment breathing hard and trying to catch his breath. Suddenly he felt very strange, almost the way he felt on trips with the old man. People walked by on the sidewalk. The sound of Christmas songs came from the stores. Soft snowflakes fell against Al's face and melted. As Al stood there, a new thought came to him. If only he had some more money, he would be able to buy Christmas presents for his sister and his mother.

"Come on," Angela said. "We'd better get home."

As they walked on the packed snow, Al kept thinking, "If only I had some more money, I would be able to buy Christmas presents."

The snow in front of Al's house was almost two feet deep. It didn't look as if Al and Angela had shoveled the walk the other day. They waded through the snow and went up the front steps. Their mother called from the kitchen. "Take your boots off and leave them in the hall."

They took off their boots. Then they brushed the snow from their jackets, hung them up and walked into the kitchen.

"Where have you been?" their mother asked. "You shouldn't be out in weather like this. They say that this is the worst snowstorm we've had in twenty years."

"It's pretty bad," Al said. "And it's still snowing out there. In fact, it's snowing harder than ever."

"Did you hear what they said about school on the radio?" his mother asked.

"No."

"They said that the schools will be closed tomorrow. And you start your Christmas vacation the day after tomorrow. So it looks as if your vacation has already started."

Al smiled, but he didn't hate school the way he had hated it before he started going to the old man's store. He had always been glad when the school closed, but he wasn't so glad now. He actually liked going to school. Why not? He was now good at schoolwork.

Al ate supper. Just after he finished eating, the doorbell rang.

"I'll get it," Al said, and went to the door.

A mailman was standing in the doorway, covered with snow. "I have a package for Al Johnson and Angela Johnson."

"That's us," Al said.

The man handed Al the package. Al thanked him and closed the door. Then he opened the package. A book titled *The Poles* was inside the package. Al knew who must have sent the book.

He sat down with Angela and started to look through the book. The first part told about people who had tried to reach the poles.

This part of the book told about interesting adventures. The people on a ship named *Endurance* had an incredible adventure trying to get to the South Pole. The ship became trapped in the ice. It drifted over five hundred miles in the ice. For nearly a year, the ship drifted. Finally the ice crushed the ship and the ship sank. But none of the men on the ship died. They all made it home.

1

The adventure of Robert Scott and four other men did not have a happy ending. They reached the South Pole. Then they started back across the mass of snow. All the men died. Fifty years later Scott's camp looked almost as it did on the day that he had left it. There was food on the tables. And the food was still good after fifty years.

C Number your paper from 1 through 18.

Skill Items

Here are 3 events that happened in the story. Write **beginning, middle** or **end** for each event.

1. The adventure of Robert Scott and four other men did not have a happy ending.
2. Now the car started moving faster and faster as it got into the tracks that other cars had made.
3. Suddenly, everything started to grow dark, and Al realized that he was back in the store on Anywhere Street.

Troops of baboons moved across the veld.

4. What word refers to **groups** of baboons?
5. What word names a large member of the monkey family?
6. What word refers to a large field in Africa?

Review Items

Write **toward** or **away from** for each blank.
During our winter, the North Pole tilts **7.** the sun and the South Pole tilts **8.** the sun.

Write **dark** or **light** for each blank.
During our winter, the North Pole is always **9.** and the South Pole is always **10.** .

11. Which picture shows where the paths of light will go after they go through the lens?
12. Which letter shows the film?
13. Which letter shows the lens?
14. Which letter shows the iris?

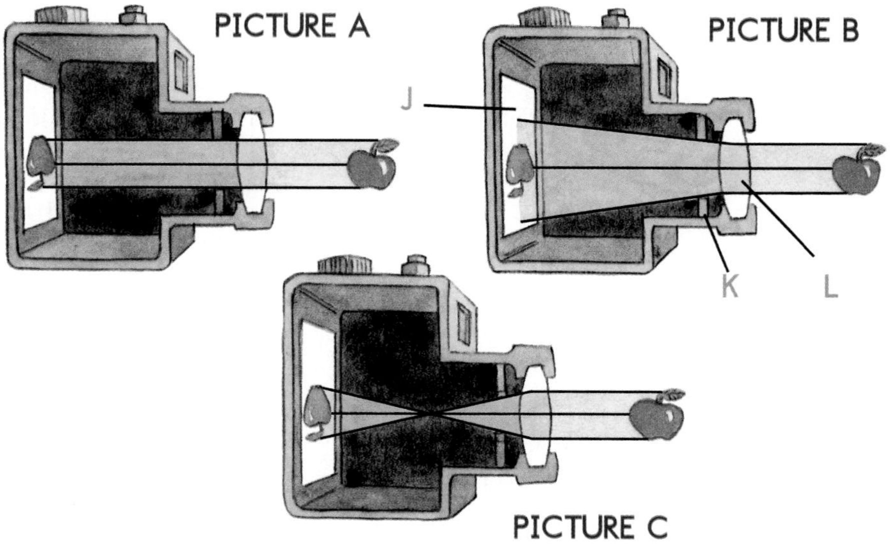

15. How many hours does it take the sun to make a full circle around a person at the North Pole?
16. What's under the snow at the North Pole?
17. How deep is the snow at the South Pole?
18. Where is the snow deeper, at the North Pole or at the South Pole?

A

1	2
1. gorilla	1. sabers
2. sweaters	2. history
3. wallet	3. leopard
4. porpoise	4. quick
	5. slices
	6. baboon

B

Animals

Here are some of the animals you are going to read about in later lessons.

The baboon is a very smart animal that lives in large groups called **troops.**

A gorilla looks something like a baboon but it is much bigger and stronger and has no tail.

A leopard is in the same family as lions and tigers. A leopard has spots.

It is no bigger than a big dog, but it is very strong and very quick.

A porpoise is in the same family as whales. All the animals in that family are warm-blooded. Some people think that the porpoise is the smartest animal in that family.

The saber-toothed tiger no longer lives on Earth. It had teeth that stuck out like sabers or swords. It lived on Earth until around 25 thousand years ago.

C

Angela and Al Buy Christmas Presents

Al looked out of the window the next morning. He couldn't see anything but snow through the window.

He went into the kitchen. His mother was setting the table. "What are you going to do today?" she asked.

"I don't know," Al said. "I thought I'd go to the library and read another book about the poles."

His mother said, "The library is closed. Most of the stores are closed. Almost everything is closed."

After breakfast Al whispered to Angela, "I wonder whether the old man's store would be open today."

"Let's see," she replied.

They put on their boots and heavy coats. As they were going outside, their mother said, "Come home before lunch time."

"Okay, Mom," they replied as they walked out the door.

Christmas songs still came from some of the stores. But there weren't many people on the streets. Al listened to the songs and started thinking about Christmas again. If only he had a few more dollars . . .

Angela and Al turned the corner at Anywhere Street and then they both stopped. The snow had been shoveled in front of all the buildings except one. The only building that had snow in front of it was the old man's store. And the snow in front of the store was over three feet deep.

"That sure is strange," Angela said.

Al and Angela walked through the snow in front of the old man's store. They opened the door. "Ding, ding." Plop—a great pile of snow fell inside. Al looked up and saw the old man standing right in front of them, holding a big snow shovel.

"Go anywhere. See anything. But first shovel my walk. I will pay you."

"You don't have to pay us," Al said.

"If you shovel my walk, I will pay you," the old man replied.

Al shoveled until he was tired. Then Angela shoveled. Then Al shoveled again.

At last the walk was shoveled. Angela and Al went inside. "Ding, ding." The old man was waiting for them. He handed two dollars to Angela and two dollars to Al.

The old man said, "Take the money to the store next door and buy your Christmas presents."

Al said, "I don't have enough money with me. I only have two dollars."

"What do you want to buy?" the old man asked.

Al whispered to the old man so that Angela wouldn't hear. "I want to buy a toaster for my mother and a wallet for my sister. But I don't have enough money with me. I only have two dollars."

The old man said, "Take your two dollars to the store next door and buy the gifts. I want Angela to stay with me while you shop."

Al was puzzled as he went to the store next door. Inside that store, a bell went ding, ding. One wall of the store was filled with wallets. There were wallets of every size and every shape. There were brown wallets and white wallets and pink wallets and black wallets. Al figured that there must have been more than two hundred wallets on that wall.

And the other wall was covered with toasters. There were big toasters and little toasters. There were silver toasters, gold toasters, red toasters. There were toasters for two slices of bread, for three slices of bread, for four slices of bread and even for eight slices of bread.

And that's all there was in the whole store—toasters and wallets.

A little old man came out of the back. "You will find anything you want in this store—as long as you want a toaster or a wallet." The old man laughed so hard that Al thought he would fall over. "What can I sell you? All wallets cost one dollar. All toasters cost one dollar. What do you want to buy?"

Al said, "That's wrong. Toasters cost a lot more than one dollar. So do those wallets."

The old man looked very angry. "This is my store," he said. "Don't tell me how much things should cost in this store."

Al picked out a big toaster and a beautiful pink wallet with many plastic windows and a secret pocket for money.

After Al came back to the old man's store, Angela went to the store next door. While she was gone, Al talked to the old man. When she came back, she said, "That's the strangest store I have ever seen. It had nothing but books and women's sweaters." Al had a pretty good idea of what he was going to get from Angela for Christmas.

D Number your paper from 1 through 20.

Skill Items

Use the words in the box to write complete sentences.

message	veld	baboons	control	troops
horizon	pulse	hollow	bedroom	single

1. A ___ star was near the ___.
2. ___ of ___ moved across the ___.

3. What is animal A?
4. What is animal B?
5. What is animal C?
6. What is animal D?
7. What is animal E?

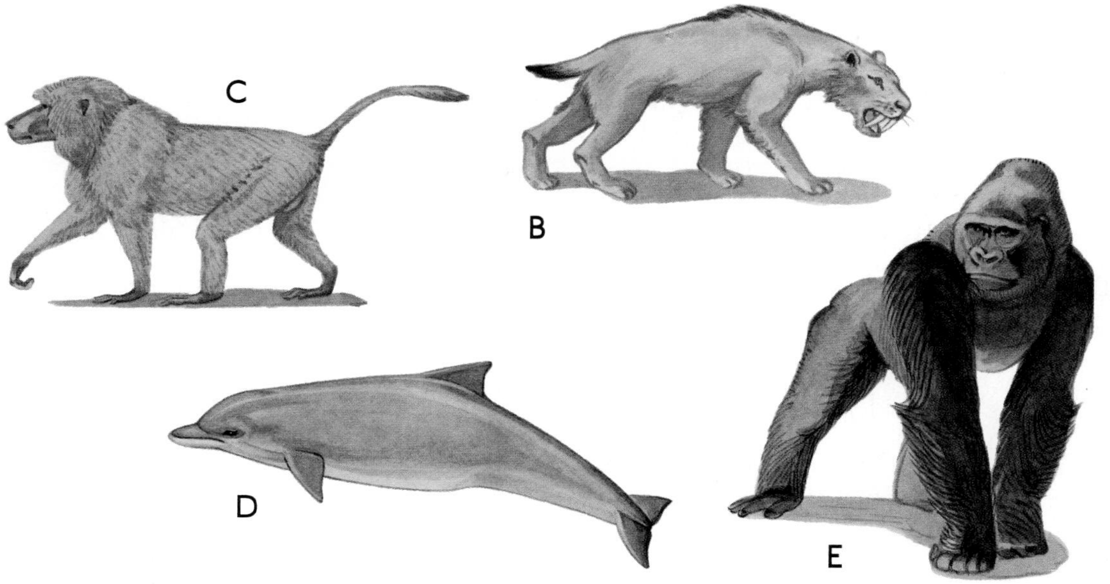

Review Items

8. How many hours does it take the sun to make a full circle around a person at the North Pole?
9. The ship named *Endurance* was stuck in ice at the _____.
10. What happened to Scott and the men with him?
11. What season do we have when the North Pole tilts **toward** the sun?
12. What season do we have when the North Pole tilts **away from** the sun?
13. During what season is it dark at the North Pole?
14. How cold does it often get during that season?
    - 200 degrees below zero
    - 100 degrees below zero
    - 60 degrees below zero

15. If you're taking a picture where it's very bright, you would set the iris of the camera so the hole is _____.

    • big • small

16. If you're taking a picture where there is very little light, you would set the iris of the camera so the hole is _____.

17. What's part A?
18. What's part B?
19. Write the letter of the part that shows a picture of what the eye sees.
20. Write the letter of the part that bends the light.

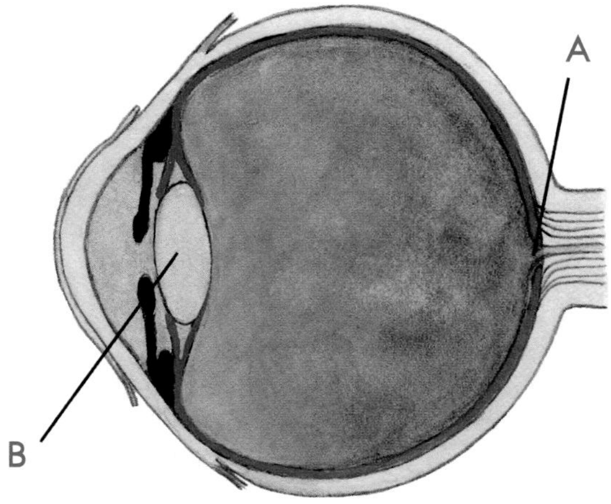

A

1

1. Plateosaurus
2. enemies
3. extend
4. history
5. typed
6. screen
7. known

B Angela and Al Go to the Library

Al and Angela were inside the old man's store. Al felt excited about the presents he had bought. He had almost forgotten that he and Angela had to take a test on their last trip.

The old man asked them many questions. Al and Angela answered all of them.

Then the old man said, "You have passed the test. But this is your last trip. I cannot take you on any more trips."

"Why not?" Al asked. "Didn't we do a good job on the tests?"

"You did a wonderful job," the old man said. Then he put his arms around Angela and Al.

The old man continued, "You don't need the trips anymore. When you first came to me, you needed to see things. You needed to learn about the world. And you needed to learn that it is fun to learn. Now you have learned these things, so you no longer need the trips. You have learned how to take a trip by reading books."

The room was silent. Al and Angela stood there looking at the old man. Al didn't know what to say. The trips were the most exciting things in Al's life. But maybe the old man was right. Al had read the book about the poles. He had learned things that he had not seen on his trip to the poles. And when Al had read the book, he had almost felt as if he was on a trip.

The old man said, "Since this is our last trip, let me choose where we will go."

"Sure," Angela said. She sounded sad.

The old man said, "Good. We will take a trip into the world of books."

Slowly the room got brighter. The walls seemed to melt. Rows and rows of books started to appear. Al realized that he and Angela were in a library—a very large library.

The old man said, "There are over three million books in this library. Think of it—over three million books. And think of how those books got here. They didn't fall out of the sky like snowflakes. Somebody wrote every book that is here. And many of these books are very, very old. Some were written by people who lived over two thousand years ago."

"Think of it," the old man said, waving his arms. "In this building is nearly everything that we have learned about our world and the things in it. The books in this building tell about science. They tell nearly everything that is known about arithmetic, and they tell about history. They tell what is known about every place in the universe from the galaxies to the bottom of the sea. They tell about music and art and about the human brain. They tell how to train your dog or how to build a rocket. And they tell almost every story that people have ever told—good stories, bad stories, old stories and new stories."

As the old man walked across the library, his shoes went "clack, clack, clack" on the floor. The old man walked into a room with rows of computers. The old man said, "And here is the brain of the library. Name anything that you want to read about. Name anything at all."

Angela said, "I like to read about all of the different kinds of animals."

"Animals," the old man said and typed the word **animals** in the computer.

Some facts appeared on the computer screen. The old man said, "The computer tells us that there are over three thousand books on animals. If you wish, the computer will list all the titles. Or you can give the computer more information about the kinds of animals you are interested in."

Angela said, "Well, I don't really care that much. I like all . . ."

Before she could finish her sentence, the old man said, "I will select some titles for you."

The old man quickly pressed some keys on the computer keyboard. Then he said, "Our books will be here in a moment."

The old man stood up and walked over to a small door in the wall. Suddenly a light over the door went on. The old man opened the door and there was a pile of books inside.

The old man picked them up and carried them over to a table. He picked up a book titled *Animals in Africa* and handed it to Al. The old man said, "Start reading for us and we'll go on a new kind of trip."

Al picked up the book and started to read.

C Number your paper from 1 through 23.

Review Items

1. Which iris is right for taking a picture in a dark place?

D

E

2. Which iris sees well in a dark place?

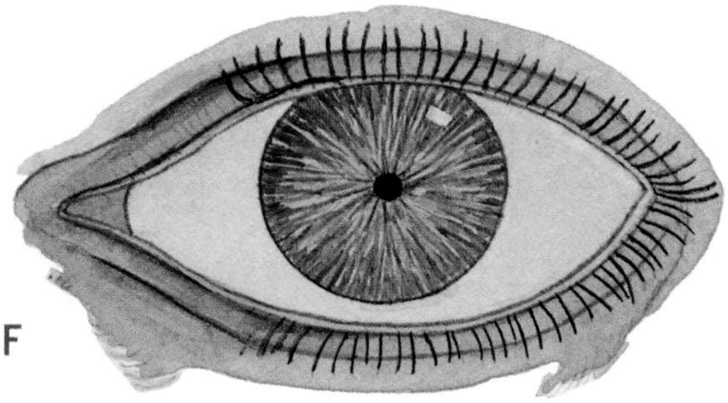

F

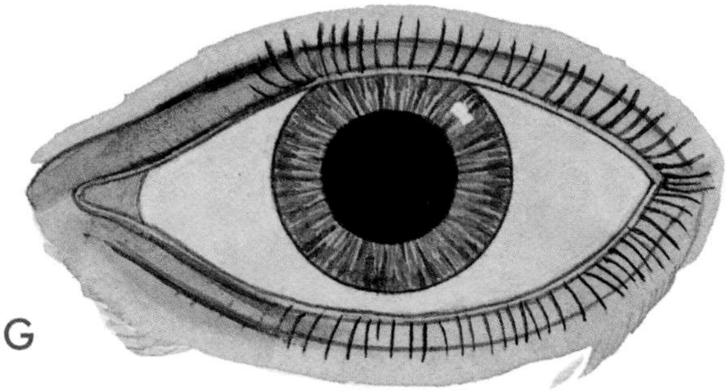

G

3. What is part A?
4. What is part B?

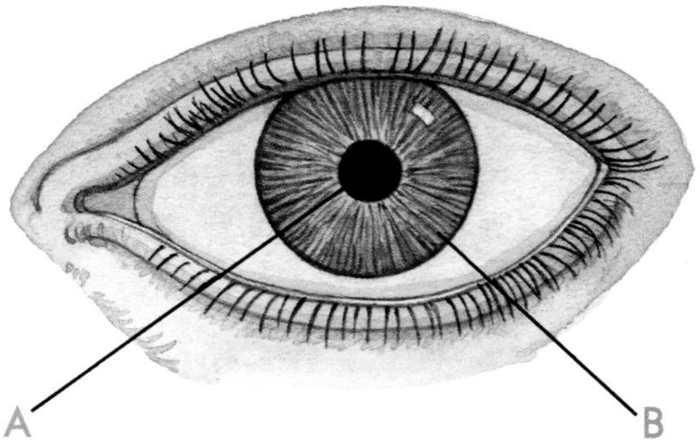

5. What's under the snow at the North Pole?
6. About how deep is the snow at the South Pole?
7. Where is the snow deeper, at the North Pole or at the South Pole?

8. What are groups of baboons called?
9. Name an animal that looks something like a baboon but is much bigger.
10. Name an animal in the cat family that is the size of a big dog.
11. Name an animal in the whale family that many people think is the smartest.
12. About how long ago did saber-toothed tigers disappear from the earth?
13. Which pole is at the top of the earth?
14. Which pole is at the bottom of the earth?

15. How many miles does light travel in one second?
16. What else travels as fast as light?

17. Which letter shows the part of the earth where it is night?
18. Which letter shows the part of the earth where it is daytime?

Write which season each Earth shows.

22.

19.

21.

20.

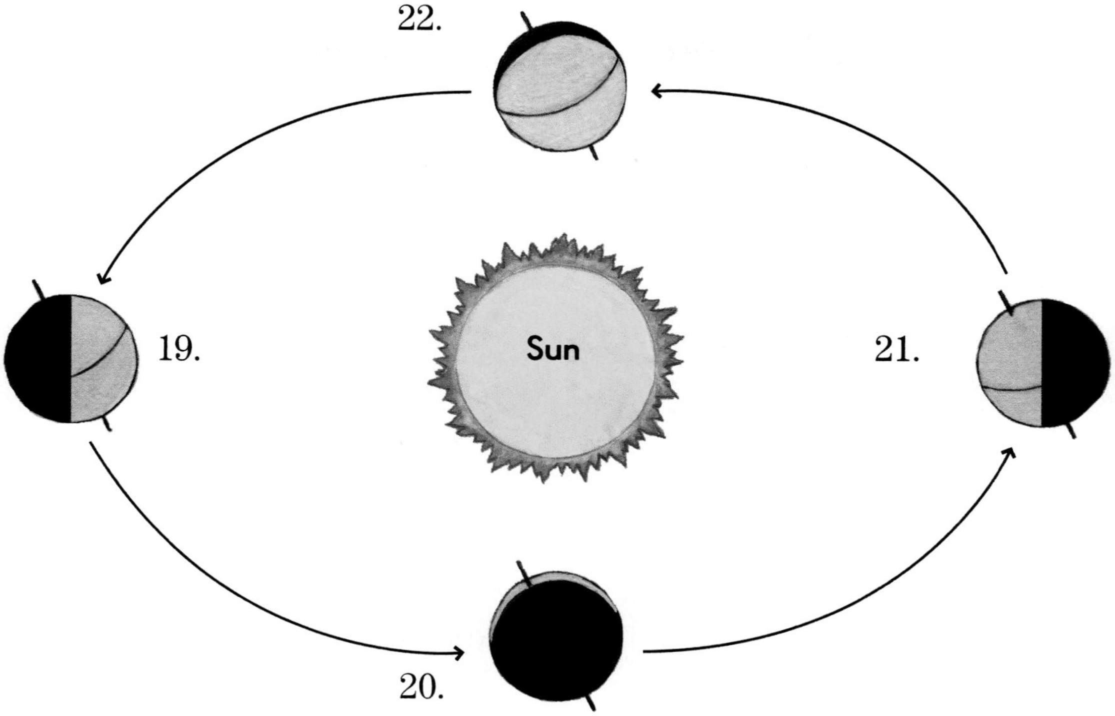

23. How much daylight is there during winter at the North Pole?

137

A

1	2
1. extends	1. era
2. giraffes	2. flat-topped
3. barks	3. next-smartest
4. enemies	4. Plateosaurus
	5. Africa

B

Angela and Al Read About Baboons

Al read the first page of the book about animals in Africa.

> Africa has a wet season and a dry season. You are in Africa during the dry season. You are on the veld. The veld is a great field of grass that extends for many miles. The veld is dry and hot and the sun is burning down on you. In the distance you can see bright blue mountains and trees with flat tops. You can also see many animals moving in long lines. They are walking to a water hole. You see a troop of baboons. You see a group of giraffes. You see a group of lions. And you see many other groups of animals.

As Al sat there in the library, he started to feel as if he was going on a trip. He could almost feel the sun and see the flat-topped trees.

Al read the first part of the next page.

> Leopards and monkeys drink from the water hole at the same time.
>
> The leopards do not kill the monkeys at the water hole because the animals come to drink, not to fight or kill. So all day long the animals wait their turn at the water hole. They drink and then they slowly walk away across the veld.

Now Angela read part of the page.

The veld has not changed much in a million years or more, but some of the animals that wait their turn at the water hole have changed. At one time the saber-toothed tiger waited in line.

Suddenly the old man took the book from Angela and said, "Perhaps you will want to come back and read the rest of this book."

Angela said, "Yes, I would like to continue reading this book right now."

The old man said, "Not now. But you can come back to the library sometime. The book is here waiting for you to read it and take you on a trip to Africa. It will teach you about many things you have never seen before."

The old man put the book down on the table and picked up another book from the pile. The title of this book was *How Animals Learn.* The old man opened the book to the first page. He said, "I will read to you." He read:

Everyone agrees that humans are smarter than other animals. Humans can do more than the other animals and humans can learn more. But which animal is the next-smartest? Some people say it is the porpoise. Others say that it is the gorilla. But I believe the baboon is the next-smartest animal.

Observe a troop of baboons. The troop is like a large family and it has many enemies—lion and leopards. So the troop has to be very smart and careful. The troop has lookouts who sit on high cliffs and watch for danger.

We see three lookouts. One is on the top of the cliff. The two other lookouts are about halfway down the cliff. There is something moving above one of the lookouts. It is a baby baboon who is sneaking up behind the lookout. The lookout turns and looks at the baby baboon. Then the lookout turns away, pretending that he does not see the baby. The baby baboon stands up on a rock just above the lookout and leaps onto the lookout.

The lookout is strong enough to kill a leopard with his hands. But the lookout falls down.

"Ahhh, ahhh," he cries and pretends that he is hurt.

The baby baboon jumps on the lookout again. "Eeeeee," the baby calls.

"Ahhh," the lookout cries.

The lookout plays with the baby baboon for a few minutes. Then the lookout sits up and barks at the baby. The baby stops playing. The lookout barks again and then slaps the baby on its behind. The baby runs away back to the troop.

"Wow!" Angela said. "That baboon was playing with the baby just like a human plays with a baby."

"Correct," the old man said.

The old man handed the book to Al. "Why don't you read a little to us?" the old man said.

Al read:

Let's do something to see just how smart baboons are. Let's put some food inside a

wooden box that is about a foot wide and a foot high. That box is very strong. We put the box out in the field near the troop.

One of the larger baboons comes up to the box and smells it. Then he calls out. Other baboons come over to the box. One starts biting at a corner of the box.

A second baboon pushes the first baboon away. The second baboon starts biting at a corner of the box.

The biggest baboon says, "Uhhhaaa, raaah." He picks up a large rock. He stands next to the box and holds the rock over his head with both hands.

He throws the rock at the box very hard. The other baboons watch for a moment. Then they pick up rocks and start throwing them at the box. Soon the box starts to break.

One of the baboons reaches inside the box and grabs a small piece of food. He quickly puts the food in his mouth. The biggest baboon hits this baboon. No other baboon tries to eat the food. They carry the food back to the troop.

The baboons used rocks as tools for opening the box. An animal must be very smart to use tools.

The old man said, "We don't have time to read more from that book."

"Too bad," Al said. "That was interesting. I never thought of a rock as a tool before."

Angela said, "I'd like to read more about baboons."

The old man said, "Come back to the library and read about them. There are a lot of books about baboons."

C Number your paper from 1 through 22.

Review Items

1. Do any two snowflakes look **exactly** alike?
2. All snowflakes are the same because they all have [redacted] spokes.
3. Which would be harder, snow that is 10 meters below the top of a pile or snow that is 15 meters below the top of the pile?
4. What part of a camera bends the light that goes through it?
5. What part of a camera lets just enough light into the camera?

6. Which picture shows where the paths of light will go after they go through the lens?
7. Which letter shows the iris?
8. Which letter shows the lens?
9. Which letter shows the film?

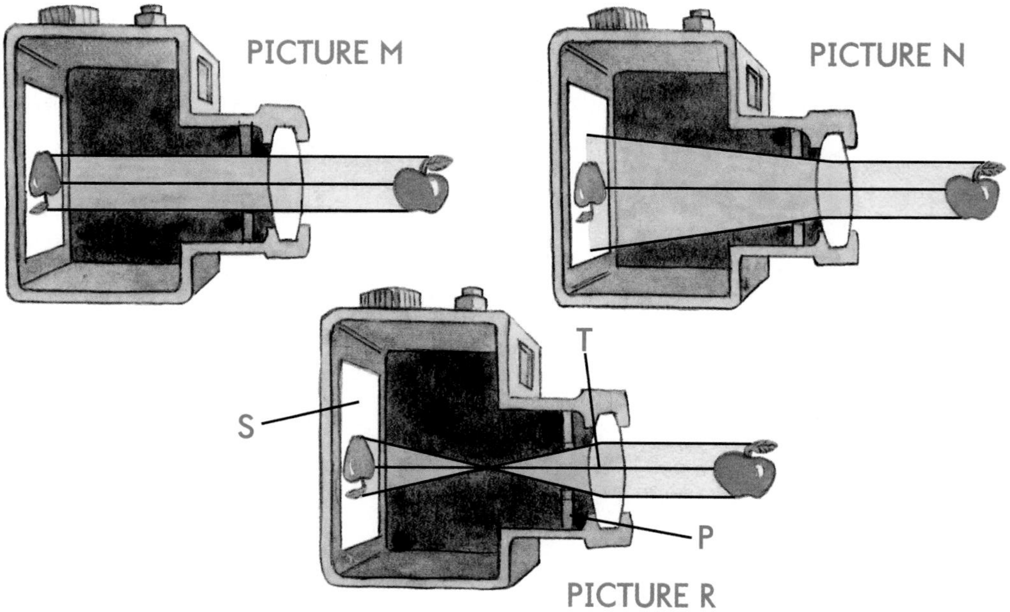

Write **toward** or **away from** for each blank.
During our winter, the North Pole tilts 10. the sun and the South Pole tilts 11. the sun.

12. How many hours does it take the sun to make a full circle around a person at the North Pole?

13. What's part X?
14. What's part Y?
15. Write the letter of the part that bends the light.
16. Write the letter of the part that shows a picture of what the eye sees.

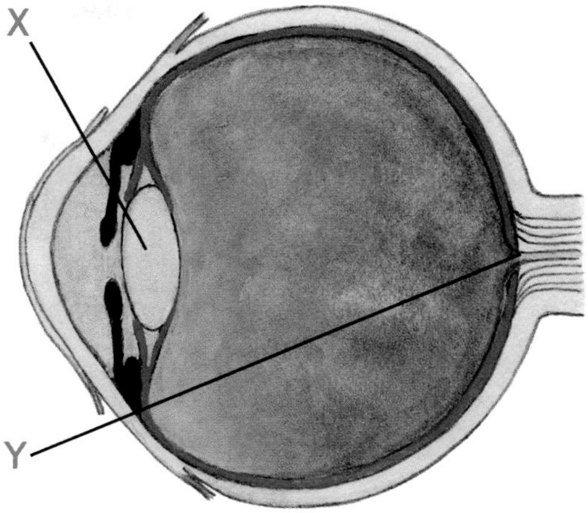

17. When you dive down 33 feet, you have ___ times the pressure on you that you have at the surface.
18. When you dive down 66 feet, you have ___ times the pressure on you that you have at the surface.
19. When you teach animals to work for new rewards, do you change the reward **quickly** or **slowly?**
20. When you teach an animal to work for a new reward, what kind of reward do you start with?
21. Then what do you do to that reward?
22. When do you stop changing the reward?

138

A

1	2
1. dragonflies	1. Plateosaurus
2. spaceships	2. rabbit
3. anytime	3. pages
4. bookstore	4. stack
5. cookbook	5. packages
	6. era

B

Angela and Al Finish Their Last Trip

Al, Angela, and the old man were in a library that had over three million books. Angela and Al had read the first few pages in two books.

The old man said, "What else do you want to read about? Where do you want to go? What do you want to see? You can go anywhere and see anything in this library."

Al said, "I always wanted to know more about dinosaurs."

So the old man went over to a computer and pressed some keys. A few minutes later the light over the little door went on. The old man opened the door, took out a pile of books and carried them to one of the tables. He announced, "This library has over six hundred books on dinosaurs. I think you'll enjoy the ones I selected."

The book on the top of the pile was *The First Dinosaurs*. The old man read the first page out loud.

> Dinosaurs lived during the Mesozoic era. The Mesozoic era started about 235 million years ago. The Mesozoic era was the time of the dinosaurs. Some dinosaurs were no bigger than a rabbit. Some ate plants. Some ate other animals. Let's go back to the beginning of the Mesozoic and look at dinosaurs that lived before Triceratops and Tyrannosaurus.

The old man read about a jungle with very strange plants, about dragonflies bigger than most birds and about bees as big as your fist.

The jungle was hot and wet and the trees and the grass were strange.

The old man read about one of the first great dinosaurs, Plateosaurus. These dinosaurs were over 20 feet long. The book had a picture of Plateosaurus.

Angela and Al took turns reading parts of other books. Every book that they started to read seemed very interesting. But the old man did not let them read very much from each book. He kept telling them, “You can find this book in your library. If you want to read it, it is there. It is waiting to take you on a trip.”

After Angela, Al and the old man had looked at books on dinosaurs, Angela said that she wanted to learn more about the planets in the solar system. She said, “I didn’t get to go on those trips.”

The old man went back to a computer. A few minutes later Angela and Al were looking at books about the solar system. Some books told about spaceships and trips to the moon. Others told about Jupiter and Saturn.

After going through the stack of books on the solar system, the old man stood up and said, “How did you like this trip? Did you like it as much as the trip to the bottom of the ocean?”

“No, I didn’t,” Al said. Angela agreed.

The old man said, “Did you like this trip as much as the trip to the poles or the human body?”

“No, I didn’t,” Angela said.

The old man smiled. Then he said, “Taking a trip from a book is not as easy as taking a real trip. You have to use your imagination to take a trip from a book. You have to think harder about what you are reading.”

The old man continued, "You can't go on real trips anymore. But you can still go back to the bottom of the sea with a book. And if you want to visit the other planets, take a trip from a book."

The old man stopped talking. The library was quiet. Al was thinking, "Maybe the trip from a book would not be as good as a real trip, but it would still be a good trip. It would be fun to take a trip to Africa and learn about the baboons. It would be fun to go back to the Mesozoic and read about Plateosaurus."

Slowly the walls of the library started to melt and everything started to become darker and darker. Al realized that he was back in the store.

The old man said, "I would like to shake your hands. I enjoyed the trips that we took together."

As the old man shook Al's hand, Al felt very sad. He wanted to say something to the old man, but he couldn't seem to talk. So he just nodded his head.

"Angela," the old man said. "I want to shake your hand, too. You're an intelligent girl and a good thinker. Just keep on learning and thinking."

As the old man shook Angela's hand, Angela nodded. Then slowly the old man stepped back into the darkness, and the inside of the store was very quiet. The old man had gone.

"Can we come back to see you sometime?" Angela asked. Her voice was high and it trembled as she talked.

There was no answer.

Angela said, "You don't have to take us on a trip. I just thought we could come back and talk to you sometime." There was no answer.

Angela and Al stood in the dark store for a long moment. Finally Al said, "He's gone."

Angela and Al picked up their packages and went outside. The bell on the door did not go ding, ding when they went outside. Angela said, "Look," and pointed to the window of the store. The sign was gone. The window was empty. Al felt very sad.

They walked past the store where they had bought the presents. "Look," Angela said. The store was empty and dark.

Angela said, "I don't understand this. Sometimes I think that I'm just having a dream. The store had lots of things in it, and now it is empty."

As Angela and Al walked home, they didn't talk very much.

It was starting to snow again. Most of the sidewalks were shoveled, but a thin layer of new snow was forming on them.

Al didn't say anything at dinner. After dinner he wrapped the presents that he had bought at the strange store. Imagine buying a beautiful toaster for only a dollar. It didn't make sense. Nothing made sense to Al on the night before Christmas.

C Number your paper from 1 through 26.

Skill Items

Write the word from the box that means the same thing as the underlined part of each sentence.

leopard	porpoise	bought	dinosaurs
history	sabers	transparent	created

1. The museum had a display of <u>swords</u>.
2. She <u>made</u> a beautiful painting.
3. We watched the <u>dolphin</u> do tricks.

Review Items

Write **dark** or **light** for each blank.
During our winter, the North Pole is ___4.___ all the time and the South Pole is ___5.___ all the time.

6. What's under the snow at the North Pole?
7. About how deep is the snow at the South Pole?
8. Where is the snow deeper, at the North Pole or at the South Pole?
9. The ship named *Endurance* was stuck in the ice at the ______.
10. What happened to Scott and the men with him?
11. What are the two kinds of seasons that Africa has?
12. What is the veld of Africa?

13. Every day during the dry season, African animals go to a place where they don't usually fight. Name that place.
14. Al and Angela read part of a book about how animals learn. Which animal did that book say is the smartest?
15. Why do troops of baboons need lookouts?

16. What is part A?
17. What is part B?

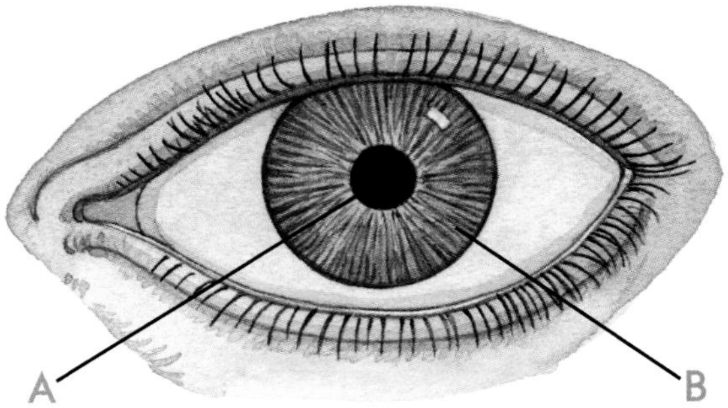

18. Which is bigger, Alaska or Japan?
19. Is Japan a **state** or a **country?**
20. How many people live in Japan?
   - 127
   - 127 million
   - 127 thousand

21. About how deep is the snow at the North Pole?
22. How much land is under the snow at the North Pole?

23. Which letter shows the South Pole?
24. Which letter shows the North Pole?

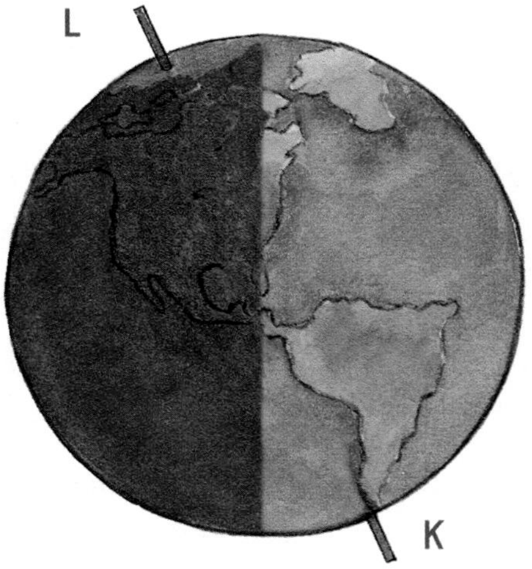

25. The arrow on the map goes from San Francisco to ______.

26. Which ocean does the arrow cross?

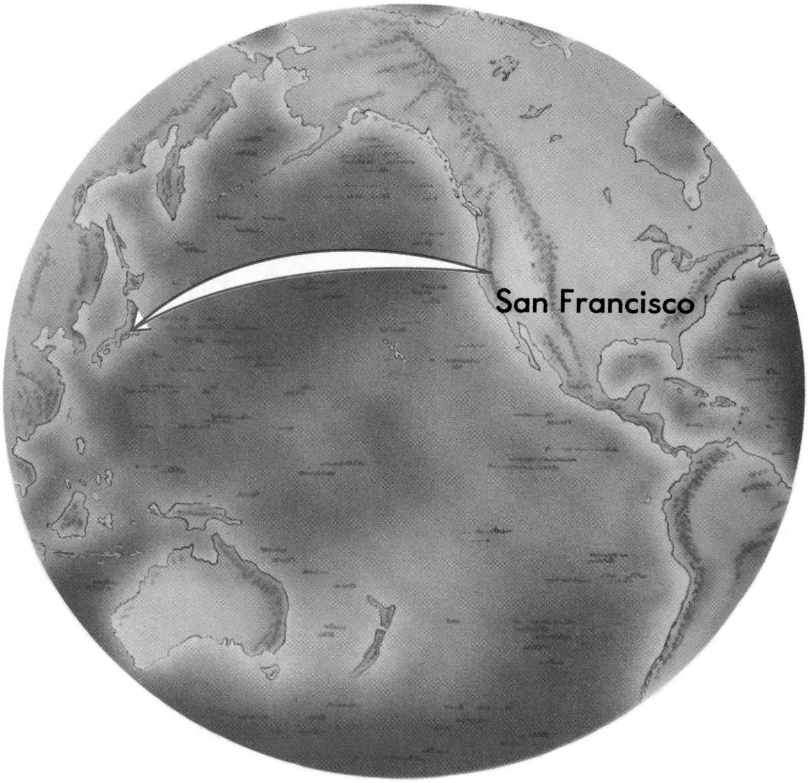

A

1

1. terrific
2. pancakes
3. cookbook
4. merry
5. bookstore
6. Anderson
7. anytime

B

Go Anywhere—See Anything With Books

Al got up early on Christmas morning. He gave the presents to his mother and Angela. His mother was so happy with the toaster that she started to cry. And Angela really liked the wallet.

Al's mother gave Al a book. She said, "We don't have much money this year, so I couldn't get you anything expensive. I noticed that you've been reading a lot of books lately, so I got you a book. I hope you like it." It was one of the books that Al had seen on his trip to the library. It was all about the animals in Africa.

"Thanks, Mama," Al said. "It's a terrific present."

After everybody had opened the presents, Al's mother fixed a big breakfast of pancakes. Al ate so many that he could hardly stand up. "I'm too full," he said.

"Me too," Angela said.

Their mother said, "I think we should go for a walk and work off our breakfast."

So everybody got dressed and went outside. It was a beautiful day. All the buildings were covered with fresh snow. They seemed to shine in the bright sunlight. Everything looked clean and white.

"Let's go this way," Al said, and pointed in the direction of the old man's store.

Soon they were walking down the street next to Anywhere Street. Angela said, "Why don't we walk down Anywhere Street?"

Al's mother said, "Anywhere Street? There's no street called Anywhere Street around here."

"Sure there is," Angela said. "It's right up there at the corner."

The street sign on the corner was covered with snow. All Al could read was the first letter in the name. It was an A.

Al said, "See—that's an A. It's the first letter in Anywhere."

Angela made a snowball and threw it at the sign. When the snowball hit the sign, the snow dropped off. Now they could read the name on the sign. But the sign did not say ANYWHERE STREET. It said ANDERSON STREET.

"I told you," their mother said. "There's no Anywhere Street in this city."

Al shook his head. He didn't know what to say.

Slowly, Al and the others started to walk down Anderson Street. The street looked a little different. Most of the stores on the street were closed. But the old man's store was open. And so was the store next to it.

Angela and Al stopped in front of the store next to the old man's store. It had many different items in the window and on the shelves. And there was a big sign in the window:

GIFT SHOP—GIFTS FOR EVERYONE.

Al said, "Wow, that's strange! The other day. . ." Al didn't finish the sentence.

Angela shrugged and smiled at Al. Then she said, "Look at the old man's store."

Al ran over to the window of the old man's store. There were two big signs in the window. One said GO ANYWHERE. SEE ANYTHING—WITH BOOKS. The other sign said BOOKSTORE.

The inside of the store looked very bright. Al could see shelves filled with books. And there was the old man sitting in a chair, reading a book.

Angela said, "Let's go inside and say hello." Before her mother could object, Angela opened the door. The bell went ding, ding.

The old man stood up and walked over to Al and the others. "Hello, hello," he said. "Go anywhere, see anything with a book. I have books that will take you to the moon or to the center of the earth. I have books on birds, books on baboons or books on bottles. Where do you want to go? What do you want to see? I have books that will take you anywhere you want to go."

"We're just looking," Al's mother said. "We don't want to buy anything."

The old man laughed. "Young woman," he said, "you are in luck. Every year I give a book to the first people who come in on Christmas Day. You are the first people here. So I will give you free books."

The old man ran over to one of the shelves and came back with a thick book. He handed the book to Al's mother. "Here is your book, young woman."

Al's mother said, "I don't read very much."

"But you will like this book."

Al's mother looked at the book.

"Oh," she exclaimed. "This is that cookbook I've been wanting for years. Oh, I can't take that. It's much too expensive."

The old man said to her, "I like to give gifts on Christmas, but I don't have a family. So you would make me very happy if you would keep the book."

Al's mother smiled. "Thank you very much," she said.

Then the old man took a great big book from the shelf. He handed the book to Al and Angela. Al read the title, *Go Anywhere. See Anything.*

The old man said, "You will really like that book. It tells all about the wonders of the world. That book will take you to places most people have never seen. It will take you to a molecule and it will take you inside the human brain. It will take you anywhere."

"Wow!" Al said.

"Thanks a lot," Angela said.

The old man talked to Al and the others for a while. Then Al's mother said, "We'd better get going. I have to cook a big Christmas dinner."

When Angela opened the door, the bell went ding, ding. The old man followed them outside. "Have a merry Christmas," he said.

Al said, "This is the best Christmas I ever had." Al felt very happy and very sad at the same time.

The old man said, "And come back and see me sometime. I have a lot of good books. Come in and read them. You don't have to buy them. Come in anytime."

"We will," Angela said.

Then they all started walking back down Anderson Street. They walked past the gift shop to the corner.

When they reached the corner, Angela turned to Al. "Did this really happen? Did we really go on all those trips? Or was it just some kind of dream?"

"I don't know," Al said. "But it sure was great. It was really great."

Later that day Al's mother fixed the best Christmas dinner Al ever had. And after dinner Angela and Al read from the book *Go Anywhere. See Anything.* It was the best book that Al had ever read. And Al had the best Christmas ever.

C Number your paper from 1 through 22.

Review Items

1. Name the part of the eye where pictures are formed.
2. If you're taking a picture where there is very little light, you would set the iris of the camera so the hole is ___.
   - small
   - big
3. If you're taking a picture where it's very bright, you would set the iris of the camera so the hole is ___.

4. Which iris sees well in a bright place?

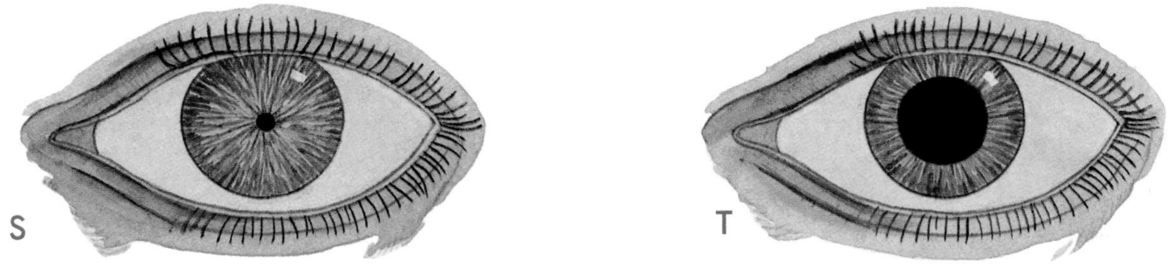

Write which season each Earth shows.

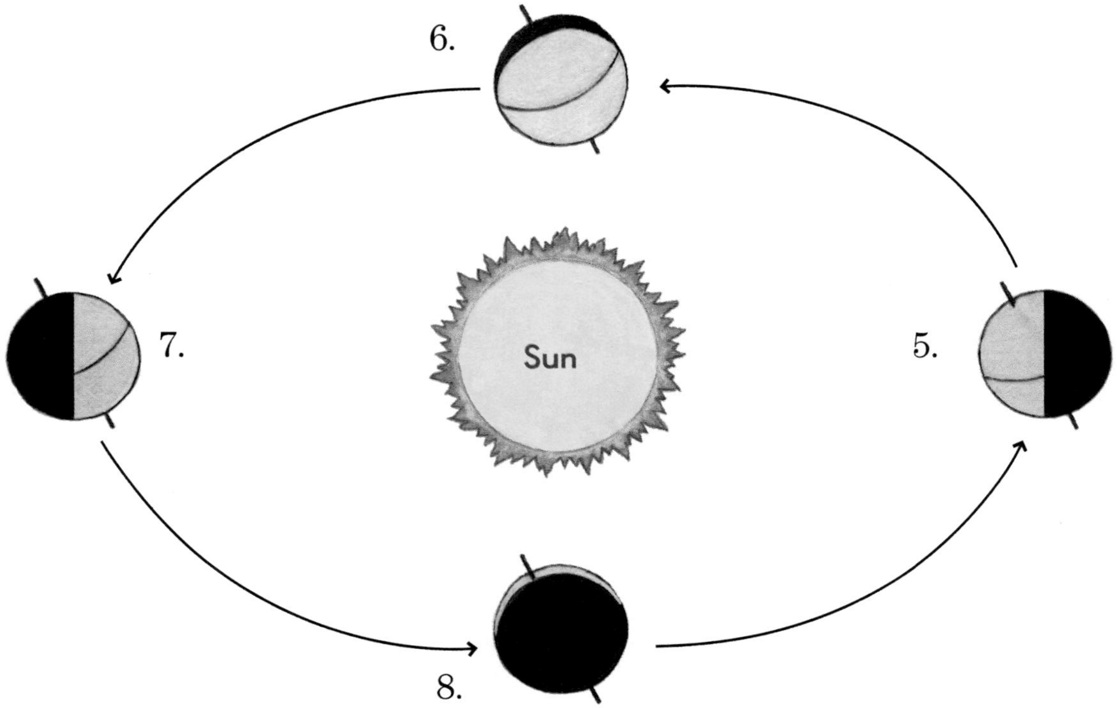

9. Name the two poles.
10. What season do we have when the North Pole tilts toward the sun?
11. What season do we have when the North Pole tilts away from the sun?
12. During what season is it dark at the North Pole?
13. How cold does it often get during that season?
    - 60 degrees
    - 60 degrees below zero
    - 100 degrees below zero

14. What is the name of the hole at the front of the eye?
15. What color is that part?
16. What part of the eye is just behind the hole?

17. What's strange about the images that are formed in your eye?
18. How long does it take light to travel from the sun to Earth?
19. How much daylight is there during winter at the North Pole?
20. The more water the glass has, the ___ the sound it makes.
    - lower
    - higher

21. Write the letter of the glass that will make the lowest ring.
22. Write the letter of the glass that will make the highest ring.

A B C D E F

140

TEST 14

Number your paper from 1 through 35.

1. About how deep is the snow at the North Pole?
2. What is under the snow at the North Pole?
3. What's under the snow at the South Pole?
4. Name the part of the eye where pictures are formed.
5. What part of a camera bends the light that goes through it?
6. What part of a camera lets just enough light into the camera?
7. If you're taking a picture where it's very bright, you would set the iris of the camera so the hole is ____.
   - large
   - small
8. If you're taking a picture where there is very little light, you would set the iris of the camera so the hole is ____.
9. What is part C?
10. What is part D?

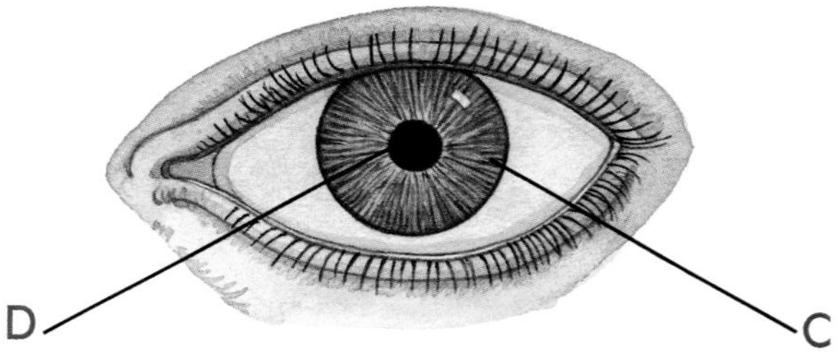

11. Name an animal in the cat family that is the size of a big dog.
12. Name an animal in the whale family that many people think is the smartest.
13. What are the 2 kinds of seasons that Africa has?
14. What is the veld of Africa?
15. Dinosaurs lived during the ____.
16. Which dinosaur lived earlier, Plateosaurus or Tyrannosaurus?
17. About how long was Plateosaurus?
18. Write 3 things that you would see in the jungle where the first dinosaurs lived.

19. Which picture shows where the paths of light will go after they go through the lens?
20. Which letter shows the film?
21. Which letter shows the lens?
22. Which letter shows the iris?

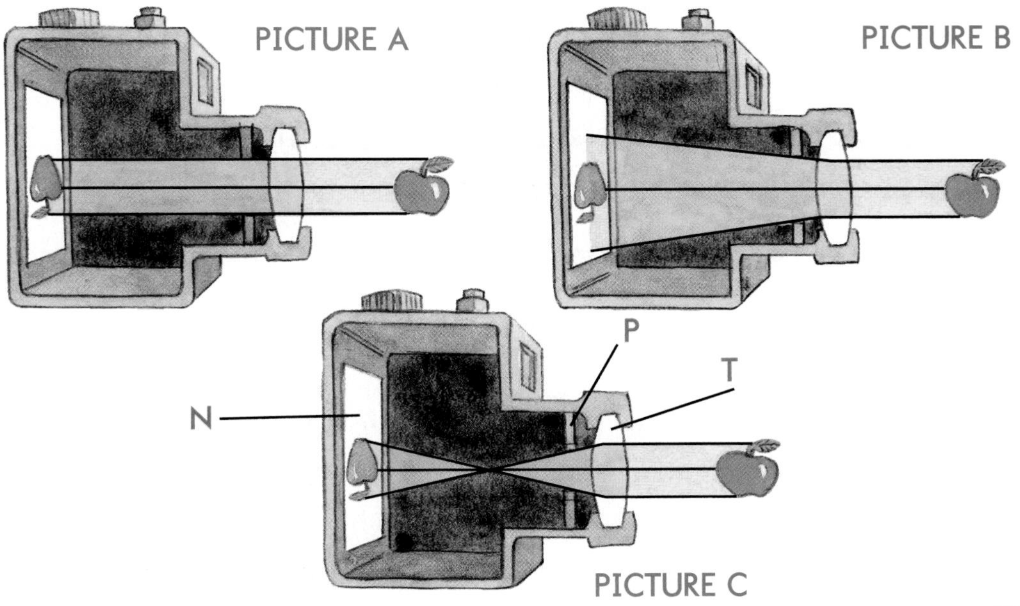

23. What is animal A?
24. What is animal B?
25. What is animal C?
26. What is animal D?
27. What is animal E?

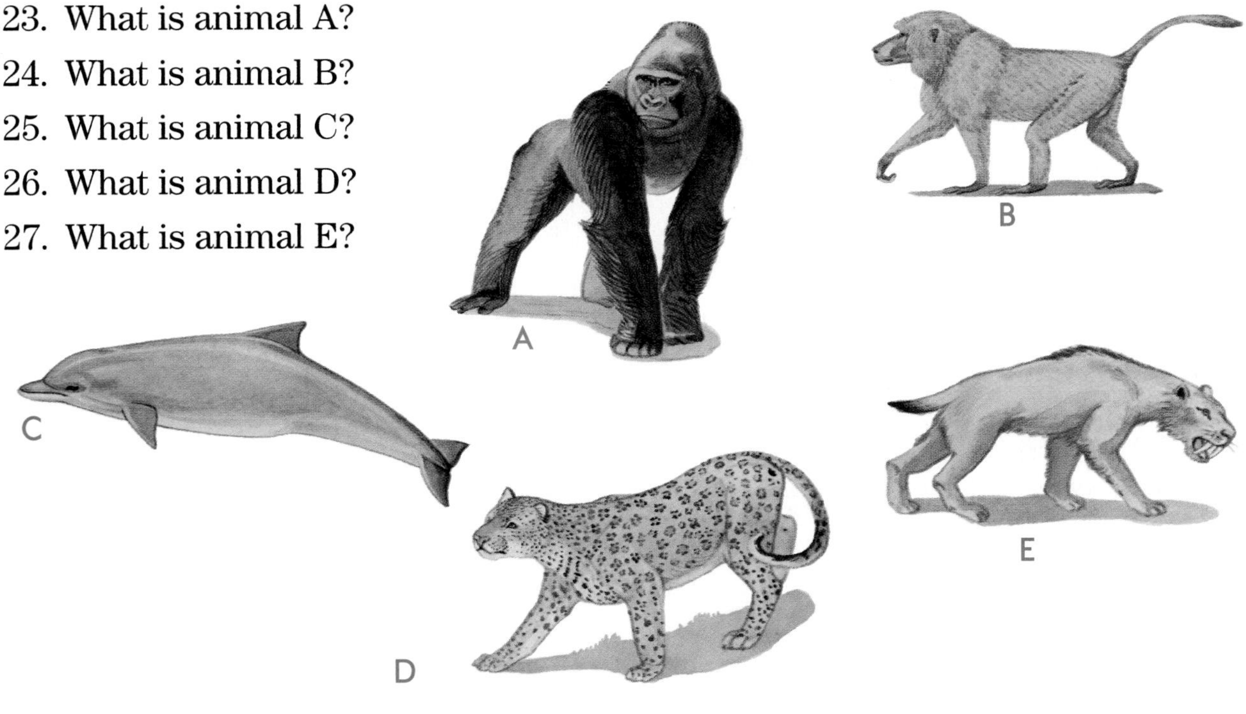

Write **toward** or **away from** for each blank.

During our winter, the North Pole tilts **28.** , the sun and the South Pole tilts **29.** the sun.

30. How many hours does it take the sun to make a full circle around a person who is at the North Pole?

Skill Items

For each item, write the underlined word or words from the sentences in the box.

A single star was near the horizon.
Troops of baboons moved across the veld.

31. What underlining refers to **groups** of baboons?
32. What underlining means **one?**
33. What underlining names large members of the monkey family?
34. What underlining names the line between the earth and the sky?
35. What underlining refers to a large field in Africa?

END OF TEST 14

SPECIAL PROJECT

Here are the last places that Al and Angela visited:

- ✦ The human body
- ✦ The poles
- ✦ The Milky Way

Pick one of those three places. Go to the library and find a book that tells about the place and that has good pictures that you could show to the class.

Find a part of the book that is very interesting. Show the class one or two pictures from that part. Tell at least three facts that the book gave about each picture you show.

Fact Game Answer Key

Lesson 80

2. a. top
   b. bottom
3. a. B
   b. C
4. a. Greeley; Denver
   b. Salt Lake City
5. a. Rocky Mountains
   b. west
6. a. slowly
   b. Idea: When it becomes a new reward
7. a. when it does the trick
   b. when it doesn't do the trick
8. a. Idea: The reward the animal will work for
   b. Idea: Slowly change it
9. A–Utah
   B–Colorado
10. lower
11. a. no
    b. Idea: It stops trying.
    c. Idea: Trying to do the trick
12. planet X

Lesson 90

2. a. skeletons
   b. reef
3. a. Idea: How deep it is
   b. barracuda
4. a. T
   b. K
5. a. Idea: It goes down.
   b. bubbles
6. a. Atlantic Ocean
   b. 1000
7. a. 2 times
   b. 3 times
8. a. bends
   b. bubbles
   c. less pressure
9. a. 1100
   b. 10 days
10. a. Alaska
    b. Anchorage
    c. Nome
11. a. no
    b. cooler
    c. dark
12. a. air
    b. Idea: The diver floats.
    c. Idea: The diver sinks.

Lesson 100

2. a. They fall off.
   b. Ideas: The dog's blood cannot circulate around the paws; the dog's ankles swell up.
3. a. even
   b. 16
4. a. Idea: Carry it on the sled to the next checkpoint
   b. 5
   c. 24, 8
5. a. Libby Riddles
   b. 1985
6. a. 2 pounds
   b. an injured dog
7. a. wheel dogs
   b. lead dogs
   c. swing dogs
8. a. haw
   b. gee
   c. mush
9. a. Susan Butcher
   b. 17
   c. 4
10. enough food for a day; a good sleeping bag; snowshoes; an ax
11. a. airplanes
    b. 50 miles
    c. usually 24
12. a. Idea: It can't run in the Iditarod.
    b. Idea: None

Lesson 110

2. a. molecules
   b. 3
3. a. gas
   b. solid
   c. liquid
4. a. Idea: Heat it.
   b. Idea: Cool it.
5. a. gas
   b. gas
6. a. 186 thousand
   b. Idea: Nothing
7. a. 5 seconds
   b. 8 minutes
8. wood, rock, glass
9. air, stream
10. a. light
    b. racing car
11. a. liquid
    b. solid
    c. gas
12. a. solid
    b. liquid
    c. gas

Lesson 120

2. a. solid
   b. Saturn
3. a. warm-blooded
   b. no
4. a. F
   b. H
5. a. triceps
   b. biceps
   c. patent
6. a. triceps
   b. biceps
7. a. gas
   b. solid
8. a. Milky Way
   b. 100 billion
9. a. gas
   b. solid
10. a. 40 feet deep
    b. 60 feet deep
11. milk, water, tea
12. A–blue whale
    B–squid
    C–killer whale

Lesson 130

2. a. feel
   b. move
3. spinal cord
4. a. retina
   b. pupil
   c. lens
5. a. 4
   b. 2
   c. 2
6. a. small
   b. big
7. a. lungs
   b. heart
   c. Idea: All parts of the body
8. a. (bright) red
   b. black
   c. lungs
9. a. 206
   b. Idea: Make the body strong and protect body parts
10. a. air; oxygen
    b. black to (bright) red
11. a. Idea: They are hollow.
    b. Idea: They are upside down.
12. a. cerebrum
    b. back

Lesson 140

2. a. Plateosaurus
   b. 20 feet
3. a. 70 feet
   b. 24
4. a. water; ice
   b. land; rock
5. a. lens
   b. iris
6. a. K
   b. H
   c. J
7. away from, toward
8. a. pupil
   b. iris
9. a. small
   b. big
10. A–baboon
    B–porpoise
    C–gorilla
11. D–saber-toothed tiger
    E–leopard
12. a. wet, dry
    b. Mesozoic

VOCABULARY SENTENCES

Lessons 1–70

1. The horses became restless on the dangerous route.
2. Scientists do not ignore ordinary things.
3. She actually repeated that careless mistake.
4. The smell attracted flies immediately.
5. The rim of the volcano exploded.
6. The new exhibit displayed mysterious fish.
7. She automatically arranged the flowers.
8. They were impressed by her large vocabulary.
9. He responded to her clever solution.
10. The patent attorney wrote an agreement.
11. The applause interrupted his speech.
12. She selected a comfortable seat.
13. Without gravity, they were weightless.
14. She demonstrated how animals use oxygen.
15. Lava erupted from the volcano's crater.
16. The incredible whales made them anxious.
17. The boring speaker disturbed the audience.

VOCABULARY SENTENCES

Lesson 71–140

18. A lot of folks mobbed the cute singer.
19. The tour to the islands was a fantastic experience.
20. She will contact the person we want to hire.
21. I have confidence that we can avoid a long conversation.
22. The scuba diver and her partner surfaced near the reef.
23. The veterinarian gave the dogs a thorough examination.
24. Visibility was miserable in the fierce blizzard.
25. At midnight, he saw a familiar galaxy.
26. The crystal contained more than a billion molecules.
27. The poem they created was nonsense.
28. The squid wriggled its tentacles.
29. The triceps muscle is bigger than the biceps muscle.
30. The injury to his spinal cord paralyzed him.
31. A single star was near the horizon.
32. Troops of baboons moved across the veld.

Glossary

absolutely *Absolutely* is another word for *totally or completely.*

according If you do something that follows the rules, you do that thing *according* to the rules.

addressed When letters are *addressed* to you, they have your name and address on them.

admission The amount you pay to get into a show is the *admission* for that show.

aimlessly When you do things *aimlessly,* you don't have a plan about what you're doing.

amuse When something *amuses* a person, it makes the person laugh.

anchor An *anchor* is a weight that is attached to a boat.

Anchorage *Anchorage* is the name of a city in Alaska.

arrangements When you make *arrangements* to do something, you make a plan to do that thing.

assistant An *assistant* is somebody who helps the person who is in charge.

attractive *Attractive is* another word for *pretty.*

avoid When you *avoid* something, you stay away from that thing.

award An *award* is something you receive for doing something special.

baboon *Baboons* are a kind of monkey.

backbone The bones that run from your skull down the middle of your back are called the *backbone.*

balanced When things are *balanced* on a point, they don't tip one way or the other way.

bare When something is *bare,* it has no coverings.

barracuda A *barracuda* is a large arrow-shaped fish with sharp teeth.

beak The bill of a bird is called a *beak.*

beware *Beware* is another word for *watch out.*

biceps The *biceps* is the muscle on the front of the upper arm.

billion A *billion* is a thousand million.

blizzard A *blizzard* is a snowstorm that is windy and very cold.

blood vessel A *blood vessel* is a tube that carries blood through the body.

briskly *Briskly* means *fast and peppy.*

buoyancy device A *buoyancy device* is something a diver wears to control how buoyant the diver is underwater.

buoyant Things that are *buoyant* float.

cell *Cells* are the smallest parts of your body.

cerebrum The part of the brain that lets you think is called the *cerebrum.*

certificate A *certificate* is a paper that proves something.

challenging Another word for *very difficult* is *challenging.*

chamber Special rooms are called *chambers.*

chant When you *chant,* you say the same thing over and over.

chilly *Chilly* means *sort of cold.*

comment When you *comment* about something, you tell about that thing.

compass A *compass* is a tool that shows the directions north, south, east and west.

compete Things that *compete* with each other are in a contest with each other.

confidence When you have *confidence* about something, you are *sure* about it.

congratulate When you *congratulate* somebody, you praise the person for something the person did well.

conversation When people talk to each other about something, they have a *conversation* about that thing.

coral The shells of animals that cover rocks in the ocean are called *coral.*

courage Another word for *bravery* is *courage.*

create *Create* is another word for *make.*

cruel *Cruel* is another word for *very mean.*

crystal A *crystal* is a shiny material that has flat sides and sharp edges.

curious When you are *curious* about something, you want to know about that thing.

cute Something that is good-looking and charming is *cute.*

dart When things move very fast, they *dart.*

deadly fear A *deadly fear* is a great fear.

deathly If something reminds you of death, that thing is *deathly.*

decorate When you *decorate* something, you add things to make it look prettier.

dedicated If something is *dedicated* to a person, it is done out of respect for that person.

demand When you *demand* something, you insist on that thing.

Denali *Denali* is the name of a huge mountain in Alaska.

deserve Something you *deserve* is something you should receive.

disk A flat circle is a *disk.*

dragonflies *Dragonflies* are insects with wings that you can see through.

emergency brake An *emergency brake* is a brake you use if the regular brake does not work.

endurance *Endurance* tells how long you can keep doing something.

especially *Especially* is another word for *really.*

examination An *examination* is a checkup.

exchange *Exchange* is another word for *trade.*

exclaim When you *exclaim,* you say something as if it is very important.

experience Each thing you do is an *experience.*

extend When you *extend* something, you stretch it out.

familiar Things that are well-known to you are *familiar* to you.

fantastic Another word for *fantastic* is *wonderful.*

feat Amazing things that people do are *feats.*

fierce Something that is very wild is *fierce.*

flail When you *flail* your arms, you swing them around in all directions.

flop If something is a *flop,* that thing did not work well.

folks *Folks* is another word for *people.*

forearem The *forearm* is the part of the arm that goes from the elbow to the wrist.

galaxy A *galaxy* is a group of millions and millions of stars.

gear The supplies and equipment that you take with you are called your *gear.*

gorilla A *gorilla* is a huge member of the ape family.

grasp If you *grasp* something, you grab it and hold on to it.

Greeley *Greeley* is a city in Colorado.

guide A *guide* is a person who shows the way.

gust A *gust* of wind is a strong wind that starts suddenly and doesn't last long.

harnessed When a sled-dog team is attached to a sled, the team is *harnessed* to the sled.

health Your *health* refers to how well your body is.

hero A *hero* is somebody we admire for having great courage or doing great things.

hip joint The place where the leg joins the hip is the *hip joint.*

history *History* is the study of the past.

horizon The *horizon* is the line where the earth ends and the sky begins.

husky A *husky* is a strong sled dog that survives well in very cold weather.

Iditarod The *Iditarod* is a sled-dog race that is run every year in Alaska.

image An *image* is a picture.

imagination Your *imagination* is the part of your mind that can think of things that might happen.

include When you *include* something, you let it inside something else.

indeed *Indeed* is another word for *certainly.*

injured *Injured* is another word for *hurt.*

injury If a person has an *injury,* that person is seriously hurt.

insist When you keep arguing that you must have something, you *insist* on that thing.

instructor Another word for *teacher* is *instructor.*

intelligent *Intelligent* is another word for *smart.*

iris The *iris* of the eye is the part that is colored.

iron *Iron* is a heavy metal that magnets stick to.

jammed *Jammed* is another word for *crowded.*

kennel A *kennel* is a place where dogs are kept.

Knik *Knik* is the name of a town in Alaska.

lantern A lamp that sends out light in all directions is a *lantern.*

leopard A *leopard* is a member of the cat family that lives in Africa.

level When something is *level,* it is flat.

limp The opposite of *stiff* is *limp.*

lungs Your *lungs* are the organs in your chest that you use when you breathe.

magnifying Something that is *magnified* is made larger.

mass A *mass* of things is a large number of those things crowded together.

midnight *Midnight* is the middle of the night.

miserable *Miserable* is another word for *terrible.*

mob When people crowd around something, they *mob* that thing.

molecule *Molecules* are the smallest parts of a material.

muscles *Muscles* are attached to bones and move those bones so you can move.

musher A *musher* is a person who drives a sled-dog team.

nerve *Nerves* are like wires that carry messages to the brain and the body.

nightmare A *nightmare* is a bad, bad dream.

Nome *Nome* is a very small city in Alaska.

nonsense *Nonsense* means *no sense at all.*

o'clock *O'clock* tells about the hour of the day.

official An *official* is somebody who can judge if things are done as they are supposed to be done.

overcome When you *overcome* a problem, you solve it.

panic When you *panic,* you become so afraid that your mind doesn't work well.

paralyzed If a body part is *paralyzed,* it can't move.

parka A *parka* is a warm jacket with a hood.

partner A *partner* is somebody you do something with.

peer When you look at something as hard as you can, you *peer* at that thing.

permit When you let something happen, you *permit* it to happen.

Plateosaurus *Plateosaurus* was the very first dinosaur.

platform A *platform* is a level place that is above the places around it.

plunge If something *plunges* into the water, it dives into the water.

porpoise A *porpoise* is sometimes called a dolphin.

prevent When you *prevent* something, you make sure it doesn't happen.

protect When you *protect* something, you don't let anything hurt it.

prove When you *prove* something, you show that it has to be true.

pulse When something *pulses,* it beats.

purpose If you do something on *purpose,* you do something the way you planned to do it.

rapidly Another word for *quickly* is *rapidly.*

recently If something happened not long ago, that thing happened *recently.*

reef A *reef* is a ridge that forms underwater.

regular *Regular* is another word for *usual* or *ordinary.*

reins *Reins* are the straps that are attached to horses.

relax When you *relax,* you take it easy.

retina The *retina* is the part of the eye where pictures are formed.

saber A *saber* is a kind of sword.

scene If you look at something with many things or parts to it, you're looking at a *scene.*

scent Another word for the *smell* of something is the *scent* of something.

science The careful study of anything in the world is a *science.*

scuba diver A *scuba diver* goes underwater wearing a mask and a tank of air.

separated Things that are *separated* are no longer together.

sheltered Things that are *sheltered* are protected.

shortly Another word for *soon* is *shortly.*

single *Single* means *one.*

skull Your *skull* is the bone that covers the top of your head.

spinal cord The *spinal cord* is the bundle of nerves that goes down the middle of your backbone.

spiral A *spiral* is a circle that keeps getting bigger.

squid A *squid* is a sea animal that looks like an octopus that has ten tentacles.

straining When somebody pulls or pushes as hard as possible, the person is *straining.*

success When you have *success,* you do very well at something.

surfaces When a diver *surfaces,* the diver swims up to the surface of the water.

suspended Things that are *suspended* are hung in space.

Sweden *Sweden* is a country that's part of the land the Vikings once ruled.

swooping When birds dip down and glide back up, they are *swooping.*

tarp A *tarp* is a large covering made of canvas or plastic.

tempted If you are *tempted* to do something, part of you wants to do it but another part doesn't.

tentacles A squid's *tentacles* are its ten arms.

terrific *Terrific* is another word for *wonderful.*

thorough Something is *thorough* if it doesn't overlook anything.

tightrope A *tightrope* is a rope high above the ground that circus people walk on.

tour When you go on a *tour,* you take a trip to several places.

trails If something *trails,* it follows behind something else.

transparent If something is *transparent,* you can see things clearly through it.

triceps The *triceps* is the muscle on the back of the upper arm.

troop A *troop* is a group of baboons that are related.

trudge When you *trudge,* you walk along slowly.

tune A *tune* is a song.

twilight *Twilight* is the time just after the sun goes down.

unbearable If you can't stand something, that thing is *unbearable.*

universe The *universe* is everything there is—all the galaxies and everything in them.

usual Things that are *usual* are things that happen most of the time.

veld The *veld* is a large open plain or field in Africa that goes for miles and miles.

veterinarian A *veterinarian* is an animal doctor.

vibrate When something *vibrates,* it moves back and forth so fast you can hardly see it move.

victory Another word for a *win* is a *victory.*

visibility *Visibility* is how well you can see things.

volunteer A *volunteer* is a person who does a job without pay.

waste When we *waste* something, we use it the wrong way.

weary Another word for *very tired* is *weary.*

white-capped A *white-capped* wave is a wave with white foam on top of it.

woman's Something that belongs to a woman is the *woman's.*

wriggle When something *wriggles,* it squirms and moves in all directions.

x-ray An *x-ray* is a photograph that shows someone's bones.

yucky Things that are unpleasant or foul or slimy are *yucky.*

Index